Lyndsey Dyer would like to thank the following:

- Her colleague, Maria Evans, for volunteering her free time to read initial draft of this book.
- Andrew Bruff for his comments on the final draft- he is a patient man!
- Her colleagues Rachel Kerrigher and Tracey Kennedy for always offering the very best advice.
- Her husband, Liam, and dog, Max, for their patience and understanding during the writing process.
- A very important thank you goes to both Ciara Rock for kindly allowing her work to be featured as an example in this guide and to Natalie Masala for offering examiner-style comments on Ciara's work.
- And last, but definitely not least, a final thank you goes to the English department at South Axholme Academy, Epworth for helping her find her love of teaching (and her job) again.
- Sam Perkins and Sunny Ratilal, for designing the front cover.

CONTENTS:

PART 1a: THE ORIGINS OF THE PLAY

You are probably already familiar with the fact that William Shakespeare often based his plays on existing stories. For those of you whose excitement about studying *Othello* stems from your love of Disney's Aladdin (yes, seriously) you can be forgiven (kind of) for recounting your knowledge of the infamous Jafar and his sidekick Iago as a 'warm-up' analysis for your study of this play. Here's why:

The Tragedy of Othello, the Moor of Venice is widely believed to have been written by Shakespeare and first performed in 1604 and was based on a story called *Un Capitano Moro* (A Moorish Captain) by Cinthio (Giovanni Battista Giraldi) written in 1565. In Cinthio's story, his Moorish general is deceived by his ensign into believing his wife is unfaithful, giving Shakespeare one of the main tragic elements of his plot. However, Cinthio cannot be credited entirely with the plot. *Un Capitano Moro* is said to be based on *The Tale of Three Apples* from *One Thousand and One Nights* – a collection of Middle Eastern folk tales compiled during The Islamic Golden Age (right back in the eighth to thirteenth century). In *The Tale of Three Apples*, a man wrongly kills his wife because a slave tricked him into believing she was his mistress. The slave's proof is a rare apple which the man had bought his wife. It transpires that the slave actually stole the apple from a child who had stolen it from his mother (the man's wife) to use as a toy. Throughout this story the Wazir, Ja'far (no, Walt Disney is not really a modern day Shakespeare) has to find the truth or face certain death.

Set against a backdrop of military conflict between Venice and Turkey (which took place throughout latter part of the sixteenth century) *Othello* is Shakespeare's modernised version of a tale of deception that has transcended time and cultures. In his version, Shakespeare chooses to retain Cinthio's conflict between black and white: both in skin colour and symbolism, yet his choice of a black man as protagonist was original. In Elizabethan England, the colour black was associated with moral evil and death, with a 'Moor' in Shakespeare's earlier play, *Titus Andronicus*, being a villain. However, regardless of the fact that Othello is referred to as a Moor throughout, the importance of his race on his demise is, and has always been, open to some debate. The term 'Moor' was used broadly to describe Africans from various regions as well as anybody with dark skin and, therefore, Othello's actual ethnicity can never be proved. This is exactly why you should not become preoccupied by *Othello* being a racist play; *Othello* is much more complex and disconcerting than that. *Othello* is a play about the reversal of fortune. It is a politically controversial play that challenges what it means to be a noble soldier during the 16th century. It is a domestic play that highlights the struggle between soldier and wife. It is a play exploring how patriarchal order, class, race, and pride can destroy a marriage and lead to death.

PART 1b: OTHELLO AS A TRAGEDY

Shakespeare's *Othello* is considered to be a tragedy (no, not just because it has the word 'tragedy' in its title) because it meets the majority of Aristotle's definition of tragedy. Aristotle defined tragedy as a play of direct action, told in a dramatic way, containing a character that has a serious fall from a position of high status. This fall occurs because of the character's own fatal flaw (hamartia), which in Othello's case is, arguably, jealousy. Aristotle wrote that the whole point of a tragedy is to bring about a catharsis after witnessing disaster strike the fortune of the protagonist. According to Aristotle, character is not as important as plot in a tragic play. In fact, the character never has any chance of reversing his fortune as the incidents are not always linked to his personality. Basically, the audience spend the entirety of the play willing Othello to find out the truth and for Iago to be punished, but this psychological torment is a deliberate and necessary ingredient of Aristotle's. He wants us to sympathise with the protagonist, to feel fear and pity, and then to be disappointed at the end as the mistake is realised just seconds too late. How else would we be taught a moral lesson?

Unlike many tragedies, *Othello* doesn't conform entirely to the Aristotelian tragic form. Firstly, as a black man who has converted to Christianity, Othello cannot be considered high status when compared to the white generals at the time. His commitment to Christianity, as told to us by Iago in Act 2, Scene 3, would also raise questions amongst society as Moors were Muslim. Othello openly speaks of his 'redemption' after being 'taken by the insolent foe/and sold to slavery' in Act 1, Scene 3. The redemption was possibly his conversion to Christianity. Many audience members would have been fearful of the religion he formerly followed (especially when people insinuate pagan savagery), and therefore, would question how trustworthy he is. Secondly, there are hints that Othello is not inherently 'good', nor does he have a genuine tragic flaw. It is suggested that he had an affair with Emilia (see the end of Act 1, Scene 3), and that his tragic flaw of jealousy or monomania is not a traditional flaw in personality because it is not something we can be born with – it is a trait that is developed over time. It is more likely that he is a victim of insecurity due to his differences in race, appearance, and perceived character, emphasised continuously by Roderigo, Brabantio and Iago by referring to him as 'the Moor' 'thick lips' and sarcastically as 'his Moorship'. Othello also emphasises himself how different he is by highlighting the fact that he has been a soldier since he was seven years old, '...these arms of mine had seven years' pith'. Additionally, the sub-plot of Iago exploiting money from Roderigo in the hope of receiving sexual favours from Desdemona, interspersed with the visitors from Venice, deviates from Aristotle's one time, one place, and one action unities – as does the juxtaposition of the military and the domestic backdrops.

Finally, Desdemona's murder is not 'accidental 'or committed without intent. Othello plots to commit murder by smothering her, regardless of the fact that he believes she is guilty of a crime and he was acting out of 'honour'.

Make no mistake: Shakespeare intended *Othello* to be considered a tragic hero, but he is not the same as Shakespeare's other tragic heroes. Othello is seen to be much more 'ordinary' than a European King like Macbeth; probably because his hamartia is a 'normal' human emotion in comparison to Macbeth's 'vaulting ambition'. Although he has similar military power, his skin colour and race, alongside his journey through slavery, mean he has no real status amongst Venetian society. However, he is of foreign royalty so does have some of the status required to be considered a tragic hero. And a tragic hero he is. Othello falls from his position of hero, loving husband unafraid to speak of his respect of and devotion to his wife, dignified and powerful leader, gifted and musical orator, noble and admirable man, to become a brainwashed incomprehensible puppet controlled by the jealous Iago. We are supposed to mourn his death, and feel sympathy, yet we also feel as satisfied by his demise as we are of Iago's.

It is true that not all tragedies end in death, but all of Shakespeare's do. The deaths in this tragedy seem to be a result of Iago's villainous mind-games. One of the most famous quotations about Iago comes from Coleridge who claims that Iago's soliloquies reveal 'the motive-hunting of motiveless malignity'. However, Iago claims that he has several motives. He accuses Othello of having sex with his wife; he claims he is jealous that Cassio has been promoted in his place, and he states his annoyance at the fact that Cassio is more attractive than he is. What Coleridge possibly meant was that these motives are excuses for inherent evil and the pleasure he takes from the pain and torture he inflicts on others, evidenced by a lack of a clear plan from the start of the play. Shakespeare deliberately stages most of Iago's actions in the dark or at night, suggesting a clear link to the devil, and, therefore, evidence of his desire to commit evil acts with no genuine motive other than a wish to be involved in the thrill of the deaths of others.

Although *Othello* is a play with many victims and deaths, like all good tragedies it ends with a resolution. Unfortunately, the resolution of *Othello* leaves many disturbing and uncomfortable questions with the audience. One particularly troubling question being whether or not the tragedy in *Othello* is the fact that Othello, Desdemona, Emilia, and Roderigo all die whilst the cunning Iago lives and the white and handsome Cassio restores order.

PART 2a: THE CONTEXT

You will already know from your studies of Shakespeare during GCSE English that the 16th century is a time period with a culture of customs and beliefs very different to those we hold today. European countries were beginning to expand their trade routes so were starting to come into contact with new cultures. Mauritania, found in North Africa, is the fatherland of Shakespeare's *Othello* and is one such new culture that Europeans were becoming familiar with. It is from Mauritania that the term 'Moor' is said to derive from; giving further weight to Othello's race and former religious beliefs (Mauritania has been an Islamic region since the 10th century). Othello is referred to as 'The Moor' throughout the play, but, contrary to some suggestions, this term was not meant to be negative or derogatory in any way. In fact, during the 16th century a person's job was seen to be a true reflection of their character and reputation; being in the army was a job that held prestige, and only those thought to be logical, trustworthy, loyal and courageous were appointed as generals. Therefore, the treatment of Othello as a black man needs to be carefully approached when exploring Iago's main motives. (see Act 1, Scene 1 analysis).

Brabantio, Desdemona's father, is also worth careful consideration when establishing his motive for disliking Othello's marriage to his daughter. During the 16th century the rules of marriage reflected the patriarchal society. Men made all the decisions for the family, and women were expected to be subservient and obedient. Assertive women were considered a threat to the social order. As is made very clear in Shakespeare's *Romeo and Juliet*, fathers would often choose a husband for their daughters from similar or higher social and economic rank. Marriage was considered to be much more like a business transaction and a way of improving a family's finances and status. When Desdemona marries Othello without her father's permission, she rebels against the social conventions of the time, which embarrasses her father. Eloping was not respectful or virtuous, no matter who the chosen partner was. In fact, it is this that proves that Othello's behaviour is already considered to be despicable and contemptuous before Iago begins to manipulate him, especially from a 21st century perspective. It is actually his ridiculous dependency on Iago that brings about his downfall.

The majority of the play is set during the late 16th century on the small island of Cyprus, but the plot begins in Venice. These two disparate worlds, geographically dichotomous, helped convince a 16th century audience that the rapid change in Othello and Desdemona's relationship was possible. Shakespeare's choice to set the play on the island of Cyprus amidst the imaginary destruction of the

'Turks' by a storm is not historically correct. In 1571, the 'Turks' had conquered Cyprus (about 30 years before Shakespeare wrote *Othello*) but Shakespeare's dismissal of the Turks enables the Venetians to arrive safely on the island so the plot of Iago can proceed. Shakespeare often ignored historical facts to suit his plots, his audience, and his country. The Turks were actually the terror of Europe, and Shakespeare needed a big threat to move Othello and Desdemona away from civilised Venice; he would have also scored bonus points with a Christian audience deeply suspicious of one of the most powerful forces in Europe being Islamic. Western Europeans were suspicious of the Ottoman Empire and Shakespeare set his play as a symbol of the struggle between the liberal Europeans and the savage Turks. Therefore, the shift from Venice to (the historically Turkish owned) Cyprus changes Othello. Some may also see virtue, valour and redemption in the way Othello takes his own life in Cyprus because he re-enacts his taking a Turk by the throat and killing him when he brought shame upon the state.

The moral geography is further deepened by Shakespeare's deliberate choice to have Desdemona derive from Venice: the prosperous Italian city full of white people, a city renowned for prostitution. When the English thought about Venice, they imagined a city of culture and civilisation, but also a city of corruption, conflict, and promiscuous women. The Venetian Desdemona never stood a chance. It is much easier for Othello to believe his wife could be unfaithful once Iago reminds him of the apparent behaviour of women in Venice. Additionally, Othello is a perfect oxymoron as a soldier residing on an island devoted to the Goddess of love, Venus. It is tragically ironic that a great soldier dies for love in a war zone.

Finally, to further appease the audience's view of England's power, Iago's name was carefully chosen. Spain was England's greatest enemy due to the competitive nature of colonisation. The English feared invasion by the Spanish yet continued to independently trade with northern Africa, despite Spanish protest. Iago, being a Spanish name, is quite deliberately the play's villain in order to satisfy the Western Europeans.

PART 2b: THE STRUCTURE

Othello is often recognised as being the best constructed of all Shakespearean tragedies because the action begins almost immediately and there is hardly any digression from the main plot. From the moment the play opens up, to the point of Othello's suicide, only a few days pass. The short time of such an action-packed plot was a deliberate source of engagement. Although action-packed, the structure of the plot is simple enough to avoid any confusion and Shakespeare chose to use a three-part structure true to the Aristotelian model referred to in his work on dramatic theory *Poetics*. Aristotle states that a play should contain 'a single whole action...A whole is what has a beginning and middle and end'.

The Aristotelian Model: The story has a beginning, middle, and end.

Beginning: The marriage of Othello and Desdemona

Middle: Iago's deception

End: The murder of Desdemona and the discovery of Iago's lies

Within this three-part structure are then three main ingredients:

1. Hamartia - a tragic flaw in the tragic hero's character that brings about his downfall
2. Catharsis - a purgation of emotions so the audience feel that they have learned something
3. Anagnorisis - the character's revelation of something that hasn't been realised previously.

Othello, as a protagonist, fulfils Aristotle's requirements for a tragic hero. He begins the play as a man of noble status who falls from his position of power because of his hamartia. The catharsis and anagnorisis come when Othello realises the truth about Iago and Desdemona.

Within this three-part structure, Shakespeare then uses the five recognised structural divisions of a dramatic work according to classical critical:

The Structure of Othello: Shakespeare's classic form of five acts.

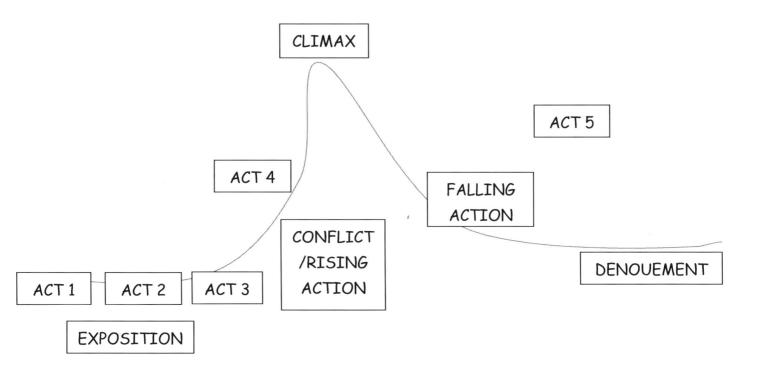

This is open to interpretation – you might map the play out in a different way and that is fine!

1. ACT 1 – <u>EXPOSITION</u>: Introduction of main characters and the meaning of the story. Othello's appearance is delayed but he is mentioned repeatedly. Iago is deliberately introduced first to allow him to manipulate the audience into believing his description of Othello as a barbarous, revolting, and threatening man, thus heightening the anticipation of Othello's arrival onstage. . Roderigo and Iago start the play by informing Brabantio of his daughter's elopement.

   ACT 2 – Brabantio complains to the Duke of Venice. Othello delivers his defence. Brabantio withdraws complaint.

   ACT 3 – Othello, Desdemona, Iago, Emilia, Cassio, and Roderigo go to Venice because of a battle with the Turks.

2. ACT 4 – <u>RISING ACTION</u>: Advancements in action occur and difficulties increase. Iago makes Othello question Desdemona's faithfulness. Iago steals the handkerchief and gives it to Cassio. Othello sees Cassio with it. Othello becomes jealous.

3. ACT 5 - <u>CLIMAX</u> – Most intense part of the story. The crisis happens late in the play to preserve the excitement until the end to keep the audience interested. Othello kills Desdemona. Emilia realises what has happened and reveals all. Iago kills Emilia. Othello realises the truth. Othello tries to kill Iago. Lodovico disarms Othello. Iago escapes.

4. <u>FALLING ACTION</u> – The characters resolve the conflict through confessing and then by dying. Othello accepts his mistake. He finds a dagger and begs to be remembered honourably.

5. <u>DENOUEMENT</u> – The conclusion of the story's tragic structure. Othello kills himself. Iago is captured. The play ends with Desdemona, Othello, and Emilia dead on the bed.

Structure – Blank Verse and Prose:

Othello is written in blank verse and prose. Blank verse is unrhymed poetry written in a meter known as iambic pentameter. Iambic pentameter consists of five 'feet' of two syllables each, an unstressed syllable followed by a stressed one. Think of it as a te-**DUM**/te-**DUM**/te-**DUM**/te-**DUM**/te-**DUM** rhythm (yes, really!).

Mr Bruff has written about this already in several of his guides, but let's revisit linked to *Othello*:

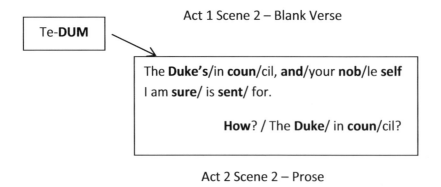

Act 1 Scene 2 – Blank Verse

> Te-**DUM**

> The **Duke's**/in **coun**/cil, **and**/your **nob**/le **self**
> I am **sure**/ is **sent**/ for.
>
>   **How**? / The **Duke**/ in **coun**/cil?

Act 2 Scene 2 – Prose

> It is Othello's pleasure, our noble and
> valiant general, that upon certain tidings
> now arrived importing the mere perdition
> of the Turkish fleet, every man put himself
> into triumph; some to dance…

So why does this really confusing stuff matter? In Shakespeare's time, verse was considered to be of higher status and moral worth than prose so carried greater significance. Prose was for everyday speech, whereas verse was more formal and usually spoken by the noble characters. If a passage or character is of no particular importance, then you may find that the text is written in prose. If a passage or character is important, then you may find that the text is rhythmic verse. So, verse = nobility and prose = commoner. Simple.

Interestingly, Iago comfortably switches between insincere blank verse and prose. He seems to adopt a manner which suits his purpose and actually chooses to use prose when manipulating others. Most of the prose spoken in *Othello* is instigated by Iago and it is this that contrasts with the blank verse. This can be seen when comparing Iago trying to convince Roderigo not to kill himself in Act 1 when he says 'Thou art sure of me: — go, make money: — I have told thee often, and I re-tell thee again and again, I hate the Moor: my cause is hearted;' to Iago's seamless transition into verse when speaking to the audience to reveal his devious plans:

'Thus do I ever make my fool my purse:
For I mine own gain'd knowledge should profane,
If I would time expend with such a snipe.
But for my sport and profit. I hate the Moor:'

There is a departure from the usual blank verse of the play...

Structure – Scene Endings:

It was common practice on the Elizabethan stage to end each scene with a rhyming couplet. This was to signify the end of a scene, signal a change, and provide entertainment.

The last two lines of Act 1 Scene 3 – Rhyming Couplets

> For if such actions may have passage **free**,
>
> Bond-slaves and pagans shall our statesmen **be**.

In Othello, a number of scenes end with iambic rhyming couplets. The first four acts end in rhyming couplets delivered by Iago as a way of creating suspense and excitement for his plan. The final rhyming couplet of the play offers a moral comment on the action and 'ties-up' the events, as well as ensures the message is memorable.

> Myself will straight aboard, and to the state
>
> This heavy act with heavy heart relate.

Symbols and Motifs

Symbols (concrete images, ideas, sounds, or words) and Motifs (recurring abstract images, ideas, sounds, or words).

Look out for the following:

- The handkerchief – a love token given to Desdemona as a symbol of love and fidelity (see Othello's explanation of its origins). It is also used as a tool of manipulation and a symbol of infidelity. Being red and white, and covered in strawberries, it could also symbolise love and loss of virginity. This red on white imagery (like their bed sheets from their marriage night) is private and precious to Othello.
- The 'Willow' song – Desdemona was taught a song by her mother's maid, Barbary, who suffered a misfortune and died singing. The lyrics suggest both sexes are unfaithful and represent Desdemona accepting her fate.
- Candles and light – symbolic of hope and life. Othello blows out a candle just before he kills Desdemona.
- Animals – often used in relation to Othello to reflect some of the racist attitudes of the characters and audience.
- Plants – Iago's speeches often involve reference to plants as a metaphor for inevitable wild natural forces.
- Poison – Iago appears to be obsessed with poison, metaphorically, in the sense that he refers to his thoughts and words as such.
- Eyes and Vision – Othello makes many demands for 'ocular proof' of Desdemona's unfaithfulness, but he often accepts stories without visual proof.

- Hell, Demons, and Monsters – Jealousy is often referred to as a monster in the play. Images of hell are constantly referred to in relation to betrayal, death, and religion.
- Locations – Venice represents civilisation, while Cyprus represents the wilderness (see chapter on context).

PART 3: TRANSLATING ACT 1 SCENE 1

ORIGINAL TEXT:	MODERN TRANSLATION:
ACT 1	**ACT 1**
SCENE I. Venice. A street.	**SCENE 1.Venice. A Street.**
Enter RODERIGO and IAGO	*Enter RODERIGO and IAGO*
RODERIGO	**RODERIGO**
Tush! never tell me; I take it much unkindly	Shush! Don't tell me; I am really annoyed
That thou, Iago, who hast had my purse	That you, Iago, who spends my money like it
As if the strings were thine, shouldst know of	belongs to you,
this.	know about this.
IAGO	**IAGO**
'Sblood, but you will not hear me:	God's blood, you will not listen to me:
If ever I did dream of such a matter, Abhor	If you ever find out I did know you can hate
me.	me.
RODERIGO	**RODERIGO**
Thou told'st me thou didst hold him in thy	You told me that you hate him.
hate.	
IAGO	**IAGO**
Despise me, if I do not. Three great ones of	Hate me if you find out I don't. Three
the city,	important people of the city,
In personal suit to make me his lieutenant,	For their own gain to make me his second in
Off-capp'd to him: and, by the faith of man,	command,
I know my price, I am worth no worse a place:	Showed admiration and respect by trying to
But he; as loving his own pride and purposes,	persuade him:
Evades them, with a bombast circumstance	I know how much I am worth. I deserve to be
Horribly stuff'd with epithets of war;	made second in charge:
And, in conclusion,	

Nonsuits my mediators; for, 'Certes,' says he,
'I have already chose my officer.'
And what was he?
Forsooth, a great arithmetician,
One Michael Cassio, a Florentine,
A fellow almost damn'd in a fair wife;
That never set a squadron in the field,
Nor the division of a battle knows
More than a spinster; unless the bookish
theoric,
Wherein the toged consuls can propose
As masterly as he: mere prattle, without
practise,
Is all his soldiership. But he, sir, had the
election:
And I, of whom his eyes had seen the proof
At Rhodes, at Cyprus and on other grounds
Christian and heathen, must be be-lee'd and
calm'd
By debitor and creditor: this counter-caster,
He, in good time, must his lieutenant be,
And I--God bless the mark!--his Moorship's
ancient.

RODERIGO
By heaven, I rather would have been his
hangman.
IAGO
Why, there's no remedy; 'tis the curse of
service,

But he is arrogant and wants to have things
his own way,
So he avoids their request with an arrogant
attitude and pompous descriptions of war;
Finally, he disregards their advice and assures
them that he
'has already chosen his second in command.'
And who has he chosen?
A man who is good with numbers,
Michael Cassio from Florence,
Whose wife's beauty is a curse to him;
He hasn't ever commanded an army,
and knows as much about battle as an old
woman; unless you count the ideas he has
from the books he's read,
That any useless person can explain just as
well as he: without even thinking about it,
But he's the one who has been chosen over
me:
And that's after he witnessed my fighting
skills and my bravery with his own eyes at
Rhodes, Cyprus and other places
Christian and not, I must act calm in front of
this numbers man.
He is going to become second in command,
And I – God bless the embarrassment! – am
going to become the Moor's flag-bearer.

RODERIGO
I swear to God, I'd rather be his executioner.

IAGO
There's nothing that can be done about it; it's
the curse of the military life,

Preferment goes by letter and affection,
And not by old gradation, where each second
Stood heir to the first. Now, sir, be judge
yourself,
Whether I in any just term am affined
To love the Moor.

RODERIGO

I would not follow him then.

IAGO

O, sir, content you;
I follow him to serve my turn upon him:
We cannot all be masters, nor all masters
Cannot be truly follow'd. You shall mark
Many a duteous and knee-crooking knave,
That, doting on his own obsequious bondage,
Wears out his time, much like his master's ass,
For nought but provender, and when he's old,
cashier'd:
Whip me such honest knaves. Others there
are
Who, trimm'd in forms and visages of duty,
Keep yet their hearts attending on
themselves,
And, throwing but shows of service on their
lords,
Do well thrive by them and when they have
lined
their coats
Do themselves homage: these fellows have
some soul;
And such a one do I profess myself. For, sir,

Promotion is based on recommendation and
who likes you,
And not because of hierarchy or because you
appear to be next in line by right. Now,
Roderigo, decide for yourself,
Whether or not I should love, respect and feel
loyal to the Moor.

RODERIGO

I wouldn't be loyal to him.

IAGO

Roderigo, you'll be pleased to know that
I am only appearing loyal so I can take
advantage of him later. We can't all be
leaders, and not all leaders are truly followed.
You will have noticed that Many dutiful and
hard-working
servants,
Who are loyal, doting, obedient and attentive,
Eventually becomes useless to his master, just
like an old donkey,
Working for nothing but food, and then
sacked when he's old:
Gullible servants should be punished.
There are others who know how to pretend
to be loyal and obedient during their service,
They have self-respect and manage to keep
focusing on themselves,
They pretend to be good servants to their
masters,
They get rich and thrive by stealing from their
masters so that they can become their own
masters

It is as sure as you are Roderigo,

Were I the Moor, I would not be Iago:

In following him, I follow but myself;

Heaven is my judge, not I for love and duty,

But seeming so, for my peculiar end:

For when my outward action doth demonstrate

The native act and figure of my heart

In compliment extern, 'tis not long after

But I will wear my heart upon my sleeve

For daws to peck at: I am not what I am.

RODERIGO

What a full fortune does the thicklips owe

If he can carry't thus!

IAGO

Call up her father,

Rouse him: make after him, poison his delight,

Proclaim him in the streets; incense her kinsmen,

And, though he in a fertile climate dwell,

Plague him with flies: though that his joy be joy,

Yet throw such changes of vexation on't,

As it may lose some colour.

RODERIGO

Here is her father's house; I'll call aloud.

These servants impress me. They are brave and bold;

And, if I do say so myself, I am just like them.

As sure as you are that you're Roderigo, If I were Othello, I wouldn't swap places. I am really following myself;

God is my judge, I am only pretending to love and honour him so that I can get what I want.

If ever my outward appearance reveals how I really feel

Or how proud I am to be born of this country

It won't be long until

I will put myself in danger if I wear my heart on my sleeve for people to attack:

I'm not who I appear to be.

RODERIGO

Big-lips will be lucky if he can do this job well!

IAGO

Let's shout to Desdemona's father,

Wake him up, constantly pester him, spoil his happiness,

We should spread rumours about him and anger the family,

And, even though his life is pleasant,

Irritate him endlessly.

His happiness is real,

But we can spoil it and anger him by causing him problems and making him view things in a different way.

RODERIGO

Here is her father's house. I'll shout to him.

IAGO

Do, with like timorous accent and dire yell
As when, by night and negligence, the fire
Is spied in populous cities.

RODERIGO

What, ho, Brabantio! Signior Brabantio, ho!

IAGO

Awake! what, ho, Brabantio! thieves! thieves!
thieves!
Look to your house, your daughter and your
bags!
Thieves! thieves!

BRABANTIO appears above, at a window

BRABANTIO

What is the reason of this terrible summons?
What is the matter there?

RODERIGO

Signior, is all your family within?

IAGO

Are your doors lock'd?

BRABANTIO

Why, wherefore ask you this?

IAGO

Do it like you are terrified of something and
shout loudly
As if you are terrified that there's a fire
In a city full of people.

RODERIGO

Hey! Hey! Brabantio! Sir Brabantio,
hey!

IAGO

Wake up! Hey, Brabantio! Thieves! Thieves!
Thieves!
They're in your house, protect your daughter
and your possessions!
Thieves! Thieves!

BRABANTIO appears above, at a window

BRABANTIO

What reason do you have for shouting at me
so loudly?
What's wrong?

RODERIGO

Sir, are all your family inside?

IAGO

Are your doors locked?

BRABANTIO

Why are asking me this question?

IAGO	**IAGO**
'Zounds, sir, you're robb'd; for shame, put on your gown;	For God's sake, sir, you've been robbed, put on your gown;
Your heart is burst, you have lost half your soul;	Your heart is broken, you have lost a part of your soul;
Even now, now, very now, an old black ram	Right now, now, right now, an old black man
Is topping your white ewe. Arise, arise;	is having sex with your beautiful and pure
Awake the snorting citizens with the bell,	daughter. Wake up, Wake up; Wake
Or else the devil will make a grandsire of you:	everybody up by ringing the alarm,
Arise, I say.	Or else the devil will make you a granddad:
	Get up!
BRABANTIO	**BRABANTIO**
What, have you lost your wits?	What, have you lost your mind?
RODERIGO	**RODERIGO**
Most reverend signior, do you know my voice?	Most noble sir, do you recognise my voice?
BRABANTIO	**BRABANTIO**
Not I what are you?	No, who are you?
RODERIGO	**RODERIGO**
My name is Roderigo.	My name is Roderigo.
BRABANTIO	**BRABANTIO**
The worser welcome:	That's worse:
I have charged thee not to haunt about my doors:	I have told you not to hang around my house:
In honest plainness thou hast heard me say	I have been really honest and you have heard me say
My daughter is not for thee; and now, in madness,	My daughter will never marry you: and now, because you are angry,
Being full of supper and distempering	And full of dinner and drink,

draughts,
Upon malicious bravery, dost thou come
To start my quiet.

RODERIGO

Sir, sir, sir,--

BRABANTIO

But thou must needs be sure
My spirit and my place have in them power
To make this bitter to thee.

RODERIGO

Patience, good sir.

BRABANTIO

What tell'st thou me of robbing? this is
Venice;
My house is not a grange.

RODERIGO

Most grave Brabantio,
In simple and pure soul I come to you.

IAGO

'Zounds, sir, you are one of those that will not
serve God, if the devil bid you. Because we
come to do you service and you think we are
ruffians, you'll have your daughter covered
with a Barbary horse; you'll have your
nephews neigh to you; you'll have coursers for
cousins and gennets for germans.

You are being malicious and brave and are
trying to annoy me.

RODERIGO

Sir, sir, sir…

BRABANTIO

But you need to be reminded
My personality and my connections are
powerful
This will turn out terrible for you.

RODERIGO

Wait, good sir.

BRABANTIO

Why are you talking about robbery? This is
Venice;
My house is not isolated in the country.

RODERIGO

I respect you, Brabantio,
I'm here out of kindness and with pure
intentions.

IAGO

For God's sake, sir, you are so stubborn that
you will not turn to seek help from God even
if the devil asks. We come to
do you a favour and you think we are
criminals, you'll have your daughter have sex
with a black man; you'll have animals for

grandsons; you'll have animals for family and your whole family will be ruined.

BRABANTIO

What profane wretch art thou?

BRABANTIO

What kind of perverted villain are you?

IAGO

I am one, sir, that comes to tell you your daughter and the Moor are now making the beast with two backs.

IAGO

I am the kind of person who has come to tell you that your daughter and the Moor are having sex like animals.

BRABANTIO

Thou art a villain.

BRABANTIO

You're an evil villain!

IAGO

You are--a senator.

IAGO

And you are a senator.

BRABANTIO

This thou shalt answer; I know thee, Roderigo.

BRABANTIO

Because I know who you are, Roderigo, you must answer me.

RODERIGO

Sir, I will answer anything. But, I beseech you,
If't be your pleasure and most wise consent,
As partly I find it is, that your fair daughter,
At this odd-even and dull watch o' the night,
Transported, with no worse nor better guard
But with a knave of common hire, a gondolier,
To the gross clasps of a lascivious Moor--
If this be known to you and your allowance,
We then have done you bold and saucy wrongs;
But if you know not this, my manners tell me
We have your wrong rebuke. Do not believe

RODERIGO

Sir, I will tell you anything. But, I beg you,
If you are happy with the arrangement and consent,
And I think you probably are, your beautiful daughter,
At this time of the night and in the dark,
Has left without anybody to protect her,
Except a hired commoner, a boatman,
To go to the disgusting embrace of the lustful Moor,
-

That, from the sense of all civility,
I thus would play and trifle with your reverence:
Your daughter, if you have not given her leave,
I say again, hath made a gross revolt;
Tying her duty, beauty, wit and fortunes
In an extravagant and wheeling stranger
Of here and everywhere. Straight satisfy yourself:
If she be in her chamber or your house,
Let loose on me the justice of the state
For thus deluding you.

If you already know about this and are allowing it,
Then we have done a disrespectful thing coming here,
But if you don't know about this, my understanding is
You are wrong to get angry at us. You should not believe
That, at risk of causing problems,
I would disturb you by pranking and confusing you:
Your daughter, if you have not allowed her to leave,
I repeat, has grossly rebelled against you, By giving her respect, beauty, wealth and intelligence to an extravagant and tricky stranger. Now see for yourself:
If she is still in her room or your house,
Then punish me according to the law
For lying to you.

BRABANTIO
Strike on the tinder, ho!
Give me a taper! call up all my people!
This accident is not unlike my dream:
Belief of it oppresses me already.
Light, I say! light!
Exit above

BRABANTIO
Light the candles!
Give me a candle! Wake all my people up!
This is similar to my dream:
I'm worried it is true.
Light! Give me some light!
Brabantio exits

IAGO
(to Roderigo)
Farewell; for I must leave you:
It seems not meet, nor wholesome to my place,

IAGO
(to Roderigo)
Goodbye; I have to go now:
It seems inappropriate, and out of place,

To be produced--as, if I stay, I shall--
Against the Moor: for, I do know, the state,
However this may gall him with some cheque,
Cannot with safety cast him, for he's embark'd
With such loud reason to the Cyprus wars,
Which even now stand in act, that, for their souls,
Another of his fathom they have none,
To lead their business: in which regard,
Though I do hate him as I do hell-pains.
Yet, for necessity of present life,
I must show out a flag and sign of love,
Which is indeed but sign. That you shall surely find him,
Lead to the Sagittary the raised search;
And there will I be with him. So, farewell.

Exit

Enter, below, BRABANTIO, and Servants with torches

For me if I am seen to be working against the
Moor: I do know, that the government,
Might reprimand him for this sort of behaviour,
But they cannot safely get rid of him, because
he's already committed to, and highly
recommended to fight the Cyprus wars,
And even if their lives and souls depended on it,
They couldn't find a man of his ability,
To lead their army: as well as him,
I hate him more than anything,
But, out of necessity of the situation,
I have got to show that I am loyal to him even
though I'm not. Wherever he is,
Lead the people to the battle;
And you will find me there with him. So, Goodbye.

Exit

Enter, below, BRABANTIO, and Servants with torches

BRABANTIO

It is too true an evil: gone she is;
And what's to come of my despised time
Is nought but bitterness. Now, Roderigo,
Where didst thou see her? O unhappy girl!
With the Moor, say'st thou? Who would be a father!
How didst thou know 'twas she? O she deceives me
Past thought! What said she to you? Get more tapers:

BRABANTIO

It is true and evil: she has gone;
And the rest of my life will be nothing but bitterness. Now,
Roderigo,
Where did you see her? Oh unhappy
Girl!
Did you say you saw her with the Moor?
Who would want to be a father!
How did you know it was her? Oh she has deceived me

Raise all my kindred. Are they married, think you?

RODERIGO

Truly, I think they are.

BRABANTIO

O heaven! How got she out? O treason of the blood!
Fathers, from hence trust not your daughters' minds
By what you see them act. Is there not charms
By which the property of youth and maidhood
May be abused? Have you not read, Roderigo,
Of some such thing?

RODERIGO

Yes, sir, I have indeed.

BRABANTIO

Call up my brother. O, would you had had her!
Some one way, some another. Do you know
Where we may apprehend her and the Moor?

RODERIGO

I think I can discover him, if you please,
To get good guard and go along with me.

So easily! What did she say to you? Get more candles;
Wake everybody up. Do you think they are married?

RODERIGO

Yes, I think they are.

BRABANTIO

Oh, heaven! How did she get out? She has betrayed this family!
Fathers, never trust your daughters' minds
Even if they seem obedient. Are there magic spells
That can lead young people and young virgins
Into rebellion? Have you ever heard, Roderigo,
Of this happening before?

RODERIGO

Yes, sir, I have indeed.

BRABANTIO

Call my brother. Now I wish that you had married her!
Some of you go one way, some the other. Do you know
Where we may find and detain her and the Moor?

RODERIGO

I think I can find him, if it's okay with you I need a group of armed men to support me.

BRABANTIO	**BRABANTIO**
Pray you, lead on. At every house I'll call;	Of course, lead the way. Stop at every house;
I may command at most. Get weapons, ho!	They'll do what I say. Get weapons,
And raise some special officers of night.	Oh!
On, good Roderigo: I'll deserve your pains.	And get the guards that work at night.
Exeunt	Let's go, Roderigo: I'll reward you for your
	troubles.
	They all exit

PART 4: ANALYSING ACT 1 SCENE 1

Themes: Appearance vs Reality, Light vs Dark, Honour, Jealousy, Manhood, Prejudice, Deception, Reputation.

The play begins theatrically in the middle of an argument (with an argumentative tone) foreshadowing the conflict that leads to the denouement:

RODERIGO

Tush! never tell me; I take it much unkindly

That thou, Iago, who hast had my purse

As if the strings were thine, shouldst know of this.

IAGO

'Sblood, but you will not hear me:

If ever I did dream of such a matter, Abhor me.

Shakespeare introduces the theme of **jealousy** by deliberately juxtaposing Roderigo's failure to marry Desdemona with Iago's failure to gain promotion. The darkness of the scene (the play opens at night) is symbolic of the evil and danger already present yet Brabantio is fooled into believing this to be the fault of Othello: 'Strike on the tinder, ho!/Give me a taper! [...] Light, I say! light!' Brabantio's repetition of the motif of **light** (used throughout the play with metaphors, personification, animalistic imagery and racial slurs) introduces the theme of good versus evil, with the light representing purity and truth. Additionally, Brabantio also introduces the idea that the light 'porcelain' skin of Desdemona is pure in contrast to Othello's black skin (something Iago develops with his animalistic descriptions). This is exactly what Iago intended in order to pacify the angry Roderigo by gaining the trust of Desdemona's father. Roderigo is angry at Iago for failing to persuade Desdemona to fall in love with him, even though he has paid him a substantial amount of money. The way in which Desdemona is presented as property to be purchased reveals the patriarchal context of the play as well as establishes Iago's misogyny. Although the opening conflict introduces us, by name, to two major characters, its purpose is to heighten the tension in anticipation for the introduction of the protagonist, Othello. Because he does not feature in the opening, Othello is a mysterious character and everything we learn about him is via Iago or Roderigo, creating dramatic interest and tension.

It appears that both men despise Othello, especially considering that he remains nameless throughout their exchange and is mainly referred to using the pronouns 'he' and 'him' alongside titles such as 'the Moor', and insults such as 'thick-lips' and 'Barbary horse', all names that appear to highlight a **prejudiced** displeasure with his race. However, Roderigo's hatred for Othello appears to be **jealousy** rather than racism (the physical description needed to be given verbally because of constraints at the time such as there being no prospect of using a black actor due to there being no professional black actors in Elizabethan England) and his insults sound stupid in contrast to Iago's fluent and venomous eloquence. Consider 'thick-lips' in comparison to 'old black ram/Is tupping your white ewe' as well as the contrast between the impolite and sexual 'tupping' with the technique of metaphor in 'white ewe'. Furthermore, Iago's intelligence and **deception** is established immediately with his cleverly timed disappearance after informing Brabantio of Desdemona's elopement. He is aware of the need not to be accused of disloyalty to Othello in order to execute his plan. In fact, Iago's intelligence and fluency allow him to turn every situation to his advantage and convince others to either become puppets in his plot or manipulate them into believing him to be a loyal subject. Iago's main 'puppet' is Roderigo.

Roderigo is in love with Desdemona and cannot accept her decision to elope to marry Othello as it is a challenge to his **manhood** and **honour**. He has already tried and failed to ask Brabantio for Desdemona's hand in marriage. Iago, on the other hand, is motivated by jealousy ('the green-eyed monster') triggered by his lack of promotion to lieutenant. He tells Roderigo he is jealous because of the way 'Preferment goes by letter and affection/And not by the old gradation.'. He hates Othello for choosing Cassio, whose **manhood** he questions, as he believes Cassio is inexperienced in battle, 'mere prattle without practice is all his soldiership'. He also claims (though this is never proved or mentioned again) that he was recommended for the job by 'great ones' of the city. This is embarrassing for Iago and he seeks to assert his **honour** and **reputation** by claiming to only serve Othello for his own self-interest to 'serve my turn upon him.'. Iago further reveals his hatred of Othello by using insulting, racist ('black ram') and sexual language ('tupping') to inform Brabantio of his daughter's elopement and to convince him that Othello is some kind of beastly animal. At the time the play was written, reducing Othello to a ram demotes him to a position below humanity in the Great Chain of Being – a strict hierarchical structure of life thought to have been decreed by God. This comparison to an animal would have been shocking for the Elizabethans who believed that God had a set order for everything, with animals being below humans. Furthermore, Elizabethans believed that black men had an animal-like, hyper-sexuality. In complete contrast, as a black man in

n of power and influence, most contemporary audiences consider Othello one of the first
es in Literature.

nile Iago, Roderigo and Brabantio's comments in Act 1 are considered racist to a contemporary audience, new historicist critics (those who consider *Othello* in relation to social and historical context) debate whether or not race was a factor in treatment of people in Shakespeare's England. It is important to note that slavery hadn't yet been fully introduced to England therefore Shakespeare and his audience were unlikely to have focussed so much on race. Therefore, when Iago deliberately challenges Brabantio's **manhood** and **honour** by highlighting the fact that his daughter has married in secret and is now having sex with an older black man, it is likely that he is reminding Brabantio that the advantage of having a daughter (a dowry) has been 'robbed' from him and the social order threatened. The verb 'robbed' alongside the description of the time of day 'At this odd-even and dull watch o' the night' suggests that Brabantio's property (his daughter) has been threatened in the dark by man whose descriptions are all linked to darkness and evil. Furthermore, Iago attempts to shock by showing Desdemona as pure and a victim with the zoomorphic 'ewe' symbolising purity, innocence, and gentleness as it has done for thousands of years in Christianity (Jesus is the lamb of God). However, his attempt fails in that it simply highlights her inequality as a woman with the reference to Desdemona preceded by the second person possessive pronoun 'your' (white ewe), reflecting the hierarchical order of women as objects or property of men. Regardless of how Desdemona is portrayed, Othello as a ram is symbolic of darkness and evil because of the choice of attributive adjective 'black'. At this point, the audience have already experienced Roderigo's pathetic need to be loved and to be guided in love as well as Iago's disturbing nature, so are not easily convinced that Othello is as Iago describes. Additionally, Iago openly admits 'I am not what I am' making the audience question the difference between **reality and appearance** from the start of the play. This utterance also echoes the statement God made to Moses in Exodus 3:14 yet is an inversion of 'I am that I am' suggesting something unnatural and un-godly. By introducing himself as a manipulator this early, Iago encourages us to sympathise with Othello. The dramatic irony established by Iago's confessions of his plot further secure Othello's position as victim and Iago as villain from the very start.

Iago's villainy is Machiavellian (using clever but often dishonest methods that deceive people so that you can win power or control- named after the apparently corrupt writer Niccolo Machiavelli) in that it appears he will not let anything stand in his way in his desire to be lieutenant. He slips away from the scene (hidden by darkness) undetected and without revealing his identity. Iago's first major manipulation is a success: Brabantio is furious with his daughter but believes she is a passive victim and accuses Othello of sorcery. His refusal to believe his daughter has deceived him by committing 'treason of the blood' by eloping reflects the stereotype of black man as sexual deviant and Desdemona as 'abused'. Furthermore, the insinuation that Othello has bewitched Desdemona further highlights social beliefs at the time. An Elizabethan audience believed in witches and they believed a black man was a descendant of Canaan, the cursed grandson of Noah, punished for his father's decision to highlight Noah's drunken nakedness (Genesis 9:25 'Cursed be Canaan; A servant of servants He shall be to his brothers.') and therefore associated with the devil. When Brabantio recalls a dream that foretold the events, this creates the sense that fate has control over the outcome of the play and not the important social figure (the father) Brabantio. He desires light in order to discover what has happened with his daughter; therefore, his utterances contain threats as well as interrogatives and reveal a weakness that Iago can manipulate. The scene ends with Brabantio declaring that Roderigo would have been the better match for his daughter, even after earlier admitting 'My daughter is not for thee', and he promises to reward him for his support.

ORIGINAL TEXT:	MODERN TRANSLATION:
SCENE II. Another street.	**SCENE II. Another street.**
Enter OTHELLO, IAGO, and Attendants with torches	*Enter OTHELLO, IAGO, and Attendants with torches*
IAGO	**IAGO**
Though in the trade of war I have slain men,	I have been to war and killed many men in battle,
Yet do I hold it very stuff o' the conscience	The murders play on my conscience
To do no contrived murder: I lack iniquity	I lack the evil and wickedness
Sometimes to do me service: nine or ten times	Sometimes to help me do it:
I had thought to have yerk'd him here under the ribs.	I have wanted to stab him under the ribs nine or ten times.
OTHELLO	**OTHELLO**
'Tis better as it is.	It is good that you didn't.
IAGO	**IAGO**
Nay, but he prated,	But he kept talking foolishly for ages,
And spoke such scurvy and provoking terms	And spoke very disrespectfully and insulted you
Against your honour	Against your honour
That, with the little godliness I have,	But, with the little bit of respect for God that I have, I restrained myself. Please tell me sir,
I did full hard forbear him. But, I pray you, sir,	Is your marriage secure? Let me assure you of this,
Are you fast married? Be assured of this,	That Brabantio is much loved,
That the Magnifico is much beloved,	And has the influence and power
And hath in his effect a voice potential	Twice as much as the duke's: he will force you to divorce;
As double as the duke's: he will divorce you;	
Or put upon you what restraint and grievance	
The law, with all his might to enforce it on,	
Will give him cable.	

	Or he will inflict upon you whatever punishment
	The law, with all his power and status, will allow him to.

OTHELLO

OTHELLO	**OTHELLO**
Let him do his spite:	Let him do his worst:
My services which I have done the signiory	The services I have done for the government
Shall out-tongue his complaints. 'Tis yet to know,--	Will speak more highly than his complaints. Nobody knows this yet
Which, when I know that boasting is an honour,	And when I know I can brag openly,
I shall promulgate--I fetch my life and being	I will announce the fact that I am related to
From men of royal siege, and my demerits	Royalty, and my faults
May speak unbonneted to as proud a fortune	Will be respected as I am as noble as
As this that I have reach'd: for know, Iago,	Desdemona. Iago,
But that I love the gentle Desdemona,	I love Desdemona,
I would not my unhoused free condition	I would never have given up my freedom if I
Put into circumscription and confine	didn't love her so much.
For the sea's worth. But, look! what lights come yond?	Look at those lights. Who's coming this way?

IAGO	**IAGO**
Those are the raised father and his friends:	That's her father and his friends. They have
You were best go in.	been woken up.
	You'd better go inside.

OTHELLO	**OTHELLO**
Not I I must be found:	No, I must face them:
My parts, my title and my perfect soul	All of my good qualities and my status as
Shall manifest me rightly. Is it they?	Desdemona's husband will protect me. Is it them?

IAGO	**IAGO**

By Janus, I think no.

Enter CASSIO, and certain Officers with torches

OTHELLO

The servants of the duke, and my lieutenant?

The goodness of the night upon you, friends!

What is the news?

CASSIO

The duke does greet you, general,

And he requires your haste-post-haste

appearance,

Even on the instant.

OTHELLO

What is the matter, think you?

CASSIO

Something from Cyprus as I may divine:

It is a business of some heat: the galleys

Have sent a dozen sequent messengers

This very night at one another's heels,

And many of the consuls, raised and met,

Are at the duke's already: you have been

hotly call'd for;

When, being not at your lodging to be found,

The senate hath sent about three several

guests

To search you out.

OTHELLO

I don't think so.

Enter CASSIO, and certain Officers with torches

OTHELLO

The servants of the duke, and my lieutenant?

I hope you are well tonight, friends!

What's going on?

CASSIO

The duke says hello, general, and he wants to see you right away.

OTHELLO

Do you know what's wrong?

CASSIO

Something about Cyprus. I think. It seems to be important: the

warships

have sent a dozen messages tonight, one after the other,

And many of the chairmen have been woken up and have met up,

They are already at the duke's: they are very anxious for you to be there;

When they couldn't find you at home

The senate sent three different search parties to find you.

OTHELLO

It is a good job that you found me.

'Tis well I am found by you.	I will speak a few words here in the house,
I will but spend a word here in the house,	Then I'll go with you.
And go with you.	*Exit*
Exit	
CASSIO	**CASSIO**
Ancient, what makes he here?	Officer, what is he doing here?
IAGO	**IAGO**
'Faith, he to-night hath boarded a land carack:	He boarded a large ship tonight:
If it prove lawful prize, he's made for ever.	If it is worth it, then he'll be set forever.
CASSIO	**CASSIO**
I do not understand.	I do not understand.
IAGO	**IAGO**
He's married.	He's married.
CASSIO	**CASSIO**
To who?	To who?
Re-enter OTHELLO	*Re-enter OTHELLO*
IAGO	**IAGO**
Marry, to--Come, captain, will you go?	Are you ready to go?
OTHELLO	**OTHELLO**
Have with you.	Yes, I'll go with you.
CASSIO	**CASSIO**
Here comes another troop to seek for you.	Here comes another group searching for you.
IAGO	**IAGO**
It is Brabantio. General, be advised;	It is Brabantio. Listen to me, sir. He is going to
He comes to bad intent.	do something horrible to you.

Enter BRABANTIO, RODERIGO, and Officers

with torches and weapons

OTHELLO

Holla! stand there!

RODERIGO

Signior, it is the Moor.

BRABANTIO

Down with him, thief!

They draw on both sides

IAGO

You, Roderigo! come, sir, I am for you.

OTHELLO

Keep up your bright swords, for the dew will

rust them.

Good signior, you shall more command with

years

Than with your weapons.

BRABANTIO

O thou foul thief, where hast thou stow'd my

daughter?

Damn'd as thou art, thou hast enchanted her;

For I'll refer me to all things of sense,

If she in chains of magic were not bound,

Whether a maid so tender, fair and happy,

So opposite to marriage that she shunned

The wealthy curled darlings of our nation,

Would ever have, to incur a general mock,

Run from her guardage to the sooty bosom

Enter BRABANTIO, RODERIGO, and Officers

with torches and weapons

OTHELLO

Hey! Stop there!

RODERIGO

Sir, it is the Moor.

BRABANTIO

Attack the thief!

They draw on both sides

IAGO

Roderigo! Come on, I'll fight you.

OTHELLO

Keep your swords looking nice, the dew will

rust them if not.

Good sir, you get more respect because of

your age than you do because of your

weapons.

BRABANTIO

You are a disgusting thief, where are you

keeping my daughter?

You are a devil and you've put a spell on her;

It is common sense

That she must be trapped by a powerful spell,

She is so beautiful and happy,

And she has refused so many offers of

marriage

From the wealthy handsome young men of

our city,

Of such a thing as thou, to fear, not to delight.

Judge me the world, if 'tis not gross in sense

That thou hast practised on her with foul charms,

Abused her delicate youth with drugs or minerals

That weaken motion: I'll have't disputed on;

'Tis probable and palpable to thinking.

I therefore apprehend and do attach thee

For an abuser of the world, a practiser

Of arts inhibited and out of warrant.

Lay hold upon him: if he do resist,

Subdue him at his peril.

OTHELLO

Hold your hands,

Both you of my inclining, and the rest:

Were it my cue to fight, I should have known it

Without a prompter. Where will you that I go

To answer this your charge?

BRABANTIO

To prison, till fit time

Of law and course of direct session

Call thee to answer.

OTHELLO

What if I do obey?

How may the duke be therewith satisfied,

That she would never, at the risk of being laughed at,

Run from my care into the arms of a black thing like you

You are a thing to fear, not to love.

It is disgusting, and obvious to everyone with sense

That you have tricked her with your horrible magic,

You have manipulated her youth with potions and drugs

That have poisoned her mind: that's probably what happened;

I am arresting you for this abuse and illegal witchcraft.

Grab hold of him: if he tries to struggle,

Use as much force as you wish.

OTHELLO

Hold on,

I don't need to be told when to fight

Where do you want me to go

To respond to these charges?

BRABANTIO

To prison, until the court is ready to call you to answer to the charges.

OTHELLO

What if I obey?

What will the duke say?

His messengers are right here next to me,

Whose messengers are here about my side,

Upon some present business of the state

To bring me to him?

First Officer

'Tis true, most worthy signior;

The duke's in council and your noble self,

I am sure, is sent for.

BRABANTIO

How! the duke in council!

In this time of the night! Bring him away:

Mine's not an idle cause: the duke himself,

Or any of my brothers of the state,

Cannot but feel this wrong as 'twere their own;

For if such actions may have passage free,

Bond-slaves and pagans shall our statesmen be.

Exeunt

They have been given reason – on state business –

To take me to him.

First Officer

It's true, most worthy sir;

The duke's in a meeting now,

He has sent for you.

BRABANTIO

The duke is in a meeting?

At this time of the night? Bring him with us:

I have reason to seize him: the duke himself,

Or any of my fellow senators,

Will understand how bad his actions are as seriously as if they were their own;

If we let crimes like this happen and people like him remain free,

Slaves and heathens will rule us all.

They all exit

PART 6: ANALYSING ACT 1 SCENE 2

Themes: Deception, Manhood and Honour, Prejudice, Society's Treatment of Outsider, Womanhood and Sexuality

Iago's **deception** and manipulation intensifies as he pretends to warn Othello about the danger that Brabantio poses, as well as pretending to want to stab Roderigo for being disrespectful about Othello. Othello is a happily married man ('I love the gentle Desdemona') and confidently believes that he has the status from his military prowess to protect him against Brabantio: 'parts...title, and ... perfect soul [....] will manifest me rightly). The audience may expect to be greeted by a savage barbarian, but Othello is presented as an authoritative, calm and secure man with a desire to avoid conflict (the polar opposite to Iago) and will not be provoked by Iago when he says 'Let him do his spite [....] I must be found'. These two brief utterances suggest Othello desires to resolve any conflict and is willing to accept full responsibility for Desdemona's elopement. Rather than being the man that Iago described in Act 1, Othello is presented as honest and dignified. He proudly defends his **honour** and declares his status as a successful fighter and a man free from slavery (possibly challenging new historicist theory that race and **prejudice** was not a factor) as his loyal supporters look on. Othello's status as honourable is further secured by his respectful treatment of Brabantio 'Good Sir'. Brabantio, however, is accusatory and insulting in his treatment of what society would deem the **outsider** when he repetitively refers to Othello as a 'thief' and accuses him of 'witchcraft' as he fails to believe that his daughter (his property) has been taken from him of her own free will.

To further heighten the presentation of Othello as a complete contrast to Brabantio and Iago, Shakespeare implicitly compares Othello to Jesus and Iago to Judas The allusion to Jesus can be seen in the torches and swords of Brabantio's men as they mirror the actions of the group who took Jesus to his crucifixion 'So Judas brought a band of soldiers and officers from the chief priests and Pharisees. They arrived at the garden carrying lanterns, torches, and weapons. Jesus, knowing all that was coming upon Him, stepped forward ...' (John 18:3)In the same why that Jesus told Peter to put up his sword into the sheath, Othello tells the men to 'Keep up your bright swords...' and proves himself to be a complete contrast to Iago's introduction. Again, Othello's admittance that he '[....] must be found' mirrors the action of Jesus stepping forward. Although compared to Jesus, Othello ends the play with a personal comparison to Judas (see Act 5). However, the most consistent and convincing allusion to Judas can be traced with the theme of betrayal, as Iago's loyalty is constantly revealed to be feigned in preference for the betrayal of his leader (see 1:1 'Lead to the Sagittary the raised search;/And there will I be with him').

37

Although Iago is portrayed as the villain, it is actually Brabantio, a white man of high status, who appears barbaric and **prejudice** with his accusations of witchcraft, ageist comments, and racism interleaved with his apparent disgust at interracial sex when he states Desdemona would never 'Run … to the sooty bosom/Of such a thing as thou, to fear … Judge me the world, if 'tis not gross in sense . Even after being referred to as a 'sooty…thing…' Othello maintains control of the situation and avoids imprisonment by willingly agreeing to 'obey' Brabantio's orders. Brabantio's racism appears to be an important factor in his anger. A Shakespearean audience would have sympathised with a father being angry at the elopement of his daughter (a serious offense) yet Shakespeare deliberately has Brabantio place greater emphasis on his shock that his daughter could possibly be attracted to a Moor, possibly because the Christian Elizabethan audience already associated Moors with Islam. However, it could be argued that witchcraft was a much more serious crime than elopement so Brabantio was actually being tactical. After all, his **manhood** has been challenged and his property stolen.

Another interesting challenge to a character's **manhood** comes in the reaction of Cassio to Iago's sexual humour when he states that Othello has '… boarded a land carack …' and if Desdemona as a 'lawful prize' is worth it, then he is 'made for ever' to which Cassio responds 'I do not understand'. Cassio is oblivious to Iago's reference to Othello being on top of or inside a land carack (Desdemona) and has, therefore, been presented as an inexperienced fool who trusts Iago even after he has failed to deliver Desdemona to him. By not sharing Iago's sense of humour and by starting the scene with a confident, urgent summons from the Duke, Cassio presents himself as a conflicted man who is easily manipulated because of his naivety. Iago is fully aware of Cassio's puzzlement and inexperience and, therefore, plots to (ironically) use him as the seducer of Desdemona. Iago's manipulation of and influence over the trusting male characters begins the decline into their becoming abusive and obsessed with patriarchal control.

In terms of stagecraft, Othello, who would have originally been played by a white man with blacked-up face; he would have been a visual spectacle. The man playing Othello would have starkly contrasted, in an unattractive and frightening way, to the rest of the white men on stage therefore giving weight to Brabantio and Iago's claims. However, once Othello speaks, it becomes apparent that he is a gifted orator and is able to persuade and inspire those around him. His authoritative presence and powerful language actually stops the confrontation, regardless of Iago's attempts to encourage violent conflict.

Othello

Hold your hands,

Both you of my inclining, and the rest:

Were it my cue to fight, I should have known it

Without a prompter. Where will you that I go

To answer this your charge?

> The imperative adds to the calm authority that Othello has established as a great soldier.

> Interrogative suggests a willingness to hand over his power in order to communicate reason.

Othello is the first character to speak about love contrasting the coarse imagery the audience have heard so far when he admits 'I love the gentle Desdemona) The other male characters have referred to women as possessions or sexual objects. Othello's sincere and positive view of his marriage further lessens the shock of a man appearing with a blacked-up face and allows Othello's confidence at the end of the scene not to be mistaken for arrogance. Unfortunately, regardless of Othello's honesty, postcolonial critical interpretation would suggest that Othello, as a Moor amongst the context of the Cypriot and Venetian conflict, is uncivilised and his love unnatural. There would have been no disconnect between his successes as a soldier and his ancestry. Othello's mixed marriage would have been viewed as abnormal, regardless of his declarations of love and his initial respect for his wife, the 'noble' Desdemona.

The rhyming couplet that ends the scene serves as a memorable reminder that the marriage is doomed:

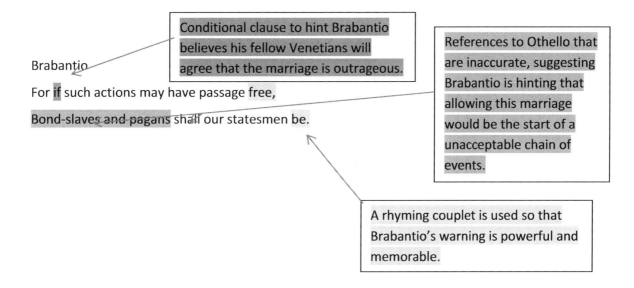

Brabantio

For if such actions may have passage free,

Bond-slaves and pagans shall our statesmen be.

> Conditional clause to hint Brabantio believes his fellow Venetians will agree that the marriage is outrageous.

> References to Othello that are inaccurate, suggesting Brabantio is hinting that allowing this marriage would be the start of a unacceptable chain of events.

> A rhyming couplet is used so that Brabantio's warning is powerful and memorable.

Turn is sombre nature

formal

ORIGINAL TEXT:	MODERN TRANSLATION:
SCENE III. A council-chamber.	**SCENE III. A council-chamber.**
The DUKE and Senators sitting at a table; *Officers attending*	*The DUKE and Senators sitting at a table;* *Officers attending*
DUKE OF VENICE There is no composition in these news That gives them credit.	**DUKE OF VENICE** There is no consistency in this news That could give it any credit. It can't be trusted.
First Senator Indeed, they are disproportion'd; My letters say a hundred and seven galleys.	**First Senator** It's true, they are inconsistent. My letters say there are a hundred and seven ships.
DUKE OF VENICE And mine, a hundred and forty.	**DUKE OF VENICE** And mine say a hundred and forty.
Second Senator And mine, two hundred: But though they jump not on a just account,-- As in these cases, where the aim reports, 'Tis oft with difference--yet do they all confirm A Turkish fleet, and bearing up to Cyprus.	**Second Senator** And mine say two hundred: But even though they are different accounts These reports are just estimates, They often have differences – yet they all confirm the same thing: A Turkish fleet is advancing on Cyprus.
DUKE OF VENICE Nay, it is possible enough to judgment: I do not so secure me in the error,	**DUKE OF VENICE** Yes, I understand the message: Even though the messages are different, the main message is clear,

educated

mathematical
+ debate

Had to formalise unhad. issue in trad. old religion place

Brabantius values This power will be in over his favour but black man progressive move

Cyprus = chaos
Venice = order/balance

But the main article I do approve

In fearful sense.

Sailor

[Within] What, ho! what, ho! what, ho!

First Officer

A messenger from the galleys.

Enter a Sailor

DUKE OF VENICE

Now, what's the business?

Sailor

The Turkish preparation makes for Rhodes;

So was I bid report here to the state

By Signior Angelo.

DUKE OF VENICE

How say you by this change?

First Senator

This cannot be,

By no assay of reason: 'tis a pageant,

To keep us in false gaze. When we consider

The importance of Cyprus to the Turk,

And let ourselves again but understand,

That as it more concerns the Turk than Rhodes,

So may he with more facile question bear it,

For that it stands not in such warlike brace,

But altogether lacks the abilities

That Rhodes is dress'd in: if we make thought of this,

We must not think the Turk is so unskilful

And it is frightening.

Sailor

[Offstage] Hello! Hey, hello! Hey, hello!

First Officer

It's a messenger from the warships.

A Sailor Enters

DUKE OF VENICE

What news do you bring to me?

Sailor

The Turkish ships are on their way to Rhodes;

So I was told to come and report this to you

by Sir Angelo.

DUKE OF VENICE

What do you think about this change?

First Senator

This can't be true,

It doesn't make sense. It's a trick,

To confuse us.

Consider how important Cyprus is to the Turks,

And think about how much more Cyprus concerns the Turks than Rhodes does,

So if we keep these things in mind,

It is less well defended than Rhodes,

And lacks the same abilities

That Rhodes has: and think about this,

We should not think that the Turks are so stupid and incompetent

To leave that latest which concerns him first,
Neglecting an attempt of ease and gain,
To wake and wage a danger profitless.

DUKE OF VENICE

Nay, in all confidence, he's not for Rhodes.

First Officer

Here is more news.

Enter a Messenger

Messenger

The Ottomites, reverend and gracious,
Steering with due course towards the isle of
Rhodes,
Have there injointed them with an after fleet.

First Senator

Ay, so I thought. How many, as you guess?

Messenger

Of thirty sail: and now they do restem
Their backward course, bearing with frank
appearance
Their purposes toward Cyprus. Signior
Montano,
Your trusty and most valiant servitor,

---

as to leave the more important target until
later instead of first,
Neglecting something so easy and profitable
to do something dangerous, when they are
unlikely to gain anything.

DUKE OF VENICE

No, I think we can be confident that the Turks
aren't headed for Rhodes.

First Officer

Here is more news.

Enter a Messenger

Messenger

The respected and gracious Ottomite ships
are heading towards the isle of Rhodes,
They have joined another fleet.

First Senator

Yes, that's what I thought. How many do you
think there are?

Messenger

Thirty ships and now they have turned around
and are clearly heading towards Cyprus.
Sir Montano,
your brave and loyal servant gives you this
information freely and recommends that you
believe him and send reinforcements.

With his free duty recommends you thus,

And prays you to believe him.

DUKE OF VENICE

'Tis certain, then, for Cyprus.

Marcus Luccicos, is not he in town?

First Senator

He's now in Florence.

DUKE OF VENICE

Write from us to him; post-post-haste
dispatch.

First Senator

Here comes Brabantio and the valiant Moor.

*Enter BRABANTIO, OTHELLO, IAGO,
RODERIGO, and Officers*

DUKE OF VENICE

Valiant Othello, we must straight employ you

Against the general enemy Ottoman.

To BRABANTIO

I did not see you; welcome, gentle signior;

We lack'd your counsel and your help tonight.

BRABANTIO

So did I yours. Good your grace, pardon me;

Neither my place nor aught I heard of business

Hath raised me from my bed, nor doth the

general care

Take hold on me, for my particular grief

DUKE OF VENICE

I am certain that they are heading for Cyprus.

Is Marcus Luccicos in town?

First Senator

No, he's now in Florence.

DUKE OF VENICE

Write to him immediately. Hurry.

First Senator

Here comes Brabantio and the brave Moor.

*Enter BRABANTIO, OTHELLO, IAGO,
RODERIGO, and Officers*

DUKE OF VENICE

Brave Othello, I have to urgently send you to
fight the enemy,

the Ottomans.

To BRABANTIO

I did not see you; welcome, gentle sir;

We missed your help and advice tonight.

BRABANTIO

I could have used yours too. Forgive me, your
grace;

Neither my position as a senator or official

business

Is of so flood-gate and o'erbearing nature

That it engluts and swallows other sorrows

And it is still itself.

DUKE OF VENICE

Why, what's the matter?

BRABANTIO

My daughter! O, my daughter!

DUKE OF VENICE Senator

Dead?

BRABANTIO

Ay, to me;

She is abused, stol'n from me, and corrupted

By spells and medicines bought of mountebanks;

For nature so preposterously to err,

Being not deficient, blind, or lame of sense,

Sans witchcraft could not.

DUKE OF VENICE

Whoe'er he be that in this foul proceeding

Hath thus beguiled your daughter of herself

And you of her, the bloody book of law

You shall yourself read in the bitter letter

After your own sense, yea, though our proper son

Stood in your action.

Has brought me here, nor has the situation

here concerned me, because I have a greater problem

It is so worrying and overwhelming

That it engulfs everything else

and is so powerful.

DUKE OF VENICE

Why, what's the matter?

BRABANTIO

My daughter! Oh, my daughter!

DUKE OF VENICE Is she dead?

BRABANTIO

She's dead to me.

She has been taken from me, and abused and corrupted

By spells and drugs bought from fraudsters;

It is not in her nature to do something like this, she's not stupid, blind or paralysed,

It must be witchcraft.

DUKE OF VENICE

Whoever he is that has used these horrible methods

To influence your daughter

And take her from you, he will pay for it and you will decide what his sentence will be

Whatever seems right to you, even if he were my own son.

BRABANTIO	**BRABANTIO**
Humbly I thank your grace.	I respect you. Thank you so much.
Here is the man, this Moor, whom now, it seems,	Here is the man, this Moor, who seems to have been personally brought here by you on state business.
Your special mandate for the state-affairs	
Hath hither brought.	
DUKE OF VENICE Senator	**DUKE OF VENICE** Senator
We are very sorry for't.	We are very sorry for it.
DUKE OF VENICE	**DUKE OF VENICE**
[To OTHELLO] What, in your own part, can you say to this?	[To OTHELLO] What do you have to say about this?
BRABANTIO	**BRABANTIO**
Nothing, but this is so.	Nothing because what I've said is true.
OTHELLO	**OTHELLO**
Most potent, grave, and reverend signiors,	Powerful, important and respected sirs,
My very noble and approved good masters,	Honourable and good masters,
That I have ta'en away this old man's daughter,	It is true that I have taken this man's daughter,
It is most true; true, I have married her:	It is definitely true that I have married her:
The very head and front of my offending	But that's the worst offence I have committed
Hath this extent, no more. Rude am I in my speech,	I haven't done anything else, nothing worse. I am not the best speaker, I am awkward and I
And little bless'd with the soft phrase of peace:	am not blessed with soft words of peace:
For since these arms of mine had seven years' pith,	Because I have (since the age of seven) always been a fighter in wars.
Till now some nine moons wasted, they have used	Until nine months ago, I have only ever known war
Their dearest action in the tented field,	I don't know much about anything else in this world so I can't speak in my defence,
And little of this great world can I speak,	But if you let me, even though I won't

More than pertains to feats of broil and battle,

And therefore little shall I grace my cause

In speaking for myself. Yet, by your gracious patience,

I will a round unvarnish'd tale deliver

Of my whole course of love; what drugs, what charms,

What conjuration and what mighty magic,

For such proceeding I am charged withal,

I won his daughter.

BRABANTIO

A maiden never bold;

Of spirit so still and quiet, that her motion

Blush'd at herself; and she, in spite of nature,

Of years, of country, credit, every thing,

To fall in love with what she fear'd to look on!

It is a judgment maim'd and most imperfect

That will confess perfection so could err

Against all rules of nature, and must be driven

To find out practises of cunning hell,

Why this should be. I therefore vouch again

That with some mixtures powerful o'er the blood,

Or with some dram conjured to this effect,

He wrought upon her.

DUKE OF VENICE

To vouch this, is no proof,

Without more wider and more overt test

Than these thin habits and poor likelihoods

Of modern seeming do prefer against him.

be able to help myself, with your patience and understanding,

I will tell you a plain, blunt, and truthful story about my love,

and I will tell you what drugs

what spells and what magic

I have used for the crime I am charged with,

To win his daughter.

BRABANTIO

She's a modest young girl;

So calm and reserved, that

She blushes at even herself; and she, in spite of her personality,

Of her age, her status, and her upbringing,

Falls in love with a man that she would

usually be too sacred to look at!

It is flawed judgement and absolutely ridiculous

Somebody that perfect

must have been forced to commit an act so against nature

that the devil must be behind it,

I say again

He must have used a powerful potion

or drugs or some such thing.

DUKE OF VENICE

To say it isn't actually proof,

Without specific evidence

Something more than just improbabilities

He cannot be condemned.

First Senator	**First Senator**
But, Othello, speak:	Othello, you tell us what happened:
Did you by indirect and forced courses	Did you deceive or force
Subdue and poison this young maid's	Drug or poison this young lady to gain her
affections?	love?
Or came it by request and such fair question	Or did it happen in a free and open way
As soul to soul affordeth?	Appropriate between two consenting people?
OTHELLO	**OTHELLO**
I do beseech you,	I beg you,
Send for the lady to the Sagittary,	Send for the lady ,
And let her speak of me before her father:	And let her speak about me in front of her
If you do find me foul in her report,	father;
The trust, the office I do hold of you,	If she says anything that suggests I have done
Not only take away, but let your sentence	wrong you can take away your trust, my
Even fall upon my life.	status, and you can sentence me to death.
DUKE OF VENICE	**DUKE OF VENICE**
Fetch Desdemona hither.	Bring Desdemona here.
OTHELLO	**OTHELLO**
Ancient, conduct them: you best know the place.	Iago, direct them: you know where she is.
Exeunt IAGO and Attendants	*IAGO and Attendants exit*
And, till she come, as truly as to heaven	Until she arrives, I will be completely honest -
I do confess the vices of my blood,	as honest as I would be when confessing my
So justly to your grave ears I'll present	sins to God, I'll tell you how I fell in love with
How I did thrive in this fair lady's love,	this beautiful lady,
And she in mine.	And how she fell in love with me.
DUKE OF VENICE	**DUKE OF VENICE**
Say it, Othello.	Tell us, Othello

47

OTHELLO	**OTHELLO**
Her father loved me; oft invited me;	Her father liked me and often invited me
Still question'd me the story of my life,	over. He questioned me about my life, the
From year to year, the battles, sieges,	battles, the sieges, the good experiences
fortunes,	I have had.
That I have passed.	I told him everything, even from my
I ran it through, even from my boyish days,	childhood,
To the very moment that he bade me tell it;	Right to the present day.
Wherein I spake of most disastrous chances,	I told him about unfortunate disasters,
Of moving accidents by flood and field	I told him about adventures on sea and land,
Of hair-breadth scapes i' the imminent deadly	of near catastrophes and dangerous
breach,	adventures,
Of being taken by the insolent foe	I told him how I was captured by the enemy
And sold to slavery, of my redemption thence	and sold to slavery, how I bought my freedom
And portance in my travels' history:	I told him where I had travelled to:
Wherein of antres vast and deserts idle,	About the vast caves and silent deserts,
Rough quarries, rocks and hills whose heads	I told him about the rough quarries, rocks and
touch heaven	hills who were so tall they reached heaven.
It was my hint to speak,--such was the	And I told him about cannibals that eat each
process;	other,
And of the Cannibals that each other eat,	I told him about the Anthropophagi and men
The Anthropophagi and men whose heads	whose heads
Do grow beneath their shoulders. This to hear	Grow beneath their shoulders.
Would Desdemona seriously incline:	Desdemona liked to listen too:
But still the house-affairs would draw her	But she would still have to complete
thence:	household duties:
Which ever as she could with haste dispatch,	However, she would complete them quickly
She'ld come again, and with a greedy ear	and come back
Devour up my discourse: which I observing,	So she could listen to more of my stories
Took once a pliant hour, and found good	And she would listen hungrily: realising this,
means	I chose a convenient time to talk to her
To draw from her a prayer of earnest heart	
That I would all my pilgrimage dilate,	

Whereof by parcels she had something heard,	That I would tell her all about my adventures
But not intentively: I did consent,	and any other parts of my stories she might
And often did beguile her of her tears,	have missed,
When I did speak of some distressful stroke	I agreed,
That my youth suffer'd. My story being done,	And found that she often wept,
She gave me for my pains a world of sighs:	When I spoke of some of the distressing
She swore, in faith, twas strange, 'twas	incidents
passing strange,	That I suffered when I was young. When I had
'Twas pitiful, 'twas wondrous pitiful:	finished my full story,
She wish'd she had not heard it, yet she wish'd	She sighed at the amount of pain I had
That heaven had made her such a man: she	endured:
thank'd me,	She told me my story was strange, very
And bade me, if I had a friend that loved her,	strange,
I should but teach him how to tell my story.	That it was sad, very wonderfully sad:
And that would woo her. Upon this hint I	She wished she had not heard it, yet she
spake:	wished
She loved me for the dangers I had pass'd,	That she had a man like me:
And I loved her that she did pity them.	She thanked me,
This only is the witchcraft I have used:	And told me that if I had a friend that loved
Here comes the lady; let her witness it.	her,
	I should teach him how to tell my
	story.
	So that he could win her heart. On this hint I
	spoke out:
	She loved me for the dangers I had
	experienced,
	And I loved her for pitying them.
	That is the only witchcraft I have used:
	Here she comes; she will confirm everything.
Enter DESDEMONA, IAGO, and Attendants	
	Enter DESDEMONA, IAGO, and Attendants
DUKE OF VENICE	**DUKE OF VENICE**

I think this tale would win my daughter too.	I think this story would win my daughter over too.
Good Brabantio,	Brabantio,
Take up this mangled matter at the best:	Make the best of this situation and accept what's happened:
Men do their broken weapons rather use	It is better to have broken weapons than bare hands in battle.
Than their bare hands.	
BRABANTIO	**BRABANTIO**
I pray you, hear her speak:	Please let her speak:
If she confess that she was half the wooer,	If she admits that she also wanted this relationship,
Destruction on my head, if my bad blame	Then I will accept it
Light on the man! Come hither, gentle mistress:	Come here, my gentle girl:
Do you perceive in all this noble company	Can you see the person in this noble company
Where most you owe obedience?	who you most owe your obedience?
DESDEMONA	**DESDEMONA**
My noble father,	My noble father,
I do perceive here a divided duty:	I am torn as I have a divided loyalty:
To you I am bound for life and education;	I will always owe you for my life and my education;
My life and education both do learn me	Both my life and education have taught me to respect you; you're the one I have to obey;
How to respect you; you are the lord of duty;	
I am hitherto your daughter: but here's my husband,	I am your daughter: but this man is my husband,
And so much duty as my mother show'd	And I owe him the same amount my mother
To you, preferring you before her father,	owed you, just as she preferred you to her own father,
So much I challenge that I may profess	So I have to do the same and give my full respect to the Moor, my husband.
Due to the Moor my lord.	
BRABANTIO	**BRABANTIO**

God be wi' you! I have done.

Please it your grace, on to the state-affairs:

I had rather to adopt a child than get it.

Come hither, Moor:

I here do give thee that with all my heart

Which, but thou hast already, with all my heart

I would keep from thee. For your sake, jewel,

I am glad at soul I have no other child:

For thy escape would teach me tyranny,

To hang clogs on them. I have done, my lord.

DUKE OF VENICE

Let me speak like yourself, and lay a sentence,

Which, as a grise or step, may help these lovers

Into your favour.

When remedies are past, the griefs are ended

By seeing the worst, which late on hopes depended.

To mourn a mischief that is past and gone

Is the next way to draw new mischief on.

What cannot be preserved when fortune takes

Patience her injury a mockery makes.

The robb'd that smiles steals something from the thief;

He robs himself that spends a bootless grief.

BRABANTIO

God bless you! I give up.

If you don't mind, Duke, let's get on with state affairs:

I'd rather adopt a child than have one of my own. Come here, Moor:

With all my heart, I give you that

Which, if you didn't already have it,

I'd try with my whole heart to keep from you.

As for you, precious,

I am really glad I don't have any other children because this would make me behave like a tyrant,

I would keep them locked up. I have finished, my lord.

DUKE OF VENICE

Let me speak like you, and tell you something,

Which, as advice, may help you forgive these lovers,

When you keep focussing on something bad that's already happened, more bad things will happen, you will always see the worst

If you keep focusing on the past, which you can't control,

You will attract more bad news.

Fortune will look after this

If a person who has been robbed can still smile then that person is superior to the thief;

But if he cries then he's wasting time.

BRABANTIO

So let the Turks steal Cyprus from us;

So let the Turk of Cyprus us beguile;

We lose it not, so long as we can smile.

He bears the sentence well that nothing bears

But the free comfort which from thence he hears,

But he bears both the sentence and the sorrow

That, to pay grief, must of poor patience borrow.

These sentences, to sugar, or to gall,

Being strong on both sides, are equivocal:

But words are words; I never yet did hear

That the bruised heart was pierced through the ear.

I humbly beseech you, proceed to the affairs of state.

DUKE OF VENICE

The Turk with a most mighty preparation makes for

Cyprus. Othello, the fortitude of the place is best

known to you; and though we have there a substitute

of most allowed sufficiency, yet opinion, a

sovereign mistress of effects, throws a more

safer voice on you: you must therefore be

content to slubber the gloss of your new fortunes with this

more stubborn and boisterous expedition.

OTHELLO

The tyrant custom, most grave senators,

Hath made the flinty and steel couch of war

We won't lose it if we keep smiling.

It's easy to say things like that if you haven't ever experienced loss

And these comforting words which he offers, show that he speaks the words but also feels the same unhappiness

These words, no matter how nice or horrible, are strong on both sides but are vague:

But words are just words; I have never heard of anybody's heart being broken by words.

I beg you, please can we continue with state matters.

DUKE OF VENICE

The well-prepared Turks are making their way towards

Cyprus. Othello, you understand the defences better

than anyone: And even though we have a

good person in charge there already,

everybody else's opinion is that you are the

best and most suitable man for the job: you

must be prepared to put a halt to your

marriage celebrations and take part in this

difficult and dangerous expedition.

OTHELLO

The effects of constant tyranny, esteemed

Senators, have made the hardships and

My thrice-driven bed of down: I do agnise

A natural and prompt alacrity

I find in hardness, and do undertake

These present wars against the Ottomites.

Most humbly therefore bending to your state,

I crave fit disposition for my wife.

Due reference of place and exhibition,

With such accommodation and besort

As levels with her breeding.

difficulties of war a soft bed for me. I do acknowledge

That I have a natural liking and prompt eagerness for the hardness of war, and accept these fights against the Ottomites.

But I humbly ask

And crave that you will offer my wife somewhere suitable to live. She needs accommodation and access to people that would suit her position and status.

DUKE OF VENICE

If you please,

Be't at her father's.

DUKE OF VENICE

She could probably stay at her father's house.

BRABANTIO

I'll not have it so.

BRABANTIO

I will not allow it.

OTHELLO

Nor I.

OTHELLO

Neither will I.

DESDEMONA

Nor I; I would not there reside,

To put my father in impatient thoughts

By being in his eye. Most gracious duke,

To my unfolding lend your prosperous ear;

And let me find a charter in your voice,

To assist my simpleness.

DESDEMONA

And neither will I; I wouldn't stay there, and upset my father by being near him. Dear Duke,

Listen to my idea with your successful ear;

And let me explain my idea and see if you can agree to it.

DUKE OF VENICE

What would You, Desdemona?

DUKE OF VENICE

What do you want to do, Desdemona?

DESDEMONA

That I did love the Moor to live with him,

My downright violence and storm of fortunes

May trumpet to the world: my heart's subdued

Even to the very quality of my lord:

I saw Othello's visage in his mind,

And to his honour and his valiant parts

Did I my soul and fortunes consecrate.

So that, dear lords, if I be left behind,

A moth of peace, and he go to the war,

The rites for which I love him are bereft me,

And I a heavy interim shall support

By his dear absence. Let me go with him.

OTHELLO

Let her have your voices.

Vouch with me, heaven, I therefore beg it not,

To please the palate of my appetite,

Nor to comply with heat--the young affects

In me defunct--and proper satisfaction.

But to be free and bounteous to her mind:

And heaven defend your good souls, that you think

I will your serious and great business scant

For she is with me: no, when light-wing'd toys

Of feather'd Cupid seal with wanton dullness

My speculative and officed instruments,

That my disports corrupt and taint my business,

Let housewives make a skillet of my helm,

And all indign and base adversities

Make head against my estimation!

DESDEMONA

When I fell in love with the Moor I wanted to live with him,

It is clear how much I wanted to be with him by how much trouble it has caused publicly: my heart belongs to him entirely

Even the part of him that is a soldier:

I saw Othello's true qualities when I saw his mind, and I gave my whole soul, life and future to his honour and bravery. So, dear lords, if I am left behind when he goes to war, I would be deprived of everything that makes me love him,

It would be extremely difficult to be without him. Let me go with him.

OTHELLO

Please give her permission.

Heaven knows, I'm not asking because I want her there for sex or to satisfy any other needs,

Not at all for my own desires – I am too old for all that and my sexual urges are dead – I want this because it is what she wants. I love her for her strong mind:

Heaven forbid that you think that I would Neglect this serious and important business If she were with me: no, if I ever let love impact my professional duties, and impact my job,

Then housewives can use my helmet as a saucepan,

And my reputation can be completely eroded!

DUKE OF VENICE

Be it as you shall privately determine,

Either for her stay or going: the affair cries

haste,

And speed must answer it.

First Senator

You must away to-night.

OTHELLO

With all my heart.

DUKE OF VENICE

At nine i' the morning here we'll meet again.

Othello, leave some officer behind,

And he shall our commission bring to you;

With such things else of quality and respect

As doth import you.

OTHELLO

So please your grace, my ancient;

A man he is of honest and trust:

To his conveyance I assign my wife,

With what else needful your good grace shall

think

To be sent after me.

DUKE OF VENICE

Let it be so.

Good night to every one.

To BRABANTIO

DUKE OF VENICE

Decide privately whether or not you think she

should stay or go: this business is urgent,

And you need to decide quickly.

First Senator

You must leave tonight.

OTHELLO

I'll leave with my full heart in this.

DUKE OF VENICE

We will meet again at nine in the morning.

Othello, get an officer to stay behind,

And he will bring your instructions to you;

He will also bring whatever else is important

to you.

OTHELLO

My lord, Iago;

He is an honest and trustworthy man:

I trust him to bring my wife to me,

And anything else that you, your good grace,

want to send to me.

DUKE OF VENICE

Then that is what will happen.

Good night everyone.

To BRABANTIO

And, noble signior, If virtue no delighted beauty lack, Your son-in-law is far more fair than black.	Noble Sir, If virtue means anything, Your son-in-law is beautiful and far more fair than black.
First Senator Adieu, brave Moor, use Desdemona well.	**First Senator** Goodbye, brave Moor, take care of Desdemona.
BRABANTIO Look to her, Moor, if thou hast eyes to see: She has deceived her father, and may thee.	**BRABANTIO** Keep your eyes on Desdemona, Moor, if you can: She has deceived her father and may deceive you too.
Exeunt DUKE OF VENICE, Senators, Officers	*The DUKE, BRABANTIO, CASSIO, SENATORS* *and officers exit.*
OTHELLO My life upon her faith! Honest Iago, My Desdemona must I leave to thee: I prithee, let thy wife attend on her: And bring them after in the best advantage. Come, Desdemona: I have but an hour Of love, of worldly matters and direction, To spend with thee: we must obey the time.	**OTHELLO** I'd bet my life that I can trust her! Honest Iago, I am leaving my Desdemona in your care. Your wife can look after her. Bring them both to Cyprus as soon as you can. Come on, Desdemona. I have only one hour to spend with you and to prepare as well as tell you what you need to do. We must hurry.
Exeunt OTHELLO and DESDEMONA	*OTHELLO and DESDEMONA exit*
RODERIGO Iago.	**RODERIGO** Iago.
IAGO What say'st thou, noble heart?	**IAGO** What do you have to say, dear friend?

RODERIGO

What will I do, thinkest thou?

IAGO

Why, go to bed, and sleep.

RODERIGO

I will incontinently drown myself.

IAGO

If thou dost, I shall never love thee after. Why, thou silly gentleman!

RODERIGO

It is silliness to live when to live is torment; and

then have we a prescription to die when death is our physician.

IAGO

O villainous! I have looked upon the world for four

times seven years; and since I could distinguish

betwixt a benefit and an injury, I never found man

that knew how to love himself. Ere I would say, I

would drown myself for the love of a guinea-hen, I

would change my humanity with a baboon.

RODERIGO

What do you think I should do?

IAGO

Go to bed and go to sleep.

RODERIGO

I'm going to drown myself.

IAGO

If you do that, I shall never respect you again. You silly man!

RODERIGO

It would be silly to stay alive when life is so hard;

Death would be the best cure right now.

IAGO

How stupid! I have been alive for twenty eight years and ever since I could

tell the difference

between good and bad, I have never met a man

that knew how to value himself properly. I would rather

be a baboon than drown myself out of the love I have for a whore.

RODERIGO

What should I do? I confess it is my shame to be so

fond; but it is not in my virtue to amend it.

IAGO

Virtue! a fig! 'tis in ourselves that we are thus or thus. Our bodies are our gardens, to the which our wills are gardeners: so that if we will plant

nettles, or sow lettuce, set hyssop and weed up thyme, supply it with one gender of herbs, or distract it with many, either to have it sterile

with idleness, or manured with industry, why, the power and corrigible authority of this lies in our wills. If the balance of our lives had not one scale of reason to poise another of sensuality, the

blood and baseness of our natures would conduct us to most preposterous conclusions: but we have reason to cool our raging motions, our carnal stings, our unbitted lusts, whereof I take this that

you call love to be a sect or scion.

RODERIGO

It cannot be.

IAGO

It is merely a lust of the blood and a permission of the will. Come, be a man. Drown thyself! Drown cats and blind puppies. I have professed me thy friend and I confess

RODERIGO

What should I do? I know it is ridiculous to be so

in love; but I can't help it. I can't control myself.

IAGO

Don't be ridiculous! Nonsense! What we are and how we behave is up to us.
Our bodies are like a garden and our willpower is the gardener. Depending on what we plant – weeds, lettuce or herb – or even one kind of herb rather than a variety, the garden will either be rich and productive with hard work or it will be useless and barren because of laziness. Whether or not the garden thrives is entirely up to us. If our lives didn't have rational thinking to balance out the emotional reactions and desires, our urges would take over and we would end up in some ridiculous situations: Thankfully, we are born with reasoning skills that calm us down and to stop us acting out our fantasies. In my opinion, I think you are experiencing lust rather than love.

RODERIGO

I don't think so.

IAGO

It is just lust. You have no willpower to control it. Come on, be a man.
Drown yourself? Drown cats and puppies instead. I have told you that You're your

me knit to thy deserving with cables of perdurable toughness; I could never better stead thee than now. Put money in thy purse; follow thou the wars; defeat thy favour with an usurped beard; I say, put money in thy purse. It
cannot be that Desdemona should long continue her love to the Moor,-- put money in thy purse,--nor he his to her: it was a violent commencement, and thou
shalt see an answerable sequestration:--put but money in thy purse. These Moors are changeable in their wills: fill thy purse with money:--the food
that to him now is as luscious as locusts, shall be to him shortly as bitter as coloquintida. She must change for youth: when she is sated with his body,
she will find the error of her choice: she must have change, she must: therefore put money in thy
purse. If thou wilt needs damn thyself, do it a more delicate way than drowning. Make all the money thou canst: if sanctimony and a frail vow betwixt
an erring barbarian and a supersubtle Venetian not too hard for my wits and all the tribe of hell, thou shalt enjoy her; therefore make money. A pox of
drowning thyself! it is clean out of the way: seek thou rather to be hanged in compassing thy joy than to be drowned and go without her.

RODERIGO

friend, and I will support you and help you as well as I can. I could never advise you better or be a better friend than now. Put some money in your purse and follow the war. Disguise yourself, get a false beard; put some money in your purse. Desdemona will not love the Moor forever. Put money in your purse. The Moor will not love her forever either. They fell in love too suddenly. You will see them break up. Put money in your purse. Moors have unstable personalities and feelings. Fill your purse with money. What seems delicious to him now will soon become as botter as crab apples. She will soon want somebody younger than him.
When she has had enough of his body, she will realise the mistake she's made. She'll want a new lover so put money in your purse.
If you want to go to hell then there is a much better way to go than to drown yourself. Make all the money you can. If
False affection and frail vows between a savage and an extremely delicate Venetian cannot get the better of me and all the evil I can muster, then you shall get to sleep with her soon. Just make some money. To hell with drowning yourself! It is out of the question. You might as well be hanged for the way in which you get the woman you want than give up and drown yourself without having her.

RODERIGO

Wilt thou be fast to my hopes, if I depend on the issue?

IAGO

Thou art sure of me:--go, make money:--I have told thee often, and I re-tell thee again and again, I hate the Moor: my cause is hearted; thine hath no

less reason. Let us be conjunctive in our revenge against him: if thou canst cuckold him, thou dost thyself a pleasure, me a sport. There are many

events in the womb of time which will be delivered.

Traverse! go, provide thy money. We will have more of this to-morrow. Adieu.

RODERIGO

Where shall we meet i' the morning?

IAGO

At my lodging.

RODERIGO

I'll be with thee betimes.

IAGO

Go to; farewell. Do you hear, Roderigo?

RODERIGO

What say you?

IAGO

If I depend on you, will you fulfil my hopes?

IAGO

You can rely on me. Go and make money. I have told you many times before, and I will tell you again and again: I hate the Moor. I'm devoted to hating him as much as you are. Let's join forces and get revenge. If you can seduce Desdemona and get her to betray him then you will get your pleasure and I will have some fun. There are lots of things we can do in the time we have.

Go! Go get your money. We will talk again tomorrow. Good bye.

RODERIGO

Where shall we meet in the morning?

IAGO

At my place.

RODERIGO

I'll be there early.

IAGO

Yes, Goodbye. One more thing, Roderigo?

RODERIGO

What is it?

IAGO

No more of drowning, do you hear?

RODERIGO

I am changed: I'll go sell all my land.

Exit

IAGO

Thus do I ever make my fool my purse:

For I mine own gain'd knowledge should profane,

If I would time expend with such a snipe.

But for my sport and profit. I hate the Moor:

And it is thought abroad, that 'twixt my sheets

He has done my office: I know not if't be true;

But I, for mere suspicion in that kind,

Will do as if for surety. He holds me well;

The better shall my purpose work on him.

Cassio's a proper man: let me see now:

To get his place and to plume up my will

In double knavery--How, how? Let's see:--

After some time, to abuse Othello's ear

That he is too familiar with his wife.

He hath a person and a smooth dispose

To be suspected, framed to make women false.

The Moor is of a free and open nature,

That thinks men honest that but seem to be so,

And will as tenderly be led by the nose

As asses are.

I have't. It is engender'd. Hell and night

No more talking about killing yourself, do you hear?

RODERIGO

I've changed my mind. I am going to sell my land.

Roderigo exits

IAGO

That's how I always get money from fools. I'd be wasting my skills and intelligence spending time with an idiot like that if I didn't get something out of it.

I will do it for money and fun. I hate the Moor.

And people abroad think he has slept with my wife.

I don't know if it is true or not but just the suspicion is enough to make me angry and want revenge.

He thinks highly of me.

That'll help me deceive him.

Cassio is a handsome man. Let's see how I can use him to hurt Othello and get his position in the army at the same time. How? How? Let's see.

After a while I'll start telling Othello that Cassio is getting too flirtatious with his wife.

Cassio is attractive and a charming man, he would be suspected of this behaviour.

The Moor is a straightforward and open man who thinks that men who seem honest are honest.

Must bring this monstrous birth to the world's light.	Stupid donkeys like him are easy to deceive.
	So I have decided. I have it all worked out.
	With some help from the devil,
Exit	I'll make sure this monstrous plan works.
	Iago exits.

PART 8: ANALYSING ACT 1 SCENE 3

Themes: Appearance vs Reality, Prejudice, Manhood and Honour, Womanhood and Sexuality, Deception, Honesty, Love, Order and Chaos.

In terms of stagecraft, this scene is much more static when compared to the movement, action, and drama of the previous two scenes because the scene takes place with the Duke and the Senators in a 'council chamber', in a very important meeting discussing their enemy. This location and occasion alongside the status of the characters creates a formal setting, formal enough to explore the idea that a woman may distract a soldier from his duty. The scene begins with the wider cultural conflict and **chaos** of the war before narrowing to return to the conflict between Othello and Brabantio, highlighting the importance of Othello trying to juggle his public duties with his private life. The historical and economic importance of the military crisis of Cyprus sets the scene, possibly as a way for Shakespeare to highlight the value of Cyprus to the Venetians. It could also be symbolic of the widespread **deception** in the world at that time, particularly because of the successes of the Turkish army. By recognising Othello first on entry and then by naming him as the 'valiant' commander of this battle 'we must straight employ you/Against the general enemy Ottoman', the Duke has publicly declared Othello's status, **honour** and importance, as well as his strength and success as a leader. From this point, Othello feels comfortable in his elopement and he says '...I have ta'en away this old man's daughter [....] I'll present/How I did thrive in this fair lady's love...'. He feels protected by his position of authority. It is clear that the Duke needs him to restore **order** so continually gives him the chance to explain himself by inviting him to speak through the interrogative 'What, in your own part, can you say to this? [....] say it, Othello' in order to be able to dismiss Brabantio's claims and focus on more important matters, such as the Turks. In fact, the constant movement between Othello justifying his **love** for Desdemona and the Duke's desire to discuss war is a deliberate structural technique employed by Shakespeare to highlight the conflict Othello will continue to face in life.

Othello's **honest** defence of his marriage and **love** for his wife is dignified, detailed, beautiful and persuasive in its rhetoric and explores the theme of **appearance vs reality in that it challenges how Iago and Brabantio have presented Othello**:

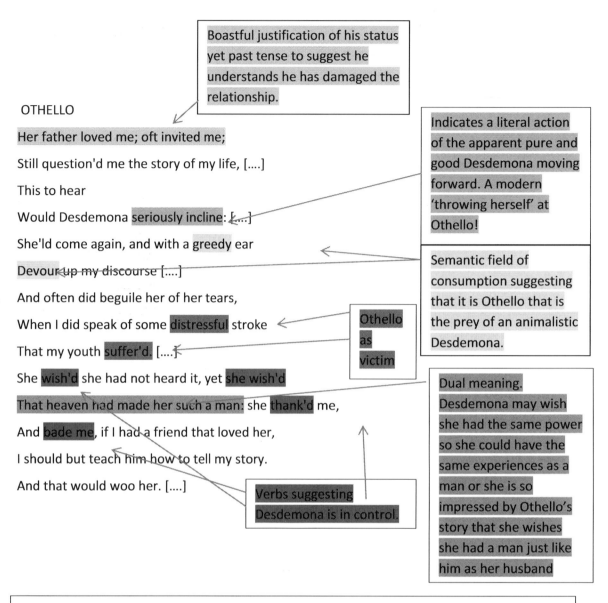

Boastful justification of his status yet past tense to suggest he understands he has damaged the relationship.

Indicates a literal action of the apparent pure and good Desdemona moving forward. A modern 'throwing herself' at Othello!

Semantic field of consumption suggesting that it is Othello that is the prey of an animalistic Desdemona.

Othello as victim

Dual meaning. Desdemona may wish she had the same power so she could have the same experiences as a man or she is so impressed by Othello's story that she wishes she had a man just like him as her husband

Verbs suggesting Desdemona is in control.

OTHELLO

Her father loved me; oft invited me;

Still question'd me the story of my life, [....]

This to hear

Would Desdemona seriously incline: [....]

She'ld come again, and with a greedy ear

Devour up my discourse [....]

And often did beguile her of her tears,

When I did speak of some distressful stroke

That my youth suffer'd. [....]

She wish'd she had not heard it, yet she wish'd

That heaven had made her such a man: she thank'd me,

And bade me, if I had a friend that loved her,

I should but teach him how to tell my story.

And that would woo her. [....]

This monologue in its entirety contains many effective oratorical devices such as alliteration, metaphor, parallelism, and repetition, supporting the fact that Othello is a powerful and skilled speaker.

Othello is aware of this seductive power of his life story and is confident that it will succeed in convincing the Duke of his innocence. He is composed, he waits his turn to speak, and he apologises before speaking for the fact that he may not be eloquent enough ('Rude am I in my speech') even though he knows he is. Othello is an intelligent man who has had many successes as an orator. However, his disingenuous apology for lack of eloquence prior to his truthful rhetoric can be forgiven when contrasted with Brabantio's irrational outbursts and Iago's lies. In fact, when Iago speaks he speaks in prose which is one of the reasons that Othello believes him to be 'honest', further suggesting that Othello knows exactly how powerful (and possibly deliberately manipulative) his rhetoric is. Unfortunately for Othello, his speech also suggests he is self-consumed and insecure because he appears to be concerned by public perceptions (later repeated in his final speech), especially with regards to his sexual relationship with Desdemona:

Othello

...Vouch with me, heaven, I therefore beg it not,

To please the palate of my appetite,

Nor to comply with heat--the young affects

In me defunct--and proper satisfaction.

But to be free and bounteous to her mind:

> Othello would rather admit to impotence than to having sex with his wife- a white woman seen to be pure.

New historicist critical reading would suggest that Othello's awareness of cultural ideologies and attitudes towards interracial marriage (possibly based on the fact that scientific racism was common during the 1600s) are the reason he publicly explains his apparently sexless marriage. It may also be admittance to not yet having consummated the marriage and, therefore, presents Desdemona and Othello's **love** as either genuinely romantic or mismatched and incapable of consummation.

Othello is keen to constantly challenge how he appears to others and knows how to generate support. The Duke's reaction to Othello's insistence that he be executed ('If you do find me foul...let your sentence...fall upon my life') for Brabantio's accusation of witchcraft further proves Othello's military importance. After initially sympathising with Brabantio and claiming that Othello and Desdemona are not compatible due to their differing races, the Duke declares that Othello's story would '...win my daughter too' giving Desdemona the stage to support Othello and switch her loyalty from her father to her husband. The Duke uses the imperative 'Fetch Desdemona hither' to further the theme of womanhood and sexuality.

Regardless of the apparent freedom of speech that Desdemona is about to have, feminist critics (those who explore the gender politics by considering the role of male and female characters in the patriarchal context of the play) suggest that the control the Duke has over Desdemona's presence is proof that she is an object to be used to her husband's advantage. Although women were expected to be silent, they were also expected to be obedient to all men due to the belief that they were inferior, both psychologically and physically. Therefore, Desdemona's defence of her actions as a

16th century women is as expected as it is courageous and disobedient, and reveals her commitment to her husband.

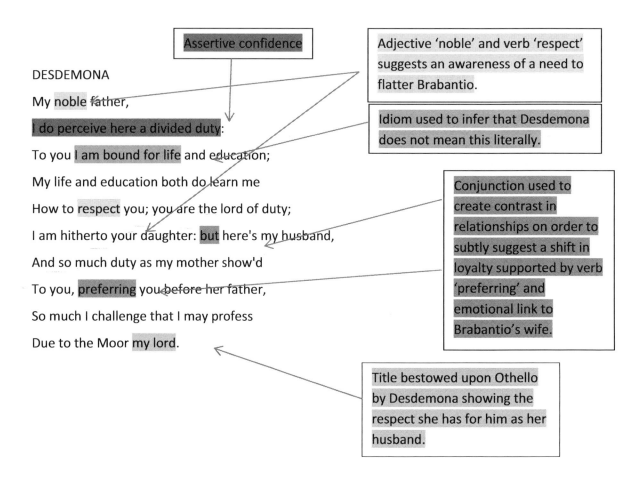

Assertive confidence

DESDEMONA

My noble father,

I do perceive here a divided duty:

To you I am bound for life and education;

My life and education both do learn me

How to respect you; you are the lord of duty;

I am hitherto your daughter: but here's my husband,

And so much duty as my mother show'd

To you, preferring you before her father,

So much I challenge that I may profess

Due to the Moor my lord.

Adjective 'noble' and verb 'respect' suggests an awareness of a need to flatter Brabantio.

Idiom used to infer that Desdemona does not mean this literally.

Conjunction used to create contrast in relationships on order to subtly suggest a shift in loyalty supported by verb 'preferring' and emotional link to Brabantio's wife.

Title bestowed upon Othello by Desdemona showing the respect she has for him as her husband.

Of course, her determination to defend her husband could be viewed as either an expectation of her role as a woman and wife, or as the brave and rebellious words of a strong woman who defies the traditional beliefs by surpassing the norms of sexual morality. Desdemona's role, although complex, certainly explores how a male-dominated society treats women, regardless of their strength and status. Brabantio began the scene by exploring Desdemona's womanhood and sexuality as demure, innocent and pure when he claimed she was a '… maiden never bold;/Of spirit so still and quiet, that her motion/Blush'd at herself…' therefore, Desdemona's admission of **deception** is a public challenge to his **manhood and honour**, creating the conflicting views that critics have and the belief that she deserves her fate. Desdemona's directness can also be seen with her request to join Othello in Cyprus 'Let me go with him' again, a socially unacceptable behaviour for a woman of the time. Desdemona's earlier claims to be a submissive wife are now contradicted by her demands to accompany Othello to Cyprus.

Brabantio shows he will never understand the relationship and calls his daughter a 'jewel', suggesting ownership.

Although it appears that Desdemona and Othello have succeeded in their justification of their marriage, Iago is not satisfied by the commitment between the lovers, regardless of Othello's reference (twice) to Iago as 'honest' and therefore trustworthy (a deliberately ironic dramatic technique to highlight Iago's manipulation and Othello's foolish trust in him). He ends the scene by directing his frustration (at having failed to cause conflict) at Roderigo calling him 'silly' as well as referring to Desdemona as a 'guinea-hen'. He reminds the audience of his evil nature by mocking Roderigo's suggestion that he is going to drown himself as 'villainous', and extorting more money (repetition of 'money' and 'purse' alongside the imperative 'Go get your money') with the promise that their plot to destroy Othello and have Desdemona fall in love with Roderigo will continue in Cyprus. Iago's metaphorical remark to Roderigo that 'Our bodies are our gardens' confirms his intention to 'grow' in power and control once he moves to Cyprus. Iago's soliloquy that ends the act introduces the idea that another reason for his hatred of Othello is that he has apparently had sex with his wife. This further indicates Iago's commitment to move on to the next stage of his plan by continuing to convince himself and others that Othello is an 'ass'. The use of blank verse to deliver the soliloquy is a demonstration of his ability to manipulate those around him (including the audience) into believing his motives.

IAGO

Thus do I ever make my fool my purse:

For I mine own gain'd knowledge should profane,

If I would time expend with such a snipe.

But for my sport and profit. I hate the Moor:

And it is thought abroad, that 'twixt my sheets

He has done my office: I know not if't be true;

But I, for mere suspicion in that kind,

Will do as if for surety. He holds me well;

The better shall my purpose work on him.

Cassio's a proper man: let me see now:

To get his place and to plume up my will

In double knavery--How, how? Let's see:--

After some time, to abuse Othello's ear

> Metaphorically referring to Roderigo as an object that is only useful to him for money. He is Iago's purse.

> Spitting anger shown by powerful and direct verb 'hate' surrounded by other monosyllabic words.

> Accusation that Othello has had sex with Iago's wife. Justification for his hatred. Possibly untrue.

> Metaphorical reference to his wife as an object. Deprives her of humanity.

> Adjective 'proper' suggests that Cassio is right and appropriate according to Venetian society. A Marxist critical view based on hierarchy. Cassio is above Iago.

That he is too familiar with his wife.

He hath a person and a smooth dispose

To be suspected, framed to make women false.

The Moor is of a free and open nature,

That thinks men honest that but seem to be so,

And will as tenderly be led by the nose

As asses are.

I have't. It is engender'd. Hell and night

Must bring this monstrous birth to the world's light.

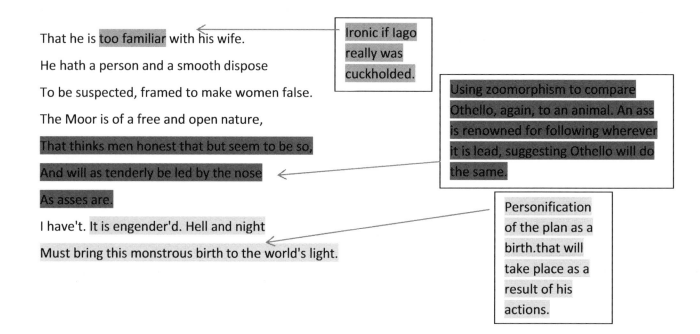

Ironic if Iago really was cuckholded.

Using zoomorphism to compare Othello, again, to an animal. An ass is renowned for following wherever it is lead, suggesting Othello will do the same.

Personification of the plan as a birth.that will take place as a result of his actions.

The play departs to a new setting – one that is not governed by law and order - where Iago's power and manipulation can intensify unchallenged.

ORIGINAL TEXT:	MODERN TRANSLATION:
SCENE I. A Sea-port in Cyprus. An open place near the quay.	**SCENE I. A Sea-port in Cyprus. An open place near the quay.**
Enter MONTANO and two Gentlemen	*Enter MONTANO and two Gentlemen*
MONTANO What from the cape can you discern at sea?	**MONTANO** What can you see out in the ocean?
First Gentleman Nothing at all: it is a highwrought flood; I cannot, 'twixt the heaven and the main, Descry a sail.	**First Gentleman** Nothing at all. The water is so high and rough that I cannot see any sails, either in the sky or in the sea.
MONTANO Methinks the wind hath spoke aloud at land; A fuller blast ne'er shook our battlements: If it hath ruffian'd so upon the sea, What ribs of oak, when mountains melt on them, Can hold the mortise? What shall we hear of this?	**MONTANO** I think the wind is deafening here on the Island. I've never known the wind to be so strong that it has badly shaken our battlements. If it is hitting the sea this powerfully what kind of ship can hold together when the waves are like mountains? What do you think is happening out there? What will happen?
Second Gentleman A segregation of the Turkish fleet: For do but stand upon the foaming shore, The chidden billow seems to pelt the clouds; The wind-shaked surge, with high and monstrous mane, seems to cast water on the burning bear,	**Second Gentleman** The Turkish ships will have broken up. Go and stand on the shore. The wind seems to be battering the clouds. The waves are so high and monstrous

And quench the guards of the ever-fixed pole:

I never did like molestation view

On the enchafed flood.

MONTANO

If that the Turkish fleet

Be not enshelter'd and embay'd, they are drown'd:

It is impossible they bear it out.

Enter a third Gentleman

Third Gentleman

News, lads! our wars are done.

The desperate tempest hath so bang'd the Turks,

That their designment halts: a noble ship of Venice

Hath seen a grievous wreck and sufferance

On most part of their fleet.

MONTANO

How! is this true?

Third Gentleman

The ship is here put in,

A Veronesa; Michael Cassio,

Lieutenant to the warlike Moor Othello,

Is come on shore: the Moor himself at sea,

And is in full commission here for Cyprus.

MONTANO

that they look as though they are drenching the stars

And putting their lights out.

I have never seen any waters so disturbed.

MONTANO

If the Turkish fleet

Isn't protected in a harbour somewhere then their men will be drowned.

It is impossible for them to survive this.

Enter a third Gentleman

Third Gentleman

I've got news. Lads! The war is over.

The terrible storm has damaged the Turks so badly

That their plans to fight are ruined. One of our ships

Has seen most of their fleet shipwrecked and probably dead.

MONTANO

What? Is this true?

Third Gentleman

The ship is sailing into harbour now. Michael Cassio from Verona, Lieutenant to the warrior Moor Othello,

Has arrived on shore. The Moor is still at sea but is on his way,

He's been commissioned to come to Cyprus.

MONTANO

I am glad on't; 'tis a worthy governor.

Third Gentleman

But this same Cassio, though he speak of comfort

Touching the Turkish loss, yet he looks sadly,

And prays the Moor be safe; for they were parted

With foul and violent tempest.

MONTANO

Pray heavens he be;

For I have served him, and the man commands

Like a full soldier. Let's to the seaside, ho!

As well to see the vessel that's come in

As to throw out our eyes for brave Othello,

Even till we make the main and the aerial blue

An indistinct regard.

Third Gentleman

Come, let's do so:

For every minute is expectancy

Of more arrivance.

Enter CASSIO

CASSIO

Thanks, you the valiant of this warlike isle,

That so approve the Moor! O, let the heavens

Give him defence against the elements,

For I have lost us him on a dangerous sea.

I'm really pleased. He will be a good general.

Third Gentleman

Although Cassio brings some comforting news

Regarding the Turks' loss, he looks really unhappy,

And is praying the Moor is safe. They were separated

By the terrible and violent storm.

MONTANO

I pray to heaven that he is ok.

I have served under him and know what an excellent soldier he is.

Let's go to the shore,

And see the ship that has just arrived and to look out for brave Othello's ship.

We will stare out to sea until our eyes become blurred and we can no longer tell the difference between the sea and the sky.

Third Gentleman

Come on. Let's do it.

We expect more ships to arrive every minute.

Enter CASSIO

CASSIO

Thanks to you brave men who defend this island,

And that respect the Moor. I hope the heavens

Protect him against the weather,

Because I lost him out on the dangerous sea.

MONTANO	**MONTANO**
Is he well shipp'd?	Is his ship strong?
CASSIO	**CASSIO**
His bark is stoutly timber'd, his pilot	It is well-built, and the pilot of the ship is very
Of very expert and approved allowance;	experienced and an expert.
Therefore my hopes, not surfeited to death,	This gives me hope that he has survived,
Stand in bold cure.	
A cry within 'A sail, a sail, a sail!'	*A cry within 'A sail, a sail, a sail!'*
Enter a fourth Gentleman	*Enter a fourth Gentleman*
CASSIO	**CASSIO**
What noise?	What's that noise?
Fourth Gentleman	**Fourth Gentleman**
The town is empty; on the brow o' the sea	The town is empty. All the people from the
Stand ranks of people, and they cry 'A sail!'	town have come to stand on the edge of the
	sea and they are shouting 'A sail!'
CASSIO	**CASSIO**
My hopes do shape him for the governor.	I really do hope it is the General.
Guns heard	*Guns heard*
Second Gentlemen	**Second Gentlemen**
They do discharge their shot of courtesy:	They have fired a greeting shot. It seems to be
Our friends at least.	a friendly ship.
CASSIO	**CASSIO**
I pray you, sir, go forth,	Please go and find out for certain who has
And give us truth who 'tis that is arrived.	arrived.

Second Gentleman

I shall.

Exit

MONTANO

But, good lieutenant, is your general wived?

CASSIO

Most fortunately: he hath achieved a maid

That paragons description and wild fame;

One that excels the quirks of blazoning pens,

And in the essential vesture of creation

Does tire the ingener.

Re-enter second Gentleman

How now! who has put in?

Second Gentleman

'Tis one Iago, ancient to the general.

CASSIO

Has had most favourable and happy speed:

Tempests themselves, high seas, and howling

winds,

The gutter'd rocks and congregated sands--

Traitors ensteep'd to clog the guiltless keel,--

As having sense of beauty, do omit

Their mortal natures, letting go safely by

The divine Desdemona.

Second Gentleman

I will.

Exit

MONTANO

Tell me, Lieutenant, is your general married?

CASSIO

Yes, and he's been very lucky to have married

the woman he did

She defies description and exaggeration.

She outshines any written word,

And is God's masterpiece. She would exhaust

anybody trying to praise her.

Re-enter second Gentleman

Well? Who has arrived?

Second Gentleman

It's Iago, ensign to the General.

CASSIO

He's done really well and made good time.

The storm, the high seas, the howling winds

The jagged rocks and the sand banks

That trap enemy ships

All appreciate the beauty that defies their

murderous nature,

They let the lovely Desdemona arrive safely.

73

MONTANO

What is she?

CASSIO

She that I spake of, our great captain's

captain,

Left in the conduct of the bold Iago,

Whose footing here anticipates our thoughts

A se'nnight's speed. Great Jove, Othello guard,

And swell his sail with thine own powerful

breath,

That he may bless this bay with his tall ship,

Make love's quick pants in Desdemona's arms,

Give renew'd fire to our extinced spirits

And bring all Cyprus comfort!

Enter DESDEMONA, EMILIA, IAGO, RODERIGO,

and Attendants

O, behold,

The riches of the ship is come on shore!

Ye men of Cyprus, let her have your knees.

Hail to thee, lady! and the grace of heaven,

Before, behind thee, and on every hand,

Enwheel thee round!

DESDEMONA

I thank you, valiant Cassio.

What tidings can you tell me of my lord?

MONTANO

Who is she?

CASSIO

She's the woman I was talking about, the

general's wife.

She was left in the care of the brave Iago, and

he has arrived here a week earlier than we

expected.

Oh God, please protect Othello,

use your breath to help his sails work to get

him here,

So that he will bless this bay with his mighty

ship,

And fall panting into Desdemona's loving

arms,

He will raise our exhausted spirits

And bring comfort to Cyprus!

Enter DESDEMONA, EMILIA, IAGO, RODERIGO,

and Attendants

Oh look,

The precious Desdemona has arrived on

shore!

Men of Cyprus, kneel before her.

Greetings, lady! May God be with you no

matter where you are!

DESDEMONA

Thank you, brave Cassio.

Can you give me any news about my husband?

CASSIO

He is not yet arrived: nor know I aught
But that he's well and will be shortly here.

CASSIO

He hasn't arrived yet As far as I am aware, he is alright and will be here soon.

DESDEMONA

O, but I fear--How lost you company?

DESDEMONA

Oh, but I am worried. How did you get separated?

CASSIO

The great contention of the sea and skies
Parted our fellowship--But, hark! a sail.

CASSIO

The storm separated us.
But look! A sail.

Within 'A sail, a sail!' Guns heard

Within 'A sail, a sail!' Guns heard

Second Gentleman

They give their greeting to the citadel;
This likewise is a friend.

Second Gentleman

They have fired a greeting shot. It is a friendly ship.

CASSIO

See for the news.

CASSIO

Go and find out the news.

Exit Gentleman

Exit Gentleman

Good ancient, you are welcome.

Good Iago, welcome.

To EMILIA
Welcome, mistress.
Let it not gall your patience, good Iago,
That I extend my manners; 'tis my breeding
That gives me this bold show of courtesy.

To EMILIA
Welcome, mistress.
I hope you don't mind if I give your wife a kiss, Iago.
It is good manners where I come from.
I was brought up to greet her this way.

Kissing her	*Kissing her*
IAGO	**IAGO**
Sir, would she give you so much of her lips	Sir, if she gave you the same amount of her lips
As of her tongue she oft bestows on me,	As she gives me of her tongue you will not want anymore.
You'll have enough.	
DESDEMONA	**DESDEMONA**
Alas, she has no speech.	She's speechless.
IAGO	**IAGO**
In faith, too much;	She usually talks too much.
I find it still, when I have list to sleep:	And it is usually when I am trying to sleep. Of course, in front of you, she stays quiet and thinks a lot instead.
Marry, before your ladyship, I grant,	
She puts her tongue a little in her heart,	
And chides with thinking.	She's scolding me silently.
EMILIA	**EMILIA**
You have little cause to say so.	You have no reason to say that.
IAGO	**IAGO**
Come on, come on; you are pictures out of doors,	Come on. You women are all exactly the same. You are as pretty as pictures when in public but in your own houses you are really noisy and act like animals. You make yourselves sound like saints but are devils when someone offends you. You don't take your role as housewives seriously and you are hussies in bed.
Bells in your parlors, wild-cats in your kitchens,	
Saints m your injuries, devils being offended,	
Players in your housewifery, and housewives' in your beds.	
DESDEMONA	**DESDEMONA**
O, fie upon thee, slanderer!	Shame on you, slanderer!

IAGO

Nay, it is true, or else I am a Turk:

You rise to play and go to bed to work.

EMILIA

You shall not write my praise.

IAGO

No, let me not.

DESDEMONA

What wouldst thou write of me, if thou

shouldst

praise me?

IAGO

O gentle lady, do not put me to't;

For I am nothing, if not critical.

DESDEMONA

Come on assay. There's one gone to the

harbour?

IAGO

Ay, madam.

DESDEMONA

I am not merry; but I do beguile

The thing I am, by seeming otherwise.

Come, how wouldst thou praise me?

IAGO

No, it is true, or I am a Turk.

You get up to play and go to bed to work.

EMILIA

You have nothing good to say about me.

IAGO

No, I don't.

DESDEMONA

What would you say about me, if you had

something

nice to say?

IAGO

Oh lovely lady, don't make me do it.

I am really critical.

DESDEMONA

Come on, try. Has someone gone down to the

harbour?

IAGO

Yes, miss.

DESDEMONA

I am not as happy as I seem to be. I am trying

my best to not show how worried I am. Come

on, what nice things would you say about

me?

IAGO

I am about it; but indeed my invention

Comes from my pate as birdlime does from frize;

It plucks out brains and all: but my Muse labours,

And thus she is deliver'd.

If she be fair and wise, fairness and wit,

The one's for use, the other useth it.

DESDEMONA

Well praised! How if she be black and witty?

IAGO

If she be black, and thereto have a wit,

She'll find a white that shall her blackness fit.

DESDEMONA

Worse and worse.

EMILIA

How if fair and foolish?

IAGO

She never yet was foolish that was fair;

For even her folly help'd her to an heir.

DESDEMONA

These are old fond paradoxes to make fools laugh i'

the alehouse. What miserable praise hast thou for

her that's foul and foolish?

IAGO

I am trying to think of something but I'm struggling to be inventive. I'm really stuck.

But I am working really hard to be creative. I've got it.

If a woman is pretty and intelligent, fair and funny

She will use it to her advantage.

DESDEMONA

Well done! What if she is smart and black?

IAGO

If she is black, and intelligent,

She will find a white man who will match her.

DESDEMONA

It just gets worse.

EMILIA

What if she's pretty but stupid?

IAGO

There isn't a pretty woman who's stupid.

Even a woman who pretends to be stupid can get a man.

DESDEMONA

These are old and stupid ideas that only make idiots laugh in

the pub. What horrible thing do you have to say about a woman who is ugly and stupid?

IAGO	**IAGO**
There's none so foul and foolish thereunto,	There's not a woman who is ugly and stupid
But does foul pranks which fair and wise ones	who is unable to get up to the same nasty
do.	tricks as the beautiful and intelligent women.
DESDEMONA	**DESDEMONA**
O heavy ignorance! thou praisest the worst	You are so ignorant! You give the best praise
best.	to the worst.
But what praise couldst thou bestow on a	But what praise would you give to the most
deserving	deserving
woman indeed, one that, in the authority of	woman, one that has no reason to worry
her merit, did justly put on the vouch of very	about what anyone said about her?
malice itself?	
IAGO	**IAGO**
She that was ever fair and never proud,	A woman that's beautiful but not proud,
Had tongue at will and yet was never loud,	Who speaks well but knows when to be quiet,
Never lack'd gold and yet went never gay,	Who dresses well but doesn't overdress,
Fled from her wish and yet said 'Now I may,'	Controls her selfish desires but knows when
She that being anger'd, her revenge being	to ask for something,
nigh,	Who, when angry, doesn't seek revenge
Bade her wrong stay and her displeasure fly,	But stays quiet and allows her anger to pass,
She that in wisdom never was so frail	A woman that was never weak with what she
To change the cod's head for the salmon's tail;	knows, and never wants to change an ugly
She that could think and ne'er disclose her	husband for a handsome one.
mind,	She who thinks deeply but never discloses her
See suitors following and not look behind,	thoughts,
She was a wight, if ever such wight were,--	She who can see that men are attracted to
	her but doesn't flirt with them – would be a
	great woman, if there was ever such a woman
	she would do…
DESDEMONA	**DESDEMONA**
To do what?	Do what?

IAGO

To suckle fools and chronicle small beer.

DESDEMONA

O most lame and impotent conclusion! Do not learn of him, Emilia, though he be thy husband. How say you, Cassio? is he not a most profane and liberal counsellor?

CASSIO

He speaks home, madam: You may relish him more in the soldier than in the scholar.

IAGO

[Aside] He takes her by the palm: ay, well said, whisper: with as little a web as this will I ensnare as great a fly as Cassio. Ay, smile upon her, do; I will gyve thee in thine own courtship.
You say true; 'tis so, indeed: if such tricks as these strip you out of your lieutenantry, it had been better you had not kissed your three fingers so oft, which now again you are most apt to play the sir in. Very good; well kissed! an excellent courtesy! 'tis so, indeed. Yet again your fingers to your lips? would they were clyster-pipes for your sake!

IAGO

Breastfeed fools and record insignificant things.

DESDEMONA

What a stupid conclusion! Do not listen to him, Emilia, even if he is your husband. What do you think, Cassio? isn't he a horrible and disgusting man?

CASSIO

He is very blunt, madam. Value him as a soldier rather than a wise man.

IAGO

[to himself] he is holding her hand. That's right, go ahead,
Whisper together.
This is exactly what I need to trap Cassio. Yes, keep smiling at her. Your charm will be your downfall.
I am sure you are saying something interesting. If you lose your job because of this, you'll wish you had never kissed your own fingers so often.
You are kissing you fingers in a courtly way, and acting like a gentleman. Well done. Well kissed. Are you putting your fingers to your lips again? I wish they were surgical instruments for your sake!

Trumpet within	*Trumpet within*
The Moor! I know his trumpet.	That's the Moor! I know his trumpet.
CASSIO	**CASSIO**
'Tis truly so.	Yes, it is.
DESDEMONA	**DESDEMONA**
Let's meet him and receive him.	Let's go and greet him.
CASSIO	**CASSIO**
Lo, where he comes!	Look, here he comes!
Enter OTHELLO and Attendants	*Enter OTHELLO and Attendants*
OTHELLO	**OTHELLO**
O my fair warrior!	My beautiful warrior!
DESDEMONA	**DESDEMONA**
My dear Othello!	My darling Othello!
OTHELLO	**OTHELLO**
It gives me wonder great as my content	It's wonderful to see you here before me. I
To see you here before me. O my soul's joy!	am so happy!
If after every tempest come such calms,	If it is this lovely after every storm then I hope
May the winds blow till they have waken'd	that every storm gets the wind to blow so
death!	hard that it will wake up the dead!
And let the labouring bark climb hills of seas	And will let the struggling ships climb hills of
Olympus-high and duck again as low	seas
As hell's from heaven! If it were now to die,	so high that they will have to dive as low as
'Twere now to be most happy; for, I fear,	hell is from heaven! If I died now
My soul hath her content so absolute	at least I would be at my happiest. I am
That not another comfort like to this	scared
Succeeds in unknown fate.	that I am so happy

	that the future couldn't possibly bring anymore happiness.
DESDEMONA	**DESDEMONA**
The heavens forbid	Heaven forbid
But that our loves and comforts should increase,	that our love and happiness should not increase
Even as our days do grow!	as each day goes by!
OTHELLO	**OTHELLO**
Amen to that, sweet powers!	Amen to that!
I cannot speak enough of this content;	I cannot tell you how happy I am anymore.
It stops me here; it is too much of joy:	It's too much. And let this be the closest we
And this, and this, the greatest discords be	ever get to fighting
Kissing her	*Kissing her*
That e'er our hearts shall make!	The closest our hearts will ever get to a fall out!
IAGO	**IAGO**
[Aside] O, you are well tuned now!	[to himself] Oh, you're happy now!
But I'll set down the pegs that make this music,	I will soon cause all the problems that will ruin your lives,
As honest as I am.	Even if I am supposed to be honest.
OTHELLO	**OTHELLO**
Come, let us to the castle.	Come on, let's go to the castle.
News, friends; our wars are done, the Turks are drown'd.	God news, friends. The war is over and the Turks have drowned.
How does my old acquaintance of this isle?	How are my old friends of this island doing?
Honey, you shall be well desired in Cyprus;	Honey, they will love you here in Cyprus.
I have found great love amongst them. O my sweet,	They have always been very good to me.

I prattle out of fashion, and I dote
In mine own comforts. I prithee, good Iago,
Go to the bay and disembark my coffers:
Bring thou the master to the citadel;
He is a good one, and his worthiness
Does challenge much respect. Come, Desdemona,
Once more, well met at Cyprus.

Exeunt OTHELLO, DESDEMONA, and Attendants

IAGO

Do thou meet me presently at the harbour.
Come hither. If thou be'st valiant,-- as, they
say, base men being in love have then a
nobility in their
natures more than is native to them--list me.
The lieutenant tonight watches on the court of
guard:--first, I must tell thee this--Desdemona
is directly in love with him.

RODERIGO

With him! why, 'tis not possible.

IAGO

Lay thy finger thus, and let thy soul be
instructed.
Mark me with what violence she first loved
the Moor,
but for bragging and telling her fantastical lies:
and will she love him still for prating? let not
thy discreet heart think it. Her eye must be

Oh, my dear,
I am babbling because I am so happy, but I am
being selfish,
Iago,
Go to the bay and get my luggage.
Bring the ship's captain to the castle.
He is a good man, and he deserves a lot of
respect. Come on,
Desdemona,
Once again, a wonderful reunion in Cyprus.

Exit OTHELLO, DESDEMONA, and Attendants

IAGO

Meet me down at the harbour.
Come here, if you are worthy. When
unworthy men are in love it apparently makes
them brave and noble in their actions more
than they usually are.
Listen to me. The lieutenant will be on guard
tonight but first I have to tell you that
Desdemona's completely in love with him.

RODERIGO

With Cassio! That's not possible.

IAGO

Be quiet and listen to me. Let me tell you this.
Remember how madly she fell in love with
the Moor
because he bragged and told her made-up
stories?

fed;

and what delight shall she have to look on the devil? When the blood is made dull with the act of sport, there should be, again to inflame it and to give satiety a fresh appetite, loveliness in favour, sympathy in years, manners and beauties; all which the Moor is defective in: now, for want of these required conveniences, her delicate tenderness will find itself abused, begin to heave the gorge, disrelish and abhor the Moor; very nature will instruct her in it and compel her to some second choice. Now, sir, this granted,--as it is a most pregnant and unforced position--who stands so eminent in the degree of this fortune as Cassio does? a knave very voluble; no further conscionable than in putting on the mere form of civil and humane seeming, for the better compassing of his salt and most hidden loose affection? why, none; why, none: a slipper and subtle knave, a finder of occasions, that has an eye can stamp and counterfeit advantages, though true advantage never present itself; a devilish knave. Besides, the knave is handsome, young, and hath all those

requisites in him that folly and green minds look after: a pestilent complete knave; and the woman hath found him already.

Did you think she would continue to love him for this chattering? Don't think that! She needs someone good-looking.

She can't like looking at Othello. He looks like the devil. When sex becomes boring she will need something else to excite her and give her lust a fresh appetite. She needs someone young and attractive. Someone who has manners and beauty, everything that the Moor does not have. Because she will want all of these things, she will not want her youthful beauty to go to waste. She will become revolted by and disgusted with the Moor. She will start to hate him. She will start to look for a second choice. Sir, if that's all true, which it obviously is, who is in a better and more fortunate position to be second choice than Cassio? He's a knave.

He is good at pretending not to be superficial. He puts on a good show and seems like a nice guy. But all of this is just so he can fulfil his lustful desires.

He is a slimy and devious knave that knows exactly how to pretend to be interested in someone. He is a devil.

But he's young and handsome and has all the qualities that young naïve and silly girls go for.

He is a bad boy and Desdemona already has her eye on him.

RODERIGO

RODERIGO

I cannot believe that in her; she's full of most blessed condition.

IAGO

Blessed fig's-end! the wine she drinks is made of grapes: if she had been blessed, she would never have loved the Moor. Blessed pudding! Didst thou
not see her paddle with the palm of his hand? didst not mark that?

RODERIGO

Yes, that I did; but that was but courtesy.

IAGO

Lechery, by this hand; an index and obscure prologue to the history of lust and foul thoughts. They met
so near with their lips that their breaths embraced together. Villanous thoughts, Roderigo! when these
mutualities so marshal the way, hard at hand comes the master and main exercise, the incorporate conclusion, Pish! But, sir, be you ruled by me: I
have brought you from Venice. Watch you to-night; for the command, I'll lay't upon you. Cassio knows you not. I'll not be far from you: do you find some occasion to anger Cassio, either by speaking too loud, or tainting his discipline; or from what
other course you please, which the time shall more favourably minister.

I can't believe that of her. She's just so lovely and blessed.

IAGO

Like hell she's lovely and blessed!
She is a person like everybody else. Is she were blessed then she would never have fallen for the Moor. Blessed? Don't be ridiculous. Didn't you see her holding Cassio's hand? Didn't you see that?

RODERIGO

Yes, I did but that was just good manners.

IAGO

They were flirting. That's just the start of lustful and disgusting thoughts; Their lips were so close that their breaths might as well have been embracing. Mischievous thoughts. Roderigo! When this type of behaviour starts to happen sex will soon follow –
the physical conclusion.
Disgusting! But, sir, let me guide you. I have brought you here from Venice.
Make sure you are on guard duty tonight. I'll show you. Cassio doesn't know you yet. I won't be that far away from you. Find something to make Cassio angry, either by speaking too loudly or by insulting him, or however else you want too in the time that we have.

RODERIGO

Well.

IAGO

Sir, he is rash and very sudden in choler, and haply may strike at you: provoke him, that he may; for even out of that will I cause these of Cyprus to

mutiny; whose qualification shall come into no true taste again but by the displanting of Cassio. So shall you have a shorter journey to your desires by

the means I shall then have to prefer them; and the impediment most profitably removed, without the

which there were no expectation of our prosperity.

RODERIGO

I will do this, if I can bring it to any opportunity.

IAGO

I warrant thee. Meet me by and by at the citadel:

I must fetch his necessaries ashore. Farewell.

RODERIGO

Adieu.

Exit

IAGO

RODERIGO

All right.

IAGO

Sir, he is bad-tempered and very easy to anger and may perhaps hit you. Provoke him. From that I can get people here in Cyprus to react. They will be so angry and will only calm down once Cassio is fired. This will be a quicker way to get what you want and I will then be able to get the obstacle out of the way. If you don't do it then things will be hopeless and we will not be successful in our plan.

RODERIGO

I will do it, if you can take advantage of the situation.

IAGO

I guarantee it. Meet me later at the castle. I have to bring Othello's luggage from the ship. Goodbye.

RODERIGO

Goodbye.

Exit

IAGO

That Cassio loves her, I do well believe it;	I think Cassio loves her. I really do believe he does.
That she loves him, 'tis apt and of great credit:	
The Moor, howbeit that I endure him not,	It is likely that she loves him too.
Is of a constant, loving, noble nature,	I hate the Moor but I have to admit
And I dare think he'll prove to Desdemona	He is reliable, loving, and a good-natured
A most dear husband. Now, I do love her too;	man. He'd be a good husband to Desdemona
Not out of absolute lust, though peradventure	A really good husband. I love her too.
I stand accountant for as great a sin,	Not out of lust but to feed my revenge
But partly led to diet my revenge,	I have a feeling that the Moor slept with my
For that I do suspect the lusty Moor	wife. The thought keeps
Hath leap'd into my seat; the thought whereof	bothering me. Like poison, it is eating me up
Doth, like a poisonous mineral, gnaw my	inside.
inwards;	
And nothing can or shall content my soul	Nothing will settle my thoughts until I get
Till I am even'd with him, wife for wife,	even with him, wife for a wife.
Or failing so, yet that I put the Moor	If I can't do that, I can make the Moor suffer
At least into a jealousy so strong	from such strong jealousy that he cannot
That judgment cannot cure. Which thing to do,	think straight.
If this poor trash of Venice, whom I trash	If that poor Venetian trash, that I am using
For his quick hunting, stand the putting on,	like a hunting dog, can do what I need him to do
I'll have our Michael Cassio on the hip,	
Abuse him to the Moor in the rank garb-	I'll have power over Michael Cassio,
For I fear Cassio with my night-cap too-Make	I will say bad things about him to the Moor. I
the Moor thank me, love me and reward me.	fear that Cassio might have seduced my wife.
For making him egregiously an ass	I'll make the Moor thank me, love me, and
And practising upon his peace and quiet	reward me.
Even to madness. 'Tis here, but yet confused:	But I will have made a fool of him.
Knavery's plain face is never seen tin used.	The plan is almost ready but not yet fully formed.
	You can never see the end of an evil plan until it is done.
Exit	*Exit*

PART 10: ANALYSING ACT 2 SCENE 1

Themes: Appearance vs Reality, Prejudice, Manhood and Honour, Womanhood and Sexuality, Deception, Honesty, Love, Order and Chaos.

This act and scene begins **chaotically** with the anticipated arrival of Othello as a violent storm rages, foreshadowing the beginning of the **chaotic** metaphorical 'storm' in the play. Structurally, Act 2 Scene 1 is the most drawn-out scene in the entire play as the build up to Othello's arrival helps to create a sense of isolation and anxiety which is then quashed with a reunion of man and wife before being re-stirred with Iago's desire to disgrace Cassio. The opening serves a narrative function as it informs the audience of the fact that the characters are now in Cyprus and that the expected military conflict of the play is now no longer part of the plot. The Elizabethan audience would have believed Cyprus to be a place of disaster and **chaos** based on the continuous wars raging between the Muslims and Christians which would have added tension to the play. However, the external threat of Cyprus as a place is soon replaced by the internal threat of Iago as the real 'storm' personified. In fact, Iago arrived in Cyprus the week before Othello after being helped by the storm suggesting Iago's future is more fortunate than Othello's.

At the start of the play, Othello appears in control, **ordered**, and completely desirable as a leader shown by Montano's fears for the safe arrival of the 'warlike Moor'. Cassio also appears to have high expectations of and admiration for Othello as he asks for him to '...bless this bay...' and 'Give renewed fire to pour extincted spirits'. Unfortunately, this excitement and respect is short-lived as there is an obvious challenge to Othello's manhood. The storm that destroys the Turks is also symbolic of the start of Othello's 'storm' and ironically he will become just as destructive and his life **chaotic**. He arrives in Cyprus as a military leader no longer needed. In fact, it is almost as though the original intended plot of Othello ends in this scene and another begins. It appears that *Othello* started as a play exploring the political yet it soon becomes a domestic tragedy. Cassio adds to the provocation of the metaphorical 'storm' by informing Iago that it is his 'breeding' that has resulted in him being promoted in place of Iago. Iago has already expressed his anger at '...letter and affection' and so feels taunted by Cassio, as well as socially inferior.

It is at this point that Iago begins to formulate a plan to involve all those who have offended him in the plot to bring about the downfall of Othello. Marxist critical readings (concerned with the economic and psychological impact of England's hierarchical social system) suggest that because Iago is subordinate to both Othello and Cassio, he is resentful and desperate for promotion. Iago's desire for a change in status is also reflective of the shifting economic system that was becoming apparent in Elizabethan England.

Cassio's adoration for Othello (as his superior) and Desdemona is immediately apparent in the opening in that he describes Desdemona in eloquent and elaborate tones as outshining '...the quirks of blazoning pens,/And in the essential vesture of creation...' and with respect as the '...captain's captain' with the demand that all the men on the island 'let her have your knees'. This praise of Desdemona is **honest**, sincere and in no way romantic. Iago joins in with some very general praise declared in rhyming couplets, making it seem insincere and humorous because of the importance placed on the form and pace rather than the words. This creates a light, playful (or even mocking) tone:

If she be fair and wise, fairness and wit,
The one's for use, the other useth it

The theme of **womanhood and sexuality** is explored through Iago's low opinion of women which appears to be a direct contrast with Othello and Cassio's opinions. It is possible that Iago, much like many Elizabethan's, struggled with the **reality** of Desdemona, an attractive aristocratic white woman, being in love with a 'Moor'. However, Iago also suggests that he dislikes his own wife when he cruelly disrespects her by stating that he only likes a woman who would 'ne'er disclose her mind' and is insulting in his metaphorical reference to women as 'clyster-pipes' (the pipe used to inject medicine into rectums). Disguised by a comic tone, Iago displays a cynical view of women, especially when conversing with Desdemona. He refers to women as 'pictures out of doors...wild-cats...devils...players...and housewives in...beds'. However, rather than show any signs of contempt towards one of her husband's soldiers, Desdemona praises 'honest' Iago for speaking bluntly even though Iago's verbal abuse and claims about women (when compared with his overtly sexual references to Desdemona and Othello's relationship in 1:1) appear to reveal a deep rooted misogyny, especially when faced with a woman of higher social class.

Desdemona's confidence, wit, and playful sexuality are refreshing to a contemporary audience, much like her elopement. Unfortunately, an Elizabethan audience would have felt uncomfortable with Desdemona's sexual awareness ('o, most lame and impotent conclusion!') and constant interrogatives directed at Iago (a man). So when Desdemona warns Emilia about Iago's choice of words, the cruel irony is that the audience would not be sympathetic when this warning becomes her own reality. This is not helped by the fact that Iago's comic tone is a deliberate attempt to manipulate others into being uncertain about his **prejudices** against women, allowing him to use this as a tool to manipulate Othello (and the audience) throughout. The apparent hatred he has for women and female **sexuality** appears to be the reasoning behind his determination to bring about Othello's downfall by ensuring that Desdemona is directly involved when he insists that 'her eye must be fed;/and what delight shall she have to look on the devil?'. It is also important to remember that Desdemona begins the play as an eloper (whose own father warns Othello not to trust) as well as a 'land carrack' according to Iago.

Iago's misogyny becomes more disparaging in the presence of Roderigo when he says Desdemona's 'eye must be fed' and when '…blood is made dull with the act of sport…' she will become unfaithful' possibly because Iago views Roderigo as his social inferior so feels at ease abusing the virtue of the Captain's wife. It is with Roderigo that the plan intensifies and he claims an affair is taking place between Desdemona and Cassio.. It is not that Iago trusts Roderigo completely, but more likely that Iago takes pleasure in the fact that Roderigo is infatuated with Desdemona and can easily be enraged and provoked to kill Cassio. To further provoke Roderigo's torment, Iago claims Desdemona drinks wine 'made of grapes' like every other woman, meaning Roderigo needs to accept that all women are the same, or at least behave in the same way that Iago believes. Iago needs Roderigo to believe in the infidelity, especially as he has also witnessed the brief touching of hands and revealed he believed it was nothing but courtesy. Othello, however, is at first a complete contrast to Iago. There is a deliberate attempt by Shakespeare to make this opening scene representative of the love and loyalty that Desdemona has for Othello and vice versa. He greets Desdemona as his 'fair warrior' suggesting not only complete devotion but equality in their skills. Iago has witnessed Desdemona be so fiercely independent and outspoken that it appears she may not need her husband to defend her physically, socially, or independently. Nevertheless, this does not in any way suggest that Desdemona could be capable of infidelity.

This act and scene also emphasises the motif of sight (referred to throughout the play with many references to perceptions) in that specific reference is made to the sight of the storm and lack of sight of Othello. However, the focus on sight shifts from literal to metaphorical with Othello's arrival. Othello arrives overjoyed at the sight of his wife before asking Iago to oversee the unloading of his ship, foreshadowing the trust he has in Iago's sight when he demands 'Ocular proof' of Desdemona's infidelity later in Act 3. Furthermore, Othello's happiness at seeing Desdemona again is quickly hindered by his open admittance that he is struggling to see a future that can ever match this positive moment when he mentions 'an unknown fate'. Desdemona, however, continues to optimistically look forward with an unobstructed vision of their positive future and growth together, 'our loves and comforts should increase/even as our days grow'. Unfortunately, Desdemona's optimism is no match for Othello's lack of sight that represents his metaphorical blindness at not being able to look beyond his hamartia (his jealousy) and anger later in the play. Regardless of the destruction about to take place, Desdemona and Othello reinforce their devotion and suitability in a poetic climax of exchanges:

OTHELLO

It gives me wonder great as my content

To see you here before me. O my soul's joy!

If after every tempest come such calms,

May the winds blow till they have waken'd death!

[....]

DESDEMONA

The heavens forbid

But that our loves and comforts should increase,

Even as our days do grow!

Unfortunately, negativity soon takes over as Othello 'fear[s]' they are experiencing 'too much joy' and his metaphorical reference to the sea when he says '...let the labouring bark climb hills of seas/Olympus-high and duck again as low/As hell's from heaven!' although an attempt to state a determination to face any challenge, actually foreshadows doom.

Part of the stagecraft in this scene is the power of the soliloquy at the end. Spoken by Iago, the final soliloquy serves as a hint that Iago will succeed in his destruction of Othello. Iago, although 'confused' about his plan, begins to mock the audience for even attempting to understand him and his motives. He continues in his arrogance by directly addressing the audience with his plan to spin an illusion by using 'reality'. The reality is that Cassio, in his courtesy, has taken Desdemona's hand to speak to her privately and Iago instantly uses this to begin the plot to sabotage Othello's life and those around him. He also uses an aside to mock the characters within the play for being so naïve to his villainous plot when he refers to himself as 'honest' immediately after he remarks that Othello is now 'well-tuned' to be deceived. The soliloquy becomes even more revealing in that it shows Iago's hatred for Othello alongside his attempt to justify his hatred with what appears to be another unfounded reference to Othello having sex with Emilia when he states 'the lusty Moor/Hath leap'd in my seat' repeating the Metaphorical reference to his wife as an object in 1:2, again depriving her of humanity. Given Iago's disdain for women from the very start of the play, his 'wife for wife' revenge that 'gnaws' at his 'inwards' seems to be nothing but an excuse to mask the jealousy he feels at having been rejected by Othello in favour of the socially superior Cassio.

ORIGINAL TEXT:	MODERN TRANSLATION:
SCENE II. A street.	**SCENE II. A street.**
Enter a Herald with a proclamation; People following	*Enter a Herald with a proclamation; People following*
Herald	**Herald**
It is Othello's pleasure, our noble and valiant general, that, upon certain tidings now arrived, importing the mere perdition of the Turkish fleet, every man put himself into triumph; some to dance, some to make bonfires, each man to what sport and revels his addiction leads him: for, besides these beneficial news, it is the celebration of his nuptial. So much was his pleasure should be proclaimed. All offices are open, and there is full liberty of feasting from this present hour of five till the bell have told eleven. Heaven bless the isle of Cyprus and our noble general Othello!	It is the pleasure of our noble and courageous Othello, that, having learned the Turks have been completely destroyed, he would like to invite every man to celebrate this victory. Some of you can come to dance. Some of you can make bonfires, and all of you can celebrate in any way you want. Besides the good news, we are also celebrating his marriage. He is very happy to announce this. There will be a feast from five o'clock until eleven clock. God bless the island of Cyprus and or noble general Othello!
Exeunt	*Exit*

PART 12: ANALYSING ACT 2 SCENE 2

93

Themes: Appearance vs Reality, Manhood and Honour.

The purpose of this very short scene is to signal a passing of time and juxtapose war and love. In terms of stagecraft, the hearld's proclamation is a verbal curtain being drawn in a modern theatre. It also acts as a division between the military start of the play and the stark contrast of the foreshadowed tragic domesticity about to follow. The fact that a feast and partying takes place at night hints that this is the beginning of Iago's plan as he had earlier proclaimed 'hell and night/Must bring this monstrous birth to the world's light'. The birth of his plan being the horror about to take place.

ORIGINAL TEXT:	MODERN TRANSLATION:
SCENE III. A hall in the castle.	**SCENE III. A hall in the castle.**
Enter OTHELLO, DESDEMONA, CASSIO, and Attendants	*Enter OTHELLO, DESDEMONA, CASSIO, and Attendants*
OTHELLO Good Michael, look you to the guard to-night: Let's teach ourselves that honourable stop, Not to outsport discretion.	**OTHELLO** Good Michael, keep a close eye on the guard tonight. Let's set an example and make sure things don't get too out of hand. Don't let the party get too wild.
CASSIO Iago hath direction what to do; But, notwithstanding, with my personal eye Will I look to't.	**CASSIO** Iago has orders about what to do. But I will make sure that I personally check that things are ok.
OTHELLO Iago is most honest. Michael, good night: to-morrow with your earliest Let me have speech with you.	**OTHELLO** Iago is a good and honest man. Goodnight, Michael. Come and speak to me tomorrow.
To DESDEMONA	*To DESDEMONA*
Come, my dear love, The purchase made, the fruits are to ensue; That profit's yet to come 'tween me and you. Good night.	Come on, my dear love. Now that we are married, we can consummate our marriage properly tonight. Good night everybody.

Exeunt OTHELLO, DESDEMONA, and Attendants	*Exeunt OTHELLO, DESDEMONA, and Attendants*
Enter IAGO	*Enter IAGO*
CASSIO	**CASSIO**
Welcome, Iago; we must to the watch.	Hello, Iago. It is time for us to guard the place.
IAGO	**IAGO**
Not this hour, lieutenant; 'tis not yet ten o' the clock. Our general cast us thus early for the love of his Desdemona; who let us not therefore blame: he hath not yet made wanton the night with her; and she is sport for Jove.	Not yet, lieutenant. It is not even ten o'clock. The general has got rid of us early so that he can be alone with Desdemona. I can't blame him for that. He has not yet spent a night with her. She is beautiful enough to be Jove's lover.
CASSIO	**CASSIO**
She's a most exquisite lady.	She's an extremely beautiful lady.
IAGO	**IAGO**
And, I'll warrant her, fun of game.	And I bet she's great in bed.
CASSIO	**CASSIO**
Indeed, she's a most fresh and delicate creature.	Yes, probably. She is young and delicate.
IAGO	**IAGO**
What an eye she has! methinks it sounds a parley of provocation.	And she has really pretty eyes! They invite you in.
CASSIO	**CASSIO**
An inviting eye; and yet methinks right modest.	Yes, she does have inviting eyes, but I think she's really modest.

IAGO

And when she speaks, is it not an alarum to love?

CASSIO

She is indeed perfection.

IAGO

Well, happiness to their sheets! Come, lieutenant, I have a stoup of wine; and here without are a brace of Cyprus gallants that would fain have a measure to the health of black Othello.

CASSIO

Not to-night, good Iago: I have very poor and unhappy brains for drinking: I could well wish courtesy would invent some other custom of entertainment.

IAGO

O, they are our friends; but one cup: I'll drink for you.

CASSIO

I have drunk but one cup to-night, and that was qualified too, and, behold, what innovation it makes here: I am unfortunate in the infirmity, and dare not task my weakness with any more.

IAGO

IAGO

And when she speaks, doesn't her voice stir up passion?

CASSIO

She is perfect.

IAGO

Well, they'll be happy tonight! Come on, lieutenant. I have a jug of wine and these two Cypriot gentlemen would like to raise a toast to the health of black Othello.

CASSIO

Not tonight, good Iago. I'm not a great drinker. I wish that there was something else to do than drink for entertainment.

IAGO

Oh, these are our friends. Just have one drink. I'll do most of the drinking for you.

CASSIO

I have already had a drink tonight, and that was watered down. Look how drunk I am. I am not a very good drinker and I daren't drink any more than I've already had.

IAGO

What, man! 'tis a night of revels: the gallants desire it.

CASSIO

Where are they?

IAGO

Here at the door; I pray you, call them in.

CASSIO

I'll do't; but it dislikes me.

Exit

IAGO

If I can fasten but one cup upon him,
With that which he hath drunk to-night already,
He'll be as full of quarrel and offence
As my young mistress' dog. Now, my sick fool Roderigo,
Whom love hath turn'd almost the wrong side out,
To Desdemona hath to-night caroused
Potations pottle-deep; and he's to watch:
Three lads of Cyprus, noble swelling spirits,
That hold their honours in a wary distance,
The very elements of this warlike isle,
Have I to-night fluster'd with flowing cups,
And they watch too. Now, 'mongst this flock of drunkards,
Am I to put our Cassio in some action
That may offend the isle.--But here they come:
If consequence do but approve my dream,

What! Tonight is a celebration. The men are waiting.

CASSIO

Where are they?

IAGO

They are waiting at the door. Please, shout them in.

CASSIO

I'll do it but I don't like it.

Exit

IAGO

If I can just tempt him to drink one more drink after what he has already drunk tonight,
Then he'll be argumentative and he'll be up for a fight just like a little dog. Now, love sick Roderigo, all twisted up with love,
has been drinking toasts to Desdemona by the gallon tonight, and he's supposed to be on guard duty.
He has also got the high-ranking lads from Cyprus, the once who easily take offence, really drunk.
I have also made sure most of the other men are drunk.
They are all watching what is happening.
I need to get Cassio to do something offensive.
Here they come.
If things turn out the way that I hope,

I will be as successful as a ship sailing freely in the wind and currents.

My boat sails freely, both with wind and stream.

Re-enter CASSIO; with him MONTANO and Gentlemen; servants following with wine

CASSIO

'Fore God, they have given me a rouse already.

MONTANO

Good faith, a little one; not past a pint, as I am a soldier.

IAGO

Some wine, ho!

Sings

And let me the canakin clink, clink;
And let me the canakin clink
A soldier's a man;
A life's but a span;
Why, then, let a soldier drink.
Some wine, boys!

CASSIO

'Fore God, an excellent song.

IAGO

I learned it in England, where, indeed, they are most potent in potting: your Dane, your German, and your swag-bellied Hollander-- Drink, ho!--are nothing to your English.

Re-enter CASSIO; with him MONTANO and Gentlemen; servants following with wine

CASSIO

Oh God, they've given me too much to drink.

MONTANO

Trust me. It was only a little one. Not more than a pint, I promise.

IAGO

Bring some more wine!

Sings

And let's clink our glasses together,
And let's clink our glasses together,
A soldier's a man,
And life is short,
So let the soldier drink.
Have some more wine, boys!

CASSIO

My God, what an excellent song.

IAGO

I learned it in England. They have a talent for drinking. The Danes, the Germans, and the Dutch are nothing compared to the English. Come on, drink!

CASSIO

Is your Englishman so expert in his drinking?

IAGO

Why, he drinks you, with facility, your Dane dead drunk; he sweats not to overthrow your Almain; he gives your Hollander a vomit, ere the next pottle

can be filled.

CASSIO

To the health of our general!

MONTANO

I am for it, lieutenant; and I'll do you justice.

IAGO

(sings)
O sweet England!
King Stephen was a worthy peer,
His breeches cost him but a crown;
He held them sixpence all too dear,
With that he call'd the tailor lown.
He was a wight of high renown,
And thou art but of low degree:
'Tis pride that pulls the country down;
Then take thine auld cloak about thee.
Some wine, ho!

CASSIO

Why, this is a more exquisite song than the other.

CASSIO

Are the English really that good at drinking?

IAGO

They can drink with the Danes until the Danes have passed out. They don't even break a sweat when drinking with the Germans. The Dutch are already vomiting when the English are asking for refills.

CASSIO

Let's drink to the health of Othello!

MONTANO

I agree with that, and I'll drink as much as you do.

IAGO

(sings)
Oh, sweet England!
King Stephen was a good king,
His pants were very cheap
He thought they were expensive,
So he called the tailor a peasant,
And that was a noble man, much higher than you are.
Pride is ruining the nation.
Be happy with your worn-out cloak
More wine!

CASSIO

That song is even better than the last one.

IAGO Will you hear't again?	**IAGO** Do you want to hear it again?
CASSIO No; for I hold him to be unworthy of his place that does those things. Well, God's above all; and there be souls must be saved, and there be souls must not be saved.	**CASSIO** No, the type of king who does those things is not worthy of his position. Oh well, God is in charge. Some people are going to heaven and some people are going to hell.
IAGO It's true, good lieutenant.	**IAGO** That's true, lieutenant.
CASSIO For mine own part,--no offence to the general, nor any man of quality,--I hope to be saved.	**CASSIO** As for me – no offence to Othello, or anybody else – I hope I am going to heaven.
IAGO And so do I too, lieutenant.	**IAGO** Me too.
CASSIO Ay, but, by your leave, not before me; the lieutenant is to be saved before the ancient. Let's have no more of this; let's to our affairs.—Forgive us our sins!--Gentlemen, let's look to our business. Do not think, gentlemen. I am drunk: this is my ancient; this is my right hand, and this is my left: I am not drunk now; I can stand well enough, and speak well enough.	**CASSIO** Okay, if you wish, but not before me. The lieutenant has to go to heaven before the ensign. Let's stop drinking and get to work. God forgive our sins! Gentleman, let's get to work. Don't be thinking I am drunk. This is my ensign. And this is my right hand and this is my left hand. I am not drunk. I can stand up and I can speak well.
All Excellent well.	**All** Yes, you are doing well.
CASSIO	**CASSIO**

Why, very well then; you must not think then that I am drunk.

Exit

MONTANO

To the platform, masters; come, let's set the watch.

IAGO

You see this fellow that is gone before;
He is a soldier fit to stand by Caesar
And give direction: and do but see his vice;
'Tis to his virtue a just equinox,
The one as long as the other: 'tis pity of him.
I fear the trust Othello puts him in.
On some odd time of his infirmity,
Will shake this island.

MONTANO

But is he often thus?

IAGO

'Tis evermore the prologue to his sleep:
He'll watch the horologe a double set,
If drink rock not his cradle.

MONTANO

It were well
The general were put in mind of it.
Perhaps he sees it not; or his good nature
Prizes the virtue that appears in Cassio,
And looks not on his evils: is not this true?

Yes, very well. So don't be thinking that I am drunk.

Exit

MONTANO

Let's go to the platform and stand guard. Come on.

IAGO

You know that man who has just left?
He is a soldier good enough to be Caesar's right-hand man. But he has a weakness.
It's the exact opposite of his strength.
Each one as powerful as the other. It's such a shame.
I am worried about the amount of trust Othello has put in him especially at the time when a mistake could be bad for Cyprus.

MONTANO

But he is often like this?

IAGO

All the time. He drinks like this every night before he goes to sleep. He'd stay up all night and all day f he didn't have a drink before bed.

MONTANO

I really think it is best
If the general were told about this.
Maybe he hasn't ever noticed because he only wants to see the good in Cassio's nature.

	Maybe he just cannot see the bad. Do you think this is true?
Enter RODERIGO	*Enter RODERIGO*
IAGO	**IAGO**
[Aside to him] How now, Roderigo!	[Aside to him] Hello, Roderigo!
I pray you, after the lieutenant; go.	Follow the lieutenant please. Go.
Exit RODERIGO	*Exit RODERIGO*
MONTANO	**MONTANO**
And 'tis great pity that the noble Moor	It really is a shame that the noble Moor
Should hazard such a place as his own second	Has chosen such an unstable man as his second-in-command
With one of an ingraft infirmity:	Especially one with such a problem.
It were an honest action to say	We should be honest with the Moor and tell him.
So to the Moor.	
IAGO	**IAGO**
Not I, for this fair island:	I'm not saying anything. I wouldn't if you offered me this whole island. I love Cassio and I want to help cure him of his drink problem. Listen! What is that noise?
I do love Cassio well; and would do much	
To cure him of this evil--But, hark! what noise?	
Cry within: 'Help! help!'	*Cry within: 'Help! help!'*
Re-enter CASSIO, driving in RODERIGO	*Re-enter CASSIO, driving in RODERIGO*
CASSIO	**CASSIO**
You rogue! you rascal!	You rogue! You villain!
MONTANO	**MONTANO**
What's the matter, lieutenant?	What's wrong, lieutenant?

CASSIO	**CASSIO**
A knave teach me my duty!	This fool has had the nerve to tell me what to do!
I'll beat the knave into a twiggen bottle.	I'll beat him until he is covered in marks.
RODERIGO	**RODERIGO**
Beat me!	You'll beat me?
CASSIO	**CASSIO**
Dost thou prate, rogue?	Are you speaking, villain?
Striking RODERIGO	*Striking RODERIGO*
MONTANO	**MONTANO**
Nay, good lieutenant;	No don't, good lieutenant.
Staying him	*Restrains him*
I pray you, sir, hold your hand.	I beg you, sir, don't hit him.
CASSIO	**CASSIO**
Let me go, sir,	Let me go, sir,
Or I'll knock you o'er the mazzard.	Or I'll hit you on the head.
MONTANO	**MONTANO**
Come, come,	Come on,
you're drunk.	You're drunk.
CASSIO	**CASSIO**
Drunk!	Drunk!
They fight	*They fight*
IAGO	**IAGO**
[Aside to RODERIGO] Away, I say; go out, and cry a mutiny.	[Aside to RODERIGO] Go and tell everybody that there's a riot happening.

Exit RODERIGO	*Exit RODERIGO*
Nay, good lieutenant,--alas, gentlemen;-- Help, ho!--Lieutenant,--sir,--Montano,--sir; Help, masters!--Here's a goodly watch indeed!	No, good lieutenant. Help, gentlemen. Help. Lieutenant, Sir, Montano. Help, men! The night guard is coming!
Bell rings Who's that which rings the bell?--Diablo, ho! The town will rise: God's will, lieutenant, hold! You will be shamed for ever.	*Bell rings* Who is ringing the bell? The whole town will wake up. For the love of God, please stop! You'll be made to feel ashamed of this forever.
Re-enter OTHELLO and Attendants	*Re-enter OTHELLO and Attendants*
OTHELLO What is the matter here?	**OTHELLO** What is the matter here?
MONTANO 'Zounds, I bleed still; I am hurt to the death.	**MONTANO** I'm bleeding. I've been mortally wounded.
Faints	*Faints*
OTHELLO Hold, for your lives!	**OTHELLO** Stop right now!
IAGO Hold, ho! Lieutenant,--sir--Montano,--gentlemen,-- Have you forgot all sense of place and duty? Hold! the general speaks to you; hold, hold, for shame!	**IAGO** Stop! Lieutenant – sir, Montano – gentlemen. Have you forgotten your duties? Stop! The general is speaking. Stop, stop, it's shameful!
OTHELLO	**OTHELLO**

Why, how now, ho! from whence ariseth this?

Are we turn'd Turks, and to ourselves do that

Which heaven hath forbid the Ottomites?

For Christian shame, put by this barbarous brawl:

He that stirs next to carve for his own rage

Holds his soul light; he dies upon his motion.

Silence that dreadful bell: it frights the isle

From her propriety. What is the matter, masters?

Honest Iago, that look'st dead with grieving,

Speak, who began this? on thy love, I charge thee.

IAGO

I do not know: friends all but now, even now,

In quarter, and in terms like bride and groom

Devesting them for bed; and then, but now--

As if some planet had unwitted men--

Swords out, and tilting one at other's breast,

In opposition bloody. I cannot speak

Any beginning to this peevish odds;

And would in action glorious I had lost

Those legs that brought me to a part of it!

OTHELLO

How comes it, Michael, you are thus forgot?

CASSIO

I pray you, pardon me; I cannot speak.

OTHELLO

How did this fighting start?

Have we all turned into the Turks and decided to behave as savagely and as brutally as them?

For God's sake, stop this savage fighting.

The next person who lashes out and cannot control his rage

Must not care about living, because the minute he lashes out, he dies.

Stop that horrible bell ringing. It is scaring the whole island.

What is wrong here, masters?

Honest Iago, you look really upset,

Speak up and tell me who started this. I command you to tell me.

IAGO

I don't know. We were all friends and having fun, as happy as a bride and groom

Taking off their clothes for bed, but then

Everything suddenly changed and it was like something had made the men insane. They started pointing their sword's at one another.

I just don't really know what happened. I would rather lose my legs in battle than be part of any of this!

OTHELLO

What made you behave like this, Michael?

CASSIO

Please excuse me. I can't speak.

OTHELLO

Worthy Montano, you were won't be civil;

The gravity and stillness of your youth

The world hath noted, and your name is great

In mouths of wisest censure: what's the matter,

That you unlace your reputation thus

And spend your rich opinion for the name

Of a night-brawler? give me answer to it.

Montano, you are supposed to be the calm one.

Ever since you were young you have been sensible. You are famous for it.

Your name is spoken

by the wisest people. What happened

to make you risk your reputation like this and become

a street brawler? Answer me.

MONTANO

Worthy Othello, I am hurt to danger:

Your officer, Iago, can inform you,--

While I spare speech, which something now offends me,--

Of all that I do know: nor know I aught

By me that's said or done amiss this night;

Unless self-charity be sometimes a vice,

And to defend ourselves it be a sin

When violence assails us.

MONTANO

Othello, I am seriously hurt.

Iago can tell you exactly what happened

While I save my breath because it really hurts to talk

I know that I didn't do anything wrong at all tonight

Unless it is wrong to defend myself when somebody violently attacks me.

OTHELLO

Now, by heaven,

My blood begins my safer guides to rule;

And passion, having my best judgment collied,

Assays to lead the way: if I once stir,

Or do but lift this arm, the best of you

Shall sink in my rebuke. Give me to know

How this foul rout began, who set it on;

And he that is approved in this offence,

Though he had twinn'd with me, both at a birth,

Shall lose me. What! in a town of war,

Yet wild, the people's hearts brimful of fear,

To manage private and domestic quarrel,

OTHELLO

For God's sake,

I'm starting to get angry.

I am about to lose my temper.

I'm tempted to lift this arm, and if I do, the best of you will suffer.

I want to know how this fight began and I want to know who started it.

Even if the guilty person were my twin brother

I would be done with him. We are in a town that has just avoided war. People are still scared,

And you are getting into fights with each other

when you should be working and guarding the place to keep it safe!

In night, and on the court and guard of safety!
'Tis monstrous. Iago, who began't?

MONTANO

If partially affined, or leagued in office,
Thou dost deliver more or less than truth,
Thou art no soldier.

IAGO

Touch me not so near:
I had rather have this tongue cut from my
mouth
Than it should do offence to Michael Cassio;
Yet, I persuade myself, to speak the truth
Shall nothing wrong him. Thus it is, general.
Montano and myself being in speech,
There comes a fellow crying out for help:
And Cassio following him with determined
sword,
To execute upon him. Sir, this gentleman
Steps in to Cassio, and entreats his pause:
Myself the crying fellow did pursue,
Lest by his clamour--as it so fell out--
The town might fall in fright: he, swift of foot,
Outran my purpose; and I return'd the rather
For that I heard the clink and fall of swords,
And Cassio high in oath; which till to-night
I ne'er might say before. When I came back--
For this was brief--I found them close
together,
At blow and thrust; even as again they were
When you yourself did part them.
More of this matter cannot I report:
But men are men; the best sometimes forget:

It's disgusting. Iago, who started it?

MONTANO

I know that you are loyal, and good friends with
Cassio, but if you don't tell the truth,
Then you are not a true soldier.

IAGO

You're offending me a bit too closely.
I would rather have my tongue cut out of my
mouth
Than say anything offensive about Michael Cassio.
But I have persuaded myself to be truthful
It won't get him into trouble. Here's the truth,
general.
Montano and I were talking,
When a man cried out for help.
Cassio was chasing after him with his sword,
He was trying to kill him. Sir, Montano stepped in
to stop Cassio and told him to put his sword away.
I followed the man who was crying for help
To stop him from scaring the rest of the people in
the town.
He was too fast and outran me.
I returned here
And I heard swords clinking
And Cassio was swearing, which I had never heard
him do before tonight
In that brief moment I saw that they were close to
killing each other until you separated them.
I don't know anything else.
But men are men. Most men lose control and
lashes out.

Though Cassio did some little wrong to him,

As men in rage strike those that wish them best,

Yet surely Cassio, I believe, received

From him that fled some strange indignity,

Which patience could not pass.

OTHELLO

I know, Iago,

Thy honesty and love doth mince this matter,

Making it light to Cassio. Cassio, I love thee

But never more be officer of mine.

Re-enter DESDEMONA, attended

Look, if my gentle love be not raised up!

I'll make thee an example.

DESDEMONA

What's the matter?

OTHELLO

All's well now, sweeting; come away to bed.

Sir, for your hurts, myself will be your surgeon:

Lead him off.

To MONTANO, who is led off

Iago, look with care about the town,

And silence those whom this vile brawl distracted.

Cassio was wrong to do what he did

Because Montano was only trying to help him.

I am sure the man who ran away had offended

Cassio and he was really angry and couldn't let it go.

OTHELLO

Iago, I know

that you are trying to make this matter sound less like Cassio's fault than it is because you love him.

Cassio, I love you

but you are never going to be one of my officers again.

Re-enter DESDEMONA, attended

Look, you've woken my wife up! I am going to make an example of you.

DESDEMONA

What's wrong?

OTHELLO

Everything is okay now, sweetheart. Go back to bed.

Montano, I'll see to it personally that your wounds are treated.

Take him away.

To MONTANO, who is led off

Iago, please go and make sure that the people in the town are calm and not upset about this vile fight.

Come, Desdemona: 'tis the soldiers' life To have their balmy slumbers waked with strife. *Exeunt all but IAGO and CASSIO* **IAGO** What, are you hurt, lieutenant? **CASSIO** Ay, past all surgery. **IAGO** Marry, heaven forbid! **CASSIO** Reputation, reputation, reputation! O, I have lost my reputation! I have lost the immortal part of myself, and what remains is bestial. My reputation, Iago, my reputation! **IAGO** As I am an honest man, I thought you had received some bodily wound; there is more sense in that than in reputation. Reputation is an idle and most false imposition: oft got without merit, and lost without deserving: you have lost no reputation at all, unless you repute yourself such a loser. What, man! there are ways to recover the general again: you are but now cast in his mood, a	Come on, Desdemona. The soldiers are used to being woken up by trouble. It's part of their lives. *Exit all but IAGO and CASSIO* **IAGO** Are you hurt, lieutenant? **CASSIO** Yes, but no doctor can help. **IAGO** Oh, God forbid. **CASSIO** My reputation – I have lost my reputation! I have lost the best and truest part of myself and all that is left is beastly. My reputation, Iago, my reputation! **IAGO** I genuinely thought you had been hurt physically. Your health is more important than your reputation. Your reputation is a pointless and fake quality invented by others. You haven't lost your reputation unless you think you have. There are lots of ways to recover from this and impress the general again. You caught him in a bad mood, that's why he has discharged you, not

110

punishment more in policy than in malice, even so as one would beat his offenceless dog to affright an imperious lion: sue to him again, and he's yours.

CASSIO

I will rather sue to be despised than to deceive so good a commander with so slight, so drunken, and so indiscreet an officer. Drunk? and speak parrot?
and squabble? swagger? swear? and discourse fustian with one's own shadow? O thou invisible spirit of wine, if thou hast no name to be known by,
let us call thee devil!

IAGO

What was he that you followed with your sword? What had he done to you?

CASSIO

I know not.

IAGO

Is't possible?

CASSIO

I remember a mass of things, but nothing distinctly; a quarrel, but nothing wherefore. O God, that men should put an enemy in their mouths to steal away
their brains! that we should, with joy, pleasance revel and applause, transform ourselves into beasts!

because he doesn't like you. He has to beat you like a weak dog to scare the stronger ones. Go to him. He will change his mind.

CASSIO

I would rather accept him despising me than to deceive such a good commander by being a drunk and stupid officer.
Drunk? Talking nonsense? Fighting? Showing-off? Swearing? Arguing with my own shadow? There's some kind of invisible spirit in wine. If you do not have a name then I will just refer to you as the devil.

IAGO

Who was chasing after you with his sword? What did he do to you?

CASSIO

I don't know.

IAGO

Is that possible?

CASSIO

I remember lots of things, but nothing clearly. I remember a fight, but I don't remember the reason we were fighting. Oh God, why do men drink and lose their minds? We party so happily and then turn into animals!

IAGO Why, but you are now well enough: how came you thus recovered?	**IAGO** But you seem to be okay now. How did you recover?
CASSIO It hath pleased the devil drunkenness to give place to the devil wrath; one unperfectness shows me another, to make me frankly despise myself.	**CASSIO** Being drunk has made me really angry. One imperfection leads to more and makes me despise myself.
IAGO Come, you are too severe a moraler: as the time, the place, and the condition of this country stands, I could heartily wish this had not befallen; but, since it is as it is, mend it for your own good.	**IAGO** Come on, you are being too hard on yourself. I do wish none of this had happened, especially because of the time and the place, but it has happened. All you can do is make the best of it.
CASSIO I will ask him for my place again; he shall tell me I am a drunkard! Had I as many mouths as Hydra, such an answer would stop them all. To be now a sensible man, by and by a fool, and presently a beast! O strange! Every inordinate cup is unblessed and the ingredient is a devil.	**CASSIO** I'll ask him to give me my job back, he will tell me that I am drunk! Even if I had lots of mouths, my answer would shut them all up. I was a sensible man, then a fool, then a beast! Oh, how strange! Every glass of alcohol is evil, and full of the devil.
IAGO Come, come, good wine is a good familiar creature, if it be well used: exclaim no more against it. And, good lieutenant, I think you think I love you.	**IAGO** Oh come on, good wine is brilliant if you don't abuse it. Don't put it down. You know I am your friend.
CASSIO	**CASSIO**

I have well approved it, sir. I drunk!

IAGO

You or any man living may be drunk! at a time, man.

I'll tell you what you shall do. Our general's wife is now the general: may say so in this respect, for that he hath devoted and given up himself to the

contemplation, mark, and denotement of her parts and graces: confess yourself freely to her; importune her help to put you in your place again: she is of so free, so kind, so apt, so blessed a disposition,

she holds it a vice in her goodness not to do more than she is requested: this broken joint between you and her husband entreat her to splinter; and, my

fortunes against any lay worth naming, this crack of your love shall grow stronger than it was before.

CASSIO

You advise me well.

IAGO

I protest, in the sincerity of love and honest kindness.

CASSIO

I think it freely; and betimes in the morning I will beseech the virtuous Desdemona to undertake for me:

I know that, sir. Me! Drunk!

IAGO

You, or any man, may get drunk from time to time! I'll tell you what to do. Othello's wife is now the general. I say that because he is besotted with her. He has given himself to her and is completely devoted to her.

Go and open up to her. Talk to her freely and ask her to help you get back to your position again. She is so kind, so generous and so willing to help that she thinks it is wrong not to help out when she can. This broken relationship that you and Othello now have could be sorted by her. And I bet everything I have that your relationship with Othello will be stronger than it was before.

CASSIO

You give me such good advice.

IAGO

I am helping because I sincerely love you and want to be honest and kind.

CASSIO

I believe you and early in the morning I'll go and visit Desdemona and beg her to help me.
I am desperate to get my job back or my future will stop here.

I am desperate of my fortunes if they cheque me here.

IAGO

You are in the right. Good night, lieutenant; I must to the watch.

CASSIO

Good night, honest Iago.

Exit

IAGO

And what's he then that says I play the villain?

When this advice is free I give and honest,

Probal to thinking and indeed the course

To win the Moor again? For 'tis most easy

The inclining Desdemona to subdue

In any honest suit: she's framed as fruitful

As the free elements. And then for her

To win the Moor--were't to renounce his baptism,

All seals and symbols of redeemed sin,

His soul is so enfetter'd to her love,

That she may make, unmake, do what she list,

Even as her appetite shall play the god

With his weak function. How am I then a villain

To counsel Cassio to this parallel course,

Directly to his good? Divinity of hell!

When devils will the blackest sins put on,

They do suggest at first with heavenly shows,

As I do now: for whiles this honest fool

Plies Desdemona to repair his fortunes

IAGO

You're doing the right thing. Good night, lieutenant. I must get to work.

CASSIO

Good night, honest Iago.

Exit

IAGO

And who can honestly say that I am being a villain? I am giving good, honest advice.

It is wise and logical and will win the Moor over. It is easy to get Desdemona on your side because she is so generous and lovely in nature.

And then she could win the Moor over in such a way that he would be willing to renounce his religion,

And religion is what saves him from sin.

He is so in love with her

that she could make him, break him, or do whatever she likes.

She manipulates his love for her.

How am I a villain

if I am giving Cassio such good advice?

When devils want to control their victims and commit their sins

They put on a heavenly show

Just like I am now. And while the fool is begging Desdemona to help repair his reputation, and while she pleads with her husband for him,

And she for him pleads strongly to the Moor,
I'll pour this pestilence into his ear,
That she repeals him for her body's lust;
And by how much she strives to do him good,
She shall undo her credit with the Moor.
So will I turn her virtue into pitch,
And out of her own goodness make the net
That shall enmesh them all.

Re-enter RODERIGO

How now, Roderigo!

RODERIGO

I do follow here in the chase, not like a hound
that hunts, but one that fills up the cry. My
money is almost spent; I have been to-night
exceedingly well
cudgelled; and I think the issue will be, I shall
have so much experience for my pains, and so,
with no money at all and a little more wit,
return again to Venice.

IAGO

How poor are they that have not patience!
What wound did ever heal but by degrees?
Thou know'st we work by wit, and not by
witchcraft;
And wit depends on dilatory time.
Does't not go well? Cassio hath beaten thee.
And thou, by that small hurt, hast cashier'd
Cassio:
Though other things grow fair against the sun,
Yet fruits that blossom first will first be ripe:

I'll speak poisonous words into Othello's ear and
tell him she is defending him out of lust
And the amount of talking she does to defend him
will cause damage between her and Othello. And
that's how I will turn her good intentions into a
trap
That will catch them all.

Re-enter RODERIGO

Hello, Roderigo!

RODERIGO

I am really tired out. The chase is too exhausting
and I am doing it for nothing. I've almost spent all
my money and I have been badly beaten tonight.
I think I will get lots of experience for my troubles,
but nothing else in return. And I'll have to return
to Venice without any money or brains left.

IAGO

People without patience are poor!
What wounds have ever healed quickly?
We work using our intelligence, not using magic.
Intelligent planning takes time.
Don't you think things are going well?
Cassio has beaten you up.
And by getting slightly hurt you have got Cassio
fired.
We need to be really patient
And we will be rewarded.

Content thyself awhile. By the mass, 'tis morning; Pleasure and action make the hours seem short. Retire thee; go where thou art billeted: Away, I say; thou shalt know more hereafter: Nay, get thee gone.	Be patient for a while. It' morning. Time flies when you are having fun. Get yourself to bed at the place where you're staying. Go on. You'll understand more later. Go on, go.
Exit RODERIGO	*Exit RODERIGO*
Two things are to be done: My wife must move for Cassio to her mistress; I'll set her on; Myself the while to draw the Moor apart, And bring him jump when he may Cassio find Soliciting his wife: ay, that's the way Dull not device by coldness and delay.	There are two things I need to do. My wife needs to persuade Desdemona to take Cassio's side. I'll get her to do that. Then I need to take the Moor to one side to talk And then make him see that Cassio is talking to his wife. I need to sort this plan soon so that it won't go cold.
Exit	*Exit*

PART 14: ANALYSING ACT 2 SCENE 3

Themes: Appearance vs Reality, Manhood and Honour, Womanhood and Sexuality, Jealousy, Reputation.

The scene begins with Cassio in a position of trust and authority, having been left to guard the party and reminded to practice self-restraint, reminding the audience of his **reputation**. It also begins with the confirmation that Othello and Desdemona are yet to consummate their marriage as they leave to retire to their marriage bed with Othello's reference to '...purchase made, the fruits are to ensue'. This contrast with the graphic suggestions about Desdemona and Othello in Act 1 Scene 1 ('tupping', 'lascivious' and 'making the beast with two backs') serves as a reminder of the deceptive and vulgar nature of Iago which continues when Iago is left alone with Cassio. Iago tries to convince Cassio in a sexually suggestive manner that Desdemona is far from modest and is 'sport for Jove' and '...full of game' but Cassio will not accept the insinuations. It is clear that Cassio will not be manipulated by Iago's rhetoric as he believes Desdemona to be pure 'fresh and delicate', 'modest' and 'perfection'. These contrasting presentations of Desdemona foreshadow the difficult choice thello will have to make later in the play when Iago presents him with his untruths.

Cassio initially rejects Iago's persuasions to drink until drunk because he has 'unhappy brains for drinking'. Cassio is presented as a sensible and rational character who appears to take his position and duties seriously, yet Othello's apparent warning to Cassio of his need to guard alongside Cassio's own comments about his drinking suggest a predisposition to recklessness, and Iago knows this and aims to skillfully capitalise on it. Iago, having failed to manipulate Cassio with words and prejudices, now turns to the audience to inform them of his plan to use alcohol as an instigator in Cassio's demise, 'If I can fasten but one cup upon him...he'll be as full of quarrel and offense/As my young mistress' dog'.

When Cassio emerges from having invited the guests in, the scene quickly becomes a contrast between the comedy of drunkenness and the anticipation of a violent brawl. Up to this point, Roderigo's rle has been that of a failed lover, however, he now becomes important structurally as he is now the first victim of Iago. Although Roderigo's demise has been carefully crafted by Iago, a sympathtic reaction is difficult based on the fact that Roderigo has been complicit in wanting to destroy the relationship between Othello and Desdemona and destroy Cassio's **reputation**.

Iago's duplicitous nature and determination to see Cassio demoted is revealed when Iago tells Montano that Cassio has issues with drinking and staying sober. His duplicity is furthered by his statement that Othello has promoted an unreliable person. Iago is a skilled manipulator and

Montano believes his claims about Cassio. His manipulation is evident from the very start in that he changes roles in order to convince his victims that he is a friend and an adviser Unfortunately, Montano's confrontation of Cassio is the start of the violent brawl that results in the demotion and loss of reputation of Cassio and the increase in trust that Othello feels for 'honest' Iago, just as Iago hoped. At this point in the play, Iago has now revealed that he is clearly obsessed with sex. His pleasure in having disturbed Othello and Desdemona during their first night together when placed alongside the excessive amount of references to sex that he has used throughout the play so far appears to suggest some kind of unnatural aversion to marital happiness. To Iago, love is a '...weak function' and because of this, he will be able to successfully destroy the marriage between Othello and Desdemona. Othello, on the other hand, has a very different opinion and his anger at being disturbed from his bed heightens his reaction to the brawl. Othello's loss of temper suggests that he is beginning to lose control, 'My blood begins my safer guides to rule'. He is also concerned that there will be political consequences as the people of Cyprus may believe they are in danger. Othello threatens execution and in his anger turns to Iago as his trusted advisor to tell him the truth about what has happened. Iago's pretence to feel uncomfortable at speaking about the brawl and preferring to have his '...tongue cut from [his] mouth...' only strengthens Othello's respect for him as a loyal friend to all. At this point, the audience become complicit in Iago's lies as we are fully aware of his manipulations and tactics. Even Othello, although still decisive, has now become deceived by Iago and become part of the plot to bring about his own downfall as Iago promises to '...pour this pestilence into his ear'. The plosive alliteration of 'p' and the sibilant 's' sounds heighten the intensity and tension by creating a violent and sinister tone. Additionally, the use of declarative further highlights Iago's confidence in his verbal powers of persuasion and his ability to manipulate and placing himself as the subject of this sentence and Othello as passive also suggests he knows he is in control.

Othello's decision to believe Iago by swiftly dismissing Cassio suggests his judgement is becoming impaired, 'never more be an officer of mine'. Furthermore, Othello's language is changing and now includes the exclamatory 'Zounds' hinting at his loss of control.

In a soliloquy to end the scene, Iago states his intention to use Cassio's desperation to re-build his reputation and Desdemona's generosity to help as the provocation of Othello. The versatility of Iago's language has finally allowed him his power to manipulate.

ORIGINAL TEXT:	MODERN TRANSLATION:
SCENE I. Before the castle.	**SCENE I. Before the castle.**
Enter CASSIO and some Musicians	*Enter CASSIO and some Musicians*
CASSIO	**CASSIO**
Masters, play here; I will content your pains;	Musicians, play here. I will pay you for your trouble.
Something that's brief; and bid 'Good morrow, general.'	Play something short and sing 'good morning, general.'
Music	*Music*
Enter Clown	*Enter Clown*
Clown	**Clown**
Why masters, have your instruments been in Naples,	Musicians, have your instruments been in Naples, because they sound really nasal?
that they speak i' the nose thus?	
First Musician	**First Musician**
How, sir, how!	What do you mean?
Clown	**Clown**
Are these, I pray you, wind-instruments?	Are these wind instruments?
First Musician	**First Musician**
Ay, marry, are they, sir.	Yes, they are.
Clown	**Clown**
O, thereby hangs a tail.	Oh, that's what the problem is.
First Musician	**First Musician**
Whereby hangs a tale, sir?	What is the problem?
Clown	**Clown**

Marry. sir, by many a wind-instrument that I know.	The many wind instruments that I know.
But, masters, here's money for you: and the general	But, here's some money for you. The general
so likes your music, that he desires you, for love's	likes your music so much that he
sake, to make no more noise with it.	would like you to stop playing now.

First Musician

Well, sir, we will not.	Well, sir, we will stop then.

Clown

If you have any music that may not be heard,	If you have any music that can't be heard
to't again: but, as they say to hear music the	then play again. But, they say the general
general does not greatly care.	doesn't like listening to music.

First Musician

We have none such, sir.	We don't have any, sir.

Clown

Then put up your pipes in your bag, for I'll away:	Then pack your instruments away. I'm going
go; vanish into air; away!	now and you should go away!

Exeunt Musicians	*Exit Musicians*

CASSIO

Dost thou hear, my honest friend?	Did you hear me, my honest friend?

Clown

No, I hear not your honest friend; I hear you.	No, I can't hear your honest friend. I can only hear you.

CASSIO

CASSIO

Prithee, keep up thy quillets. There's a poor piece of gold for thee: if the gentlewoman that attends the general's wife be stirring, tell her there's one Cassio entreats her a little favour of speech: wilt thou do this?

Clown

She is stirring, sir: if she will stir hither, I shall seem to notify unto her.

CASSIO

Do, good my friend.

Exit Clown
Enter IAGO

In happy time, Iago.

IAGO

You have not been a-bed, then?

CASSIO

Why, no; the day had broke
Before we parted. I have made bold, Iago,
To send in to your wife: my suit to her
Is, that she will to virtuous Desdemona
Procure me some access.

IAGO

I'll send her to you presently;
And I'll devise a mean to draw the Moor
Out of the way, that your converse and business
May be more free.

Please, keep it up. Here's some money for you. When the woman taking care of Desdemona wakes up, tell her that Cassio would like to speak to her. Will you do that?

Clown

She is starting to wake up, sir. If she comes over here, I'll let her know what you said.

CASSIO

Please do.

Exit Clown
Enter IAGO

Good timing, Iago.

IAGO

Have you not been to bed?

CASSIO

No, it was already morning
when we parted ways. I've been quite brave, Iago.
I have asked to speak to your wife. I am going to ask her to let me speak to Desdemona.

IAGO

I'll send her to you soon.
And I'll think of some way to get the Moor out of the way so that you can speak about things openly.

CASSIO	**CASSIO**
I humbly thank you for't.	Thank you so much for that.
Exit IAGO	*Exit IAGO*
I never knew	I never knew
A Florentine more kind and honest.	A Florentine so kind and honest.
Enter EMILIA	*Enter EMILIA*
EMILIA	**EMILIA**
Good morrow, good Lieutenant: I am sorry	Good morning, good Lieutenant. I am sorry
For your displeasure; but all will sure be well.	About your problems but I am sure things will
The general and his wife are talking of it;	be okay.
And she speaks for you stoutly: the Moor	The general and his wife are speaking about it
replies,	now.
That he you hurt is of great fame in Cyprus,	She is defending you. The Moor has replied,
And great affinity, and that in wholesome	That the man you have injured is very well-
wisdom	known and important in Cyprus,
He might not but refuse you; but he protests	He is also an important ally.
he loves you	He has no choice but to refuse to give you
And needs no other suitor but his likings	your job back, but he does keep saying that
To take the safest occasion by the front	he loves you and he doesn't want anybody
To bring you in again.	else. He is trying to find the safest
	opportunity to safely take you back.
CASSIO	**CASSIO**
Yet, I beseech you,	I am asking you,
If you think fit, or that it may be done,	If you think it is possible to organise,
Give me advantage of some brief discourse	Please get me some time alone with
With Desdemona alone.	Desdemona so I can have a brief chat with
	her.

EMILIA Pray you, come in; I will bestow you where you shall have time To speak your bosom freely. **CASSIO** I am much bound to you. *Exeunt*	**EMILIA** Please, come in. I will take you somewhere where you have time To speak freely. **CASSIO** I am really grateful to you. *Exit*

PART 16: ANALYSING ACT 3 SCENE 1

Themes: Appearance vs Reality, Manhood and Honour, Womanhood and Sexuality.

The comic relief of this scene is instantly apparent as Cassio has arranged for a group of musicians to entertain Othello and Desdemona. Unfortunately, Othello demands the musicians leave and sends a clown to mock them. An audience at the time would have reacted with some disdain at Othello's decision based on the thought that music was linked to a civilised and cultured mind. However, many Renaissance plays relied on a clown, or jester, to entertain the audience and encourage a brief pause in emotions before they were plunged deep into highly emotional scenes and could, therefore, be Shakespeare's way of introducing the clown. And a brief pause it is as Iago's plan starts to come to fruition with Cassio's request that the clown bring Emilia to him. Iago enters as the clown exits and further proves his capacity for deception by allowing his own wife to be drawn into the manipulations with a promise to Cassio that he distract Othello so that 'converse and business...may be more free'. The audience know that Iago is desperate for Cassio and Desdemona to make contact so allows Cassio and Emilia privacy to discuss his misfortunes and concoct a plan for his reinstatement. The dramatic irony is that Iago plans to guide Othello to observe this exchange. Again, Iago is the director and Emilia is completely unaware of her involvement in Iago's plan, revealing a relationship that lacks respect and love. She appears sincere in her disappointment at Cassio's demise and happily informs him of Desdemona's desire to see him reinstated and 'speaks...stoutly' to her husband about him. Rather than being satisfied by some hope that he may be forgiven by Othello, the impatient Cassio asks to speak to Desdemona alone and Iago's plan begins to gather weight.

ORIGINAL TEXT:	MODERN TRANSLATION:
SCENE II. A room in the castle.	**SCENE II. A room in the castle.**
Enter OTHELLO, IAGO, and Gentlemen	*Enter OTHELLO, IAGO, and Gentlemen*
OTHELLO	**OTHELLO**
These letters give, Iago, to the pilot; And by him do my duties to the senate: That done, I will be walking on the works; Repair there to me.	Iago, give these letters to the captain of the ship and ask him to give my reports to the senate. Once that is done, come back to me. I will be walking along the walls.
IAGO	**IAGO**
Well, my good lord, I'll do't.	Very good. I'll do it.
OTHELLO	**OTHELLO**
This fortification, gentlemen, shall we see't?	Shall we look at these fortifications, men?
Gentleman	**Gentleman**
We'll wait upon your lordship.	We will go with you.
Exeunt	*Exit*

PART 18: ANALYSING ACT 3 SCENE 2

Themes: Appearance vs Reality, Manhood and Honour.

Othello's vulnerability is revealed in this scene as his trust for Iago deepens, particularly with Iago flattering Othello with 'my good lord'. Othello is revealed to be honourable but naïve. His visit to inspect fortifications being built conveniently provides a believable amount of time for his wife to be unfaithful (we assume this is the time that Cassio uses to speak to Desdemona). The fortifications mentioned are, of course, reference to the walls built to protect a city from its enemies. However, this reference can also be seen as a metaphor for protecting himself from foreign enemies. Unfortunately, Othello fails to recognise the enemy within his walls: Iago. Iago's main role in this scene is to ensure that Othello is out of the way of Desdemona to allow Cassio to meet with her.

ORIGINAL TEXT:	MODERN TRANSLATION:
SCENE III. The garden of the castle.	**SCENE III. The garden of the castle.**
Enter DESDEMONA, CASSIO, and EMILIA	*Enter DESDEMONA, CASSIO, and EMILIA*
DESDEMONA	**DESDEMONA**
Be thou assured, good Cassio, I will do	Be assured, good Cassio, that I will do
All my abilities in thy behalf.	everything I can for you.
EMILIA	**EMILIA**
Good madam, do: I warrant it grieves my husband,	Please do. It is all really upsetting my husband,
As if the case were his.	As if it were his own direct problem.
DESDEMONA	**DESDEMONA**
O, that's an honest fellow. Do not doubt, Cassio,	Oh, you are such a good man. Don't worry, Cassio,
But I will have my lord and you again	I will make sure that you and my husband are
As friendly as you were.	As friendly as you were before all this happened.
CASSIO	**CASSIO**
Bounteous madam,	That's really generous, madam,
Whatever shall become of Michael Cassio,	Whatever happens to me,
He's never any thing but your true servant.	I will always be your true servant.
DESDEMONA	**DESDEMONA**
I know't; I thank you. You do love my lord:	I know. Thank you. You love my husband.
You have known him long; and be you well assured	You have known him a long time and you can be sure that

He shall in strangeness stand no further off Than in a polite distance.	The only reason he is acting strange and keeping away from you is for diplomatic reasons.
CASSIO Ay, but, lady, That policy may either last so long, Or feed upon such nice and waterish diet, Or breed itself so out of circumstance, That, I being absent and my place supplied, My general will forget my love and service.	**CASSIO** Yes, but, lady, That diplomacy might last a very long time, or become so watered down, Or interrupted by other things happening, That my absence and my place having been taken by somebody else Might mean the general will forget my love and commitment to the job.
DESDEMONA Do not doubt that; before Emilia here I give thee warrant of thy place: assure thee, If I do vow a friendship, I'll perform it To the last article: my lord shall never rest; I'll watch him tame and talk him out of patience; His bed shall seem a school, his board a shrift; I'll intermingle every thing he does With Cassio's suit: therefore be merry, Cassio; For thy solicitor shall rather die Than give thy cause away.	**DESDEMONA** Do not think that. It won't happen. In front of Emilia I promise you that your position is safe. If I promise something as a friend, I will make sure it is done. My husband will not get a moment's peace about it. I'll talk to him about this issue so much he will lose patience. I'll keep him up lecturing all night that his bed will feel like a school. His dinner table will feel like confession. I'll bring your name up every single time we speak. So don't worry. Cheer up. I'd rather die than give up on you.
EMILIA Madam, here comes my lord.	**EMILIA** Madam, here comes my lord.
CASSIO Madam, I'll take my leave.	**CASSIO** Madam, I'll leave now.

DESDEMONA

Why, stay, and hear me speak.

CASSIO

Madam, not now: I am very ill at ease,

Unfit for mine own purposes.

DESDEMONA

Well, do your discretion.

Exit CASSIO

Enter OTHELLO and IAGO

IAGO

Ha! I like not that.

OTHELLO

What dost thou say?

IAGO

Nothing, my lord: or if--I know not what.

OTHELLO

Was not that Cassio parted from my wife?

IAGO

Cassio, my lord! No, sure, I cannot think it,

That he would steal away so guilty-like,

Seeing you coming.

OTHELLO

DESDEMONA

Why? Stay, and hear me talk to him.

CASSIO

No, madam. I feel uneasy.

I don't feel up to it.

DESDEMONA

Well, do what you think is the best thing to

do.

Exit CASSIO

Enter OTHELLO and IAGO

IAGO

Ha! I don't like that.

OTHELLO

What?

IAGO

Oh, It's nothing, my lord. Or... No, it's nothing.

OTHELLO

Was that Cassio leaving my wife?

IAGO

Cassio, my lord! No, I don't think so,

I don't think he'd sneak away so guiltily when

he saw you coming.

OTHELLO

I do believe 'twas he.

DESDEMONA

How now, my lord!

I have been talking with a suitor here,

A man that languishes in your displeasure.

OTHELLO

Who is't you mean?

DESDEMONA

Why, your lieutenant, Cassio. Good my lord,

If I have any grace or power to move you,

His present reconciliation take;

For if he be not one that truly loves you,

That errs in ignorance and not in cunning,

I have no judgment in an honest face:

I prithee, call him back.

OTHELLO

Went he hence now?

DESDEMONA

Ay, sooth; so humbled

That he hath left part of his grief with me,

To suffer with him. Good love, call him back.

OTHELLO

I really do think it was him.

DESDEMONA

Hello, my lord!

I have been speaking to somebody who is unhappy,

A man that is suffering from your anger.

OTHELLO

Who do you mean?

DESDEMONA

Your lieutenant, Cassio.

If I have any power to influence you, please accept his apology. He is a man who truly loves you,

and has committed errors accidentally rather than maliciously,

if I'm wrong then I'm not a good judge of character.

I beg you, tell him to come back here.

OTHELLO

Did he just leave?

DESDEMONA

Yes. He feels so humiliated

That he has made me feel upset,

because of how he feels. My love, please call him back.

OTHELLO

Not now, sweet Desdemona; some other time.	Not now, sweet Desdemona; some other time.
DESDEMONA But shall't be shortly?	**DESDEMONA** But will it be soon?
OTHELLO The sooner, sweet, for you.	**OTHELLO** Very soon, just for you.
DESDEMONA Shall't be to-night at supper?	**DESDEMONA** Will it be tonight at supper?
OTHELLO No, not to-night.	**OTHELLO** No, not tonight.
DESDEMONA To-morrow dinner, then?	**DESDEMONA** Tomorrow dinner time, then?
OTHELLO I shall not dine at home; I meet the captains at the citadel.	**OTHELLO** I won't be eating at home; I am meeting the captains at the citadel.
DESDEMONA Why, then, to-morrow night; or Tuesday morn; On Tuesday noon, or night; on Wednesday morn: I prithee, name the time, but let it not Exceed three days: in faith, he's penitent; And yet his trespass, in our common reason-- Save that, they say, the wars must make examples Out of their best--is not almost a fault To incur a private cheque. When shall he	**DESDEMONA** What about tomorrow night or Tuesday morning. Or Tuesday noon, or night or Wednesday morning? I'm begging you, please name the time, and don't wait more than three days. Honestly, he's really sorry. and I believe that his offence was not something that deserves a severe punishment. I understand that you have to make an example of your best soldiers in war time.

come?

Tell me, Othello: I wonder in my soul,

What you would ask me, that I should deny,

Or stand so mammering on. What! Michael Cassio,

That came a-wooing with you, and so many a time,

When I have spoke of you dispraisingly,

Hath ta'en your part; to have so much to do

To bring him in! Trust me, I could do much,--

OTHELLO

Prithee, no more: let him come when he will;

I will deny thee nothing.

DESDEMONA

Why, this is not a boon;

'Tis as I should entreat you wear your gloves,

Or feed on nourishing dishes, or keep you warm,

Or sue to you to do a peculiar profit

To your own person: nay, when I have a suit

Wherein I mean to touch your love indeed,

It shall be full of poise and difficult weight

And fearful to be granted.

OTHELLO

I will deny thee nothing:

Whereon, I do beseech thee, grant me this,

To leave me but a little to myself.

When can he come?

Tell me, Othello. I wonder what you could ever ask of me that would make me say no,

Or make me stand muttering on. What! Michael Cassio,

Who came with you when you were trying to gain my love,

When I have criticised you,

He has always taken your side. I can't believe I am having to do so much to convince you to reinstate him. Trust me, I could do so much-

OTHELLO

Please, don't say anymore. He can come whenever he wants;

I won't refuse you anything.

DESDEMONA

This isn't a favour to me.

It is as though I am asking if I can wear your gloves when it's cold,

Or if I can eat nutritious food, or keep you warm,

Or ask you to do something for your own interest. No, when I have a request

I want out of love,

It will be much more complex and difficult to grant.

OTHELLO

I will never deny you anything.

But I beg you to do something for me.

Leave me a little time to myself.

DESDEMONA

Shall I deny you? no: farewell, my lord.

OTHELLO

Farewell, my Desdemona: I'll come to thee straight.

DESDEMONA

Emilia, come. Be as your fancies teach you;
Whate'er you be, I am obedient.

Exeunt DESDEMONA and EMILIA

OTHELLO

Excellent wretch! Perdition catch my soul,
But I do love thee! and when I love thee not,
Chaos is come again.

IAGO

My noble lord—

OTHELLO

What dost thou say, Iago?

IAGO

Did Michael Cassio, when you woo'd my lady,
Know of your love?

OTHELLO

He did, from first to last: why dost thou ask?

IAGO

DESDEMONA

Would I deny you that? No, goodbye, my lord.

OTHELLO

Goodbye, my Desdemona: I'll come see you soon.

DESDEMONA

Emilia, come on. Do whatever you want to do, and I will obey you.

Exit DESDEMONA and EMILIA

OTHELLO

Wonderful girl! God help me,
I love you! And if I stop loving you
it will be a return to chaos.

IAGO

My noble lord—

OTHELLO

What, Iago?

IAGO

When you were flirting with Desdemona, did Michael Cassio know about it?

OTHELLO

He knew about it from beginning to end: why are you asking?

IAGO

But for a satisfaction of my thought;

No further harm.

OTHELLO

Why of thy thought, Iago?

IAGO

I did not think he had been acquainted with her.

OTHELLO

O, yes; and went between us very oft.

IAGO

Indeed!

OTHELLO

Indeed! ay, indeed: discern'st thou aught in that?

Is he not honest?

IAGO

Honest, my lord!

OTHELLO

Honest! ay, honest.

IAGO

My lord, for aught I know.

OTHELLO

What dost thou think?

Just something I thought. No reason really.

OTHELLO

Why are you curious, Iago?

IAGO

I didn't realise he knew her.

OTHELLO

Yes. He often carried messages between us both.

IAGO

Really!

OTHELLO

Really! Yes, really. Is there something wrong with that?

Isn't he an honest man?

IAGO

Honest, my lord?

OTHELLO

Honest! yes, honest.

IAGO

As far as I know, sir.

OTHELLO

What are you thinking?

IAGO

Think, my lord!

OTHELLO

Think, my lord!

By heaven, he echoes me,

As if there were some monster in his thought

Too hideous to be shown. Thou dost mean something:

I heard thee say even now, thou likedst not that,

When Cassio left my wife: what didst not like?

And when I told thee he was of my counsel

In my whole course of wooing, thou criedst 'Indeed!'

And didst contract and purse thy brow together,

As if thou then hadst shut up in thy brain

Some horrible conceit: if thou dost love me,

Show me thy thought.

IAGO

My lord, you know I love you.

OTHELLO

I think thou dost;

And, for I know thou'rt full of love and honesty,

And weigh'st thy words before thou givest them breath,

Therefore these stops of thine fright me the more:

For such things in a false disloyal knave

Are tricks of custom, but in a man that's just

IAGO

What am I thinking, my lord?

OTHELLO

"Thinking, my lord!"

My God, you keep repeating me,

As if you are thinking something too horrible to say out loud.

You're thinking something:

I just heard you say that you didn't like it

When Cassio left my life. What didn't you like?

And when I told you that he was my confidant

all through my dating Desdemona, you cried 'really?'

And you pulled a face as if you had some horrible idea in your head.

If you love me

tell me what you're thinking.

IAGO

My lord, you know I love you.

OTHELLO

I think you do.

And as far as I know you are full of love and honesty,

And you are thinking carefully before you speak what's on your mind,

Therefore your hesitation scares me more.

If a stupid disloyal fool were withholding

things from me I would know it was just a

They are close delations, working from the heart

That passion cannot rule.

IAGO

For Michael Cassio,

I dare be sworn I think that he is honest.

OTHELLO

I think so too.

IAGO

Men should be what they seem;

Or those that be not, would they might seem none!

OTHELLO

Certain, men should be what they seem.

IAGO

Why, then, I think Cassio's an honest man.

OTHELLO

Nay, yet there's more in this:

I prithee, speak to me as to thy thinkings,

As thou dost ruminate, and give thy worst of thoughts

The worst of words.

IAGO

Good my lord, pardon me:

Though I am bound to every act of duty,

I am not bound to that all slaves are free to.

trick, but when a man like you acts like this then I know he is struggling with his emotions and can't help it.

IAGO

Michael Cassio,

I would swear he is honest.

OTHELLO

I think so too.

IAGO

People should be what they appear to be. If they're not honest, they shouldn't act like they are.

OTHELLO

Definitely, men should be what they appear to be.

IAGO

Okay then, I think Cassio's an honest man.

OTHELLO

No, There's more to this.

Please tell me what you are thinking.

Tell me exactly what's on your mind no matter how bad it sounds.

IAGO

My lord, forgive me.

Even though I am bound to you in every act of duty, I am not bound to utter my thoughts.

Utter my thoughts? Why, say they are vile and false;

As where's that palace whereinto foul things

Sometimes intrude not? who has a breast so pure,

But some uncleanly apprehensions

Keep leets and law-days and in session sit

With meditations lawful?

OTHELLO

Thou dost conspire against thy friend, Iago,

If thou but think'st him wrong'd and makest his ear

A stranger to thy thoughts.

IAGO

I do beseech you--

Though I perchance am vicious in my guess,

As, I confess, it is my nature's plague

To spy into abuses, and oft my jealousy

Shapes faults that are not--that your wisdom yet,

From one that so imperfectly conceits,

Would take no notice, nor build yourself a trouble

Out of his scattering and unsure observance.

It were not for your quiet nor your good,

Nor for my manhood, honesty, or wisdom,

To let you know my thoughts.

OTHELLO

What dost thou mean?

IAGO

Not even slaves have to do that. You really want me to tell you what I am thinking? What if my thoughts are vile and false?

And who doesn't have a mind that sometimes contains bad thoughts?

Who has a heart so pure

That some really bad thoughts don't live alongside side good ones?

OTHELLO

You are deceiving me, Iago

if you even think that I am being wronged and don't tell me about it.

IAGO

I am begging you to not ask me.

Maybe I am judging too harshly,

I admit that it is a fault of mine that my jealousy sometimes makes me view things the wrong way.

I am sure that you are too wise to trust the judgement of somebody like me who isn't perfect. I am sure you don't want to cause yourself too much trouble

By listening to my unsure observations.

It's not in your interest, nor is it beneficial to your peace of mind,

Or my status, honesty, or wisdom to tell you what I am thinking.

OTHELLO

What do you mean?

IAGO

137

Good name in man and woman, dear my lord,
Is the immediate jewel of their souls:
Who steals my purse steals trash; 'tis something, nothing;
'Twas mine, 'tis his, and has been slave to thousands:
But he that filches from me my good name
Robs me of that which not enriches him
And makes me poor indeed.

OTHELLO

By heaven, I'll know thy thoughts.

IAGO

You cannot, if my heart were in your hand;
Nor shall not, whilst 'tis in my custody.

OTHELLO

Ha!

IAGO

O, beware, my lord, of jealousy;
It is the green-eyed monster which doth mock
The meat it feeds on; that cuckold lives in bliss
Who, certain of his fate, loves not his wronger;
But, O, what damned minutes tells he o'er
Who dotes, yet doubts, suspects, yet strongly loves!

A good reputation in man or woman, my dear lord,
Is the most precious and valuable thing we have. Whoever steals my money steals nothing but trash – it's of no value. It was mine and now is someone else's. Money has always enslaved thousands. But the person that steals my reputation is robbing me of something that doesn't make him richer, but makes me very poor.

OTHELLO

I am going to find out what you are thinking.

IAGO

You can't. Even if you held my heart in your hand.
You will not find out my thoughts while my heart belongs to me.

OTHELLO

What?

IAGO

Beware of jealousy, my lord. It is the green-eyed monster that ridicules the victim it feeds on. The person who doesn't know he is being cheater on can live in bliss.
But the one who adores his wife, yet doubts her, suspects her and foolishly continues to love her will endure terrible unhappiness. He suspects her but he still loves her!

OTHELLO O misery!	**OTHELLO** This is awful!
IAGO Poor and content is rich and rich enough, But riches fineless is as poor as winter To him that ever fears he shall be poor. Good heaven, the souls of all my tribe defend From jealousy!	**IAGO** A person who is poor yet content is rich enough. But being extremely rich is nothing to someone who is afraid to be poor. God, help protect us from jealousy!
OTHELLO Why, why is this? Think'st thou I'ld make a lie of jealousy, To follow still the changes of the moon With fresh suspicions? No; to be once in doubt Is once to be resolved: exchange me for a goat, When I shall turn the business of my soul To such exsufflicate and blown surmises, Matching thy inference. 'Tis not to make me jealous To say my wife is fair, feeds well, loves company, Is free of speech, sings, plays and dances well; Where virtue is, these are more virtuous: Nor from mine own weak merits will I draw The smallest fear or doubt of her revolt; For she had eyes, and chose me. No, Iago; I'll see before I doubt; when I doubt, prove; And on the proof, there is no more but this,-- Away at once with love or jealousy!	**OTHELLO** Why, why are you telling me this? Do you think I would be able to live a life of jealousy? Do you think I'd cope with being tormented by new suspicions every hour? No. As soon as I have doubts I make sure I do something about it immediately. You might as well turn me into a goat if I allow my soul to suffer with the kind of accusations you are inferring. It doesn't make me jealous when someone says that my wife is beautiful, eats well, enjoys the company of others, speaks freely, sings, plays music, and dances well. When someone is virtuous these things add to her virtue. I will not doubt her faithfulness just because I doubt my own attractiveness. She can clearly see and she chose me. No, Iago. I have to see the evidence before I have any doubt about her. When I have doubts I do try to prove them. When it is proved, then that's it.

	Love and jealousy will be banished from my mind!
IAGO	**IAGO**
I am glad of it; for now I shall have reason	I am pleased to hear you say that. I now have
To show the love and duty that I bear you	reason to show you how honest and devoted
With franker spirit: therefore, as I am bound,	to you I am.
Receive it from me. I speak not yet of proof.	To be completely honest with you, as I am
Look to your wife; observe her well with	bound to be, you need to listen to me. I don't
Cassio;	have any proof of anything yet but you need
Wear your eye thus, not jealous nor secure:	to watch your wife closely. Watch her with
I would not have your free and noble nature,	Cassio. Just watch. Don't react or think with
Out of self-bounty, be abused; look to't:	jealousy. Just be objective.
I know our country disposition well;	I wouldn't want anyone to take advantage of
In Venice they do let heaven see the pranks	your nature. Just watch them.
They dare not show their husbands; their best	I know the women of Venice well.
conscience	They let God see things that they wouldn't
Is not to leave't undone, but keep't unknown.	dare let their husbands see.
	They don't avoid doing things. They would
	rather be secretive and avoid getting caught
	than not get up to any mischief.
OTHELLO	**OTHELLO**
Dost thou say so?	Do you really think so?
IAGO	**IAGO**
She did deceive her father, marrying you;	She deceived her father when she married
And when she seem'd to shake and fear your	you.
looks,	And she seemed to love you most when she
She loved them most.	appeared to be afraid of you.
OTHELLO	**OTHELLO**
And so she did.	Yes, she did.

IAGO

Why, go to then;

She that, so young, could give out such a seeming,

To seal her father's eyes up close as oak-

He thought 'twas witchcraft--but I am much to blame;

I humbly do beseech you of your pardon

For too much loving you.

OTHELLO

I am bound to thee for ever.

IAGO

I see this hath a little dash'd your spirits.

OTHELLO

Not a jot, not a jot.

IAGO

I' faith, I fear it has.

I hope you will consider what is spoke

Comes from my love. But I do see you're moved:

I am to pray you not to strain my speech

To grosser issues nor to larger reach

Than to suspicion.

OTHELLO

I will not.

IAGO

Should you do so, my lord,

My speech should fall into such vile success

IAGO

That's your proof then.

Even though she was very young

she still managed to deceive her father and

make him believe it was witch craft!

I am really sorry that I have said all this.

Please forgive me for loving you too much.

OTHELLO

I am forever grateful to you.

IAGO

I can see this has upset you.

OTHELLO

Not at all, not at all.

IAGO

Really, I think it has.

I hope that you understand that I have only

said all of this because I love you. I can see

that this has bothered you.

I am praying that you do not ask me to tell

you anything worse – anything that goes

beyond suspicion.

OTHELLO

I won't.

IAGO

If you do ask me to, my lord,

As my thoughts aim not at. Cassio's my worthy
friend--
My lord, I see you're moved.

OTHELLO

No, not much moved:
I do not think but Desdemona's honest.

IAGO

Long live she so! and long live you to think so!

OTHELLO

And yet, how nature erring from itself,--

IAGO

Ay, there's the point: as--to be bold with you--
Not to affect many proposed matches
Of her own clime, complexion, and degree,
Whereto we see in all things nature tends--
Foh! one may smell in such a will most rank,
Foul disproportion thoughts unnatural.
But pardon me; I do not in position
Distinctly speak of her; though I may fear
Her will, recoiling to her better judgment,
May fall to match you with her country forms
And happily repent.

OTHELLO

I will say things that are awful- things I don't
mean.
Cassio's a good friend of mine –
My lord, I can see you are upset.

OTHELLO

No. I'm not too upset.
I am sure that Desdemona is honest.

IAGO

And I hope she always will be! And I hope you
always think like that!

OTHELLO

But, I am thinking about how sometimes good
things can go wrong.

IAGO

Yes, that's the point I am trying to make. To
be honest with you, the fact that she rejected
all those young men from her own country,
with the same skin colour, with a similar
status (which would be the most natural thing
for her) suggests that something isn't right.
Ugh! One may think that she is too strong-
willed, or has unnatural thoughts.
But forgive me. I do not mean to talk about
her specifically, even if I do fear her nature.
I worry that she might go back to her natural
urges one day and start comparing you to the
other men from her country.
She might regret marrying you.

OTHELLO

Farewell, farewell:

If more thou dost perceive, let me know more;

Set on thy wife to observe: leave me, Iago:

IAGO

[Going] My lord, I take my leave.

OTHELLO

Why did I marry? This honest creature doubtless

Sees and knows more, much more, than he unfolds.

IAGO

[Returning] My lord, I would I might entreat your honour

To scan this thing no further; leave it to time:

Though it be fit that Cassio have his place,

For sure, he fills it up with great ability,

Yet, if you please to hold him off awhile,

You shall by that perceive him and his means:

Note, if your lady strain his entertainment

With any strong or vehement importunity;

Much will be seen in that. In the mean time,

Let me be thought too busy in my fears-As

worthy cause I have to fear I am--

And hold her free, I do beseech your honour.

OTHELLO

Fear not my government.

IAGO

Goodbye. Goodbye.

If you notice anything else then please let me know.

Ask your wife to watch her. Leave me, Iago.

IAGO

[Going] My lord, I'm going.

OTHELLO

Why did I get married? Honest Iago obviously knows more, much more, than he wants to tell me.

IAGO

[Returning] My lord, I would really like you not to think about this anymore.

Time will tell us more.

It is right to give Cassio his job back.

He is very good at his role.

But, if you hold back for a little while then you might be able to watch him closely to see how he tries to get it back. Notice whether your wife pleads passionately with you to reinstate him.

That will tell you a lot. In the meantime, just think of me as being too interfering, but for a reason.

I beg you to believe she is honest.

OTHELLO

Don't worry about how I choose to deal with it.

IAGO

I once more take my leave.	I am going again.
Exit	*Exit*
OTHELLO	**OTHELLO**
This fellow's of exceeding honesty,	This man is really honest and good,
And knows all qualities, with a learned spirit,	And he truly understands human behaviour.
Of human dealings. If I do prove her haggard,	If she is proven to be a cheat then I will send
Though that her jesses were my dear	her away, even though it will break my heart.
heartstrings,	Maybe this is happening to me because I am
I'd whistle her off and let her down the wind,	black
To pray at fortune. Haply, for I am black	and don't speak softly or have the same good
And have not those soft parts of conversation	manners as the other gentlemen.
That chamberers have, or for I am declined	Maybe it is because I am getting old, but I am
Into the vale of years,--yet that's not much--	not that much older.
She's gone. I am abused; and my relief	She's gone. I have been cheated on. I have no
Must be to loathe her. O curse of marriage,	choice but to hate her. This marriage is a
That we can call these delicate creatures ours,	curse.
And not their appetites! I had rather be a	How can we call these delicate women ours if
toad,	their desires are focussed elsewhere! I'd
And live upon the vapour of a dungeon,	rather be a toad and live in a disgusting
Than keep a corner in the thing I love	dungeon
For others' uses. Yet, 'tis the plague of great	Than keep a woman that I love if she is used
ones;	by other men. This is the curse of important
Prerogatived are they less than the base;	men: our wives betray us. We suffer more
'Tis destiny unshunnable, like death:	than men who are poor.
Even then this forked plague is fated to us	It's our destiny, like death is.
When we do quicken. Desdemona comes:	We are destined to suffer as soon as we are
	born. Desdemona is coming.
Re-enter DESDEMONA and EMILIA	*Re-enter DESDEMONA and EMILIA*
If she be false, O, then heaven mocks itself!	If she is lying, then heaven is fake.
I'll not believe't.	I won't believe it.

DESDEMONA	**DESDEMONA**
How now, my dear Othello!	How are you, my dear Othello!
Your dinner, and the generous islanders	Dinner is ready and the generous Islanders
By you invited, do attend your presence.	that you have invited are waiting for you.
OTHELLO	**OTHELLO**
I am to blame.	It's my fault.
DESDEMONA	**DESDEMONA**
Why do you speak so faintly?	Why are you whispering?
Are you not well?	Are you ill?
OTHELLO	**OTHELLO**
I have a pain upon my forehead here.	I have a headache.
DESDEMONA	**DESDEMONA**
'Faith, that's with watching; 'twill away again:	That's because you are tired. It'll go away.
Let me but bind it hard, within this hour	Let me wrap up your head and it will feel
It will be well.	better within an hour.
OTHELLO	**OTHELLO**
Your napkin is too little:	Your handkerchief is too small.
He puts the handkerchief from him; and it drops	*He puts the handkerchief from him; and it drops*
Let it alone. Come, I'll go in with you.	Leave it. Come on. Let's go.
DESDEMONA	**DESDEMONA**
I am very sorry that you are not well.	I am really sorry that you aren't feeling very well.
Exeunt OTHELLO and DESDEMONA	*Exeunt OTHELLO and DESDEMONA*

EMILIA	**EMILIA**
I am glad I have found this napkin:	I'm glad I've found her handkerchief.
This was her first remembrance from the Moor:	This was her first gift from the Moor.
My wayward husband hath a hundred times	My mischievous husband has asked me to
Woo'd me to steal it; but she so loves the token,	steal this a hundred times but she loves it so much and Othello has always told her to keep
For he conjured her she should ever keep it,	it with her at all times.
That she reserves it evermore about her	She always has it with her. She keeps it near
To kiss and talk to. I'll have the work ta'en out,	to kiss it and talk to it.
And give't Iago: what he will do with it	I'll have the pattern copied
Heaven knows, not I;	And give that one to Iago. Heaven knows
I nothing but to please his fantasy.	what he is going to do with it.
	I just try to satisfy his thoughts.
Re-enter Iago	*Re-enter Iago*
IAGO	**IAGO**
How now! what do you here alone?	What are you doing here alone?
EMILIA	**EMILIA**
Do not you chide; I have a thing for you.	Do not have a go at me. I have something for you.
IAGO	**IAGO**
A thing for me? it is a common thing—	Something for me? It is a normal thing...
EMILIA	**EMILIA**
Ha!	What?
IAGO	**IAGO**
To have a foolish wife.	I have a stupid wife.
EMILIA	**EMILIA**

O, is that all? What will you give me now

For the same handkerchief?

IAGO

What handkerchief?

EMILIA

What handkerchief?

Why, that the Moor first gave to Desdemona;

That which so often you did bid me steal.

IAGO

Hast stol'n it from her?

EMILIA

No, 'faith; she let it drop by negligence.

And, to the advantage, I, being here, took't up.

Look, here it is.

IAGO

A good wench; give it me.

EMILIA

What will you do with 't, that you have been

so earnest

To have me filch it?

IAGO

[Snatching it] Why, what's that to you?

EMILIA

If it be not for some purpose of import,

Give't me again: poor lady, she'll run mad

When she shall lack it.

Oh, is that all? What will you give me for this

handkerchief?

IAGO

What handkerchief?

EMILIA

What handkerchief?

The one the Moor first gave to Desdemona.

The one that you have begged me to steal.

IAGO

Have you stolen it?

EMILIA

No. She dropped it by accident. Luckily I was

there to pick it up.

Here it is.

IAGO

Good girl. Give it to me.

EMILIA

What are you going to do with it?

Why have you been so desperate for me to

steal it?

IAGO

[Snatching it] what has it got to do with you?

EMILIA

If you don't need it for some important

reason then you need to give it back to me.

IAGO

Be not acknown on 't; I have use for it.
Go, leave me.

Exit EMILIA

I will in Cassio's lodging lose this napkin,
And let him find it. Trifles light as air
Are to the jealous confirmations strong
As proofs of holy writ: this may do something.
The Moor already changes with my poison:
Dangerous conceits are, in their natures,
poisons.
Which at the first are scarce found to distaste,
But with a little act upon the blood.
Burn like the mines of Sulphur. I did say so:
Look, where he comes!

Re-enter OTHELLO

Not poppy, nor mandragora,
Nor all the drowsy syrups of the world,
Shall ever medicine thee to that sweet sleep
Which thou owedst yesterday.

OTHELLO

Ha! ha! false to me?

IAGO

Why, how now, general! no more of that.

Poor lady, she will go mad when she notices it
is missing.

IAGO

Don't say anything about it. I have a use for it.
Go away.

Exit EMILIA

I will leave this handkerchief in Cassio's house
and let him find it. Little things like this look
like absolute proof to a jealous man. This will
be useful to me.
The Moor's mind has already changed based
on my poisonous words.
Ideas can be poisonous and dangerous.
At first the ideas are dismissed,
But once they begin to be believed they burn
like through the blood like sulphur.
Here he comes!

Re-enter OTHELLO

No drugs or sleeping pills will ever give you
back the restful sleep which you had
yesterday.

OTHELLO

Argh! Is she being unfaithful to me?

IAGO

Come on, general! Let's not hear any more of
that.

OTHELLO

Avaunt! be gone! thou hast set me on the rack:

I swear 'tis better to be much abused

Than but to know't a little.

IAGO

How now, my lord!

OTHELLO

What sense had I of her stol'n hours of lust?

I saw't not, thought it not, it harm'd not me:

I slept the next night well, was free and merry;

I found not Cassio's kisses on her lips:

He that is robb'd, not wanting what is stol'n,

Let him not know't, and he's not robb'd at all.

IAGO

I am sorry to hear this.

OTHELLO

I had been happy, if the general camp,

Pioners and all, had tasted her sweet body,

So I had nothing known. O, now, for ever

Farewell the tranquil mind! farewell content!

Farewell the plumed troop, and the big wars,

That make ambition virtue! O, farewell!

Farewell the neighing steed, and the shrill trump,

The spirit-stirring drum, the ear-piercing fife,

The royal banner, and all quality,

Pride, pomp and circumstance of glorious war!

OTHELLO

Go away! Get out! You have tortured me with these ideas.

It would have been better if you'd have just told me everything rather than only tell me small details.

IAGO

What's wrong, my lord?

OTHELLO

I had no idea that she was being unfaithful.

I never saw it or even suspected it, so it never affected me.

I slept well and I was happy.

I didn't even sense Cassio's kisses on her lips.

A man that doesn't miss what has been stolen from him hasn't really been robbed at all.

IAGO

I am sorry to hear this.

OTHELLO

I would have been happy if everybody in the army had had sex with her, even if the lowest-ranking men had also had sex with her as long as I didn't know about it. Goodbye to my peaceful mind! Goodbye to my happiness! Goodbye to soldiers and the big wars that make us assets! Oh, goodbye!

Goodbye to all the horses and the trumpets, and the exciting drums, the extremely loud flutes,

And, O you mortal engines, whose rude throats

The immortal Jove's dead clamours counterfeit,

Farewell! Othello's occupation's gone!

IAGO

Is't possible, my lord?

OTHELLO

Villain, be sure thou prove my love a whore,

Be sure of it; give me the ocular proof:

Or by the worth of man's eternal soul,

Thou hadst been better have been born a dog

Than answer my waked wrath!

IAGO

Is't come to this?

OTHELLO

Make me to see't; or, at the least, so prove it,

That the probation bear no hinge nor loop

To hang a doubt on; or woe upon thy life!

IAGO

My noble lord,--

OTHELLO

If thou dost slander her and torture me,

Never pray more; abandon all remorse;

On horror's head horrors accumulate;

Do deeds to make heaven weep, all earth amazed;

The royal banners, and all the proud displays

of glorious war!

And, the deadly shouts of soldiers whose voices sound like deathly thunder

Goodbye! Othello's career is over.

IAGO

Is this possible, my lord?

OTHELLO

You villain, you'd better be able to prove my wife's a whore,

Be sure of it. Get me proof that I can see. Or you will wish you had been born a dog rather than answer my rage!

IAGO

Has it come to this?

OTHELLO

Let me see the proof with my own eyes, or, at least, prove it.

If you cannot prove it then your life is worthless!

IAGO

My noble lord -

OTHELLO

If you're slandering her just to torture me then praying won't save you. Neither will saying you're sorry.

Horrors will pile up on you.

You could do many more appalling acts to shock everybody, because there's nothing

For nothing canst thou to damnation add
Greater than that.

IAGO

O grace! O heaven forgive me!
Are you a man? have you a soul or sense?
God be wi' you; take mine office. O wretched
fool.
That livest to make thine honesty a vice!
O monstrous world! Take note, take note, O
world,
To be direct and honest is not safe.
I thank you for this profit; and from hence
I'll love no friend, sith love breeds such
offence.

OTHELLO

Nay, stay: thou shouldst be honest.

IAGO

I should be wise, for honesty's a fool
And loses that it works for.

OTHELLO

By the world,
I think my wife be honest and think she is not;
I think that thou art just and think thou art
not.
I'll have some proof. Her name, that was as
fresh
As Dian's visage, is now begrimed and black
As mine own face. If there be cords, or knives,

you could do that could be worse than what
you've done.

IAGO

Oh, heaven help me and forgive me!
Are you a rational man? Do you have any
sense at all? God be with you. Goodbye. I
resign from my post. I am such an idiot. My
honesty is my downfall.
What a horrible world! Listen, listen,
everybody.
It is not safe to be direct and honest.
Thank you for teaching me this lesson. From
now on,
I will never try to help a friend that I love if it
hurts him too much.

OTHELLO

No, stay: you should always be honest.

IAGO

I should be more wise. Being honest is foolish
and destroys friendships.

OTHELLO

I am so confused,
I think my wife is honest but I also think she
isn't;
One minute I think you are trustworthy and
then I don't.
I need some proof. Her reputation was as
pure as the goddess of the moon's and it is
now as dirty and as black as my own face.

151

Poison, or fire, or suffocating streams,

I'll not endure it. Would I were satisfied!

IAGO

I see, sir, you are eaten up with passion:

I do repent me that I put it to you.

You would be satisfied?

OTHELLO

Would! nay, I will.

IAGO

And may: but, how? how satisfied, my lord?

Would you, the supervisor, grossly gape on--

Behold her topp'd?

OTHELLO

Death and damnation! O!

IAGO

It were a tedious difficulty, I think,

To bring them to that prospect: damn them then,

If ever mortal eyes do see them bolster

More than their own! What then? how then?

What shall I say? Where's satisfaction?

It is impossible you should see this,

Were they as prime as goats, as hot as monkeys,

As salt as wolves in pride, and fools as gross

As ignorance made drunk. But yet, I say,

If imputation and strong circumstances,

As long as there are ropes and knives, poison and fire, or streams to drown in, I won't put up with this. I just wish I knew the truth.

IAGO

I see, sir, that you are consumed with emotion. I am sorry that I said anything. Do you want to proof?

OTHELLO

Want? Yes, and I will.

IAGO

You might, but how? How much proof do you want?

Would you hide and crudely watch them have sex?

OTHELLO

Oh! Death and damnation!

IAGO

I think it would be far too difficult to arrange that.

They would be eternally damned

if anyone sees them in bed together!

What then? How shall we do this?

What can I say? Where's the proof?

It would be impossible for you to see this,

even if they were as horny as animals in heat

Or as stupid as drunks. But still, if

circumstantial evidence, strong enough to

lead to the truth,

Were to be accepted by you, you can have it.

Which lead directly to the door of truth,

Will give you satisfaction, you may have't.

OTHELLO

Give me a living reason she's disloyal.

IAGO

I do not like the office:

But, sith I am enter'd in this cause so far,

Prick'd to't by foolish honesty and love,

I will go on. I lay with Cassio lately;

And, being troubled with a raging tooth,

I could not sleep.

There are a kind of men so loose of soul,

That in their sleeps will mutter their affairs:

One of this kind is Cassio:

In sleep I heard him say 'Sweet Desdemona,

Let us be wary, let us hide our loves;'

And then, sir, would he gripe and wring my hand,

Cry 'O sweet creature!' and then kiss me hard,

As if he pluck'd up kisses by the roots

That grew upon my lips: then laid his leg

Over my thigh, and sigh'd, and kiss'd; and then

Cried 'Cursed fate that gave thee to the Moor!'

OTHELLO

O monstrous! monstrous!

IAGO

Nay, this was but his dream.

OTHELLO

Give me a good reason to prove that she is disloyal.

IAGO

I do not like what you are asking me to do.

But since I have gotten myself involved this far,

Because of my foolish honesty and love for you, I'll tell you. I stayed with Cassio recently, and because I had raging toothache, I couldn't sleep.

There are some people that have so much hidden that they talk in their sleep.

Cassio is one of these people.

I heard him say 'sweet Desdemona,

Let's be very careful and hide our love.'

And then he grabbed my hand,

and cried out, 'Oh sweet creature!' and then he kissed me hard,

As if he were trying to suck my lips off.

Then he put his leg over my thigh, and sighed and kissed me;

And then he cried 'damn fate for giving you to the moor!'

OTHELLO

Oh that's horrible! Just horrible!

IAGO

No, it was just a dream.

OTHELLO

But this denoted a foregone conclusion:

OTHELLO

But it shows that something might have already happened.

IAGO

'Tis a shrewd doubt, though it be but a dream.
And this may help to thicken other proofs
That do demonstrate thinly.

IAGO

It's only a dream but it is reason for suspicion.
And it might help support any other proof
that may not be very strong.

OTHELLO

I'll tear her all to pieces.

OTHELLO

I'll tear her to pieces.

IAGO

Nay, but be wise: yet we see nothing done;
She may be honest yet. Tell me but this,
Have you not sometimes seen a handkerchief
Spotted with strawberries in your wife's hand?

IAGO

No, be smart about it. We don't have any proof yet.
She may actually be honest. Just tell me something. Have you ever seen your wife with a handkerchief
Decorated with strawberries?

OTHELLO

I gave her such a one; 'twas my first gift.

OTHELLO

I gave her one just like that. It was my first gift to her.

IAGO

I know not that; but such a handkerchief--
I am sure it was your wife's--did I to-day
See Cassio wipe his beard with.

IAGO

I don't know anything about that; but I have seen a handkerchief like that – I'm sure it was your wife's – I saw Cassio wipe his beard on it today.

OTHELLO

If it be that—

OTHELLO

If it is that same one...

IAGO	**IAGO**
If it be that, or any that was hers,	If it was that one, or any other that is hers, it
It speaks against her with the other proofs.	adds to the other proof we have.
OTHELLO	**OTHELLO**
O, that the slave had forty thousand lives!	Oh, I'd kill that Cassio forty thousand times if I
One is too poor, too weak for my revenge.	could!
Now do I see 'tis true. Look here, Iago;	Killing him once is not enough to get revenge.
All my fond love thus do I blow to heaven.	Now I see that it's true. Iago, all my love for
'Tis gone.	her is gone, vanished towards heaven.
Arise, black vengeance, from thy hollow cell!	It's gone.
Yield up, O love, thy crown and hearted	Wake up from your cell, black vengeance!
throne	Go away, love! Give up your crown and
To tyrannous hate! Swell, bosom, with thy	throne to hate! My heart is full of poisonous
fraught,	snakes' tongues!
For 'tis of aspics' tongues!	
IAGO	**IAGO**
Yet be content.	Calm down.
OTHELLO	**OTHELLO**
O, blood, blood, blood!	I want blood, blood, blood!
IAGO	**IAGO**
Patience, I say; your mind perhaps may	I am telling you to be patient. You might
change.	change your mind later.
OTHELLO	**OTHELLO**
Never, Iago: Like to the Pontic sea,	Never, Iago. My thoughts of revenge are
Whose icy current and compulsive course	flowing like an icy sea, compulsive in its thrust
Ne'er feels retiring ebb, but keeps due on	Never relaxing, but keeps pushing on, forcing
To the Propontic and the Hellespont,	its way through narrow openings
Even so my bloody thoughts, with violent	To the huge Black Sea.
pace,	

Shall ne'er look back, ne'er ebb to humble love,
Till that a capable and wide revenge
Swallow them up. Now, by yond marble heaven,

Kneels

In the due reverence of a sacred vow
I here engage my words.

IAGO

Do not rise yet.

Kneels

Witness, you ever-burning lights above,
You elements that clip us round about,
Witness that here Iago doth give up
The execution of his wit, hands, heart,
To wrong'd Othello's service! Let him command,
And to obey shall be in me remorse,
What bloody business ever.

They rise

OTHELLO

I greet thy love,
Not with vain thanks, but with acceptance bounteous,
And will upon the instant put thee to't:
Within these three days let me hear thee say
That Cassio's not alive.

IAGO

My friend is dead; 'tis done at your request:
But let her live.

My bloody and violent thoughts will never look back.
They will never return to the calm love I felt
Until a huge revenge
Swallows them up. Now, by heaven above,

Kneels

I swear to God I will get my revenge.

IAGO

Don't get up yet.

Kneels

Let heaven and the elements be my witness
also, I swear that I, Iago, surrender my mind,
hands, and heart to wronged Othello's control!
Let him command me,

And I will do whatever he asks me to, no
matter how violent and whatever it may be.

They rise

OTHELLO

I accept your love,
Not superficially, but completely,

And I will put it to the test immediately.
Within the next three days I want to hear you
tell me that Cassio is dead.

IAGO

My friend Cassio is dead. It's done, because
you ask it to be.

	But let Desdemona live.
OTHELLO	**OTHELLO**
Damn her, lewd minx! O, damn her!	Damn that evil whore! Damn her!
Come, go with me apart; I will withdraw,	Come with me. I am going to find a really
To furnish me with some swift means of death	quick way of killing that beautiful devil.
For the fair devil. Now art thou my lieutenant.	You are my lieutenant now.
IAGO	**IAGO**
I am your own for ever.	I am yours forever.
Exeunt	*They exit*

PART 20: ANALYSING ACT 3 SCENE 3

Themes: Appearance vs Reality, Prejudice, Manhood and Honour, Womanhood and Sexuality, Deception, Honesty, Jealousy, Love, Order and Chaos.

Often referred to as the 'temptation scene', Act 3 Scene 3 is the longest scene in the play and quite possibly the most important. Ironically, in terms of stagecraft, the curtains for this act part to reveal the most beautiful scene in the play. Desdemona is sitting in a stunning Cypriot garden and is taking a political stand against her husband (mirroring her earlier stance in response to her father's reaction to her marriage) by speaking to Cassio and offering to persuade her husband to reinstate him. Desdemona's final lines to Cassio are prophetic as she states she would 'rather die/than give [his] cause away'. Of course, Desdemona is speaking metaphorically here but it is this determined persistence that eventually results in her death, as fate would have it. Shakespeare's portrayal of the female Desdemona may appear noble to a contemporary audience, but a Jacobean audience would have viewed Desdemona's determination and independence as improper behaviour for a **woman** and, therefore, ill-fated.

Unfortunately, the beauty of the setting is contrasted with Iago's manipulation of Othello and Othello's curtness to Desdemona once he realises he has seen Cassio leave his wife's room in a hurry. Iago knows that he can convince Othello to believe that there is something suspicious between Cassio and Desdemona so begins to plant the seeds of doubt in Othello's mind when he responds to Othello's question as to whether or not it was Cassio who had just left with 'I cannot think it/That he would steal away so guilty-like/Seeing you coming'. Iago feigns difficulty believing his own comments, reminds Othello of Desdemona's successful **deception** of her own father in marrying Othello and warns Othello of the dangers of 'the green-eyed monster'. Coined by Shakespeare for *Othello*, the idiom is believed to allude to the Greek belief that jealousy occurred due to an overproduction of bile, which turned the skin a shade of green. It is also believed to allude to the eyes of cats- (often green) an animal that teases and tortures their prey before killing it. Iago is deeply **dishonest** but is able to manipulate Othello due to his natural, simple, direct, and 'honest' language and his raising of the topic of 'Good name in man and woman' reminding Othello (and the audience) of the importance of wife's chastity being connected to her husband's masculine honour. Iago's language in Act 3 Scene 3 is at its most manipulative as he is able to mirror Othello's eloquent style from the start of the play. Iago also deliberately echoes Othello by repeating his Othello's words as interrogatives, 'honest, my lord? ... think, my lord?', which provokes Othello to further question Iago and demand answers as he believes he is hiding the **truth**. Because of the emotional turmoil, Othello begins to struggle to speak in verse (or even sentences) as doubt about Desdemona begins to take over his thoughts, 'Death and damnation! O!' The breakdown of his speech represents the breakdown of his mind. Furthermore, the contradictory, 'I think my wife to be honest, and think she is not' reveals Othello's confusion and disjointed thoughts. The once calm and noble Othello allows **jealousy** to consume him and his speech becomes violent with references to 'poison, or fire, or suffocating streams' and his threat to 'tear' Desdemona 'to pieces'. Othello's hamartia, his extreme **jealousy**, turns him into a typical Jacobean villain of a revenge tragedy. He is now a protagonist pursuing vengeance against those he believes have done him wrong.

Unfortunately for Desdemona, her childish pestering of her desire to have her husband reinstate Cassio couldn't have happened at a worse time. Her timing, although completely innocent, helps to add weight to Iago's claims of her love for Cassio. Othello becomes annoyed, 'prithee, no more; let him come when he will,/I will deny thee nothing.' His abruptness appears to suggest that he is already suspicious of Desdemona and believes Iago even after her insistence that she will be 'obedient'. Iago finalises the embedding of his plan by convincing Othello to trust only what he sees. Once alone, Othello begins to lose his sense of **manhood** and begins to become sensitive to racial **prejudices** and insecurities with his age, 'Haply, for I am black/And have not those soft parts of conversation/...I am declined/Into the vale of years...' . (He later becomes concerned about his reputation as the husband of a dishonest woman, 'Farewell! Othello's occupation's gone!'). Iago's plan is working.

Othello's vulnerability and fears intensify when Desdemona re-enters the scene. As Desdemona attempts to comfort Othello by using the handkerchief he gave her as a gift, Othello's manner has changed and he watches her intently until pushing her handkerchief away, 'Your napkin is too little:/Let it alone.'. His rejection of the handkerchief is also a rejection of Desdemona herself. The handkerchief is a symbol of Othello and Desdemona's relationship, love, and fidelity as it was his own mother's tool to ensure his father was faithful. It is also a symbol of respect towards Othello's (mysterious) heritage linked to charms and spells (think back to Brabantio's obsession with Othello having put a spell on Desdemona). Furthermore, it is also a symbol of virginity and chastity as Othello explains the strawberries have been dyed red with the blood from the blood of virgins (nice!). He believes that as long as this handkerchief is in his wife's possession then she will remain chaste. His implication that invisible horns (the traditional symbol of the cuckold) are growing out of his head is Othello's admittance that he believes his wife has been unfaithful. He is in pain emotionally and physically but is not yet prepared to confront his wife.

Iago knows that Othello views the handkerchief as symbolically important and knows it has a lot of sentimental value, as well as holding important status in society. . During the Renaissance, handkerchiefs were associated with decorous behaviour and played an important role in the pursuit of cleanliness. Cleanliness carried moral implications and conferred dignity as well as nobility. To the public, a clean handkerchief was representative of a clean marriage and good behaviour therefore Iago uses it as evidence of Desdemona's infidelity and lack of respect and love for her husband The handkerchief could also be symbolic of Emilia's treatment at the hands of her husband. She feels proud that she has finally retrieved the item after her '...wayward husband hath a hundred times / wooed [her] to steal it' as she appears desperate to please her husband or at least eager to avoid any further unpleasant treatment at his hands. Emilia is not completely oblivious to Iago's intentions as she plans to make a copy of the handkerchief rather than give her husband the real version. Unfortunately, her plan fails as Iago sees her with the handkerchief. Emilia does attempt to remain in control by questioning Iago's need to possess it. Unfortunately, Emilia's attempt to have any control of the situation is instantly quashed with Iago's aggressive snatching of the item and demand that Emilia leaves the room. Not only does Iago retain control over his wife, but he also retains control of Othello's downfall. Feminist critical readings would explore the honouring of the patriarchal dictum that both Desdemona and Emilia show. Both obey their husbands' wishes and appear constrained throughout this scene. A feminist perspective would also focus on how this scene demonstrates male insecurity about female sexuality as well as a fear of infidelity.

On Othello's return to the stage it appears that he has now become consumed by jealousy. His speech has become even more frenzied demonstrated by two exclamatory gasps in quick succession, 'Avaunt! Be gone! Thou hast set me on the rack:' and he returns to the theme of sight as he turns on Iago with a savage demand for 'ocular proof' that Desdemona is unfaithful. Iago's reputation for honesty is enough to convince Othello that his circumstantial evidence about Desdemona and Cassio is true. Iago claims to have witnessed Cassio having a sexual dream asking 'Sweet Desdemona' to '...hide our loves'. His apparent hesitation to suggest infidelity or to jeopardise his public reputation by being incorrect further manipulates Othello into reassuring him that he is trusted and 'full of love and honesty'. The dramatic irony is that the audience know from Iago's conversation with Cassio about reputation (in 2:3) that he actually has no concerns about how he is perceived and views reputation as '...idle and most false...' and not the 'jewel' he now claims it to be. Shakespeare again returns to religious imagery to further strengthen the depths Iago will go to manipulate Othello as his claim to 'love' Othello echoes Peter's declaration of 'love' to Christ in John 21:15-16 'Yes, Lord; you know that I love you" in a word-for-word mockery of false love. Iago also reminds Othello that

Cassio and Desdemona have known each other for a long time as Cassio helped Othello court her as well as stating that as a Venetian woman, Desdemona is likely to be unfaithful (see context).

At this point, the manipulation of Othello has been achieved and he makes an oath (using the Pontic Sea simile) not to forgive his wife and to ensure that she meets a violent end. Othello's **manhood** has been challenged and he feels he has no option but to punish Desdemona with death. Chillingly, Iago's final words in this scene echo the language of love in an almost marriage-like pledge in that he claims to be Othello's 'own forever' and Othello claims to be '...bound to [him] forever'. This theatrical moment reflects the climax of Iago's plan as Othello's mental agony results in him crying out in anguish and making Iago his new lieutenant. Othello's opinion of himself has now become consumed by irrational thoughts of self-loathing which is enough for him to demand the death of both Cassio and Desdemona.

The structure of the scene is less clear than the others because it is occupied by dialogue between Othello and Iago, but some other characters are present at certain points and some action does take place. The structure of the dialogue is important in showing the dominance that Iago displays. He speaks more than Othello and both characters finish each other's lines, showing how closely connected they are becoming through Iago's power. In terms of plot, the scene begins with Othello completely in love with Desdemona but ends with him being tormented by jealousy and anger with demands of proof of his wife's infidelity. Desdemona innocently attempts to have Cassio reinstated but that gives Iago the ammunition to convince Othello that she is besotted with Cassio. The climax from this point in the play seems inevitable.

ORIGINAL TEXT:	MODERN TRANSLATION:
SCENE IV. Before the castle.	**SCENE IV. Before the castle.**
Enter DESDEMONA, EMILIA, and Clown	*Enter DESDEMONA, EMILIA, and Clown*
DESDEMONA	**DESDEMONA**
Do you know, sirrah, where Lieutenant Cassio lies?	Do you know which room Cassio lies in?
Clown	**Clown**
I dare not say he lies any where.	I daren't say that he lies.
DESDEMONA	**DESDEMONA**
Why, man?	Why not?
Clown	**Clown**
He's a soldier, and for one to say a soldier lies, is stabbing.	He's a soldier. If I accused a soldier of lying, he'd stab me.
DESDEMONA	**DESDEMONA**
Go to: where lodges he?	Oh stop it. Where is he staying?
Clown	**Clown**
To tell you where he lodges, is to tell you where I lie.	To tell you where he is staying is like telling you where I am staying.
DESDEMONA	**DESDEMONA**
Can any thing be made of this?	Can anybody understand this?
Clown	**Clown**

I know not where he lodges, and for me to devise a lodging and say he lies here or he lies there, were to lie in mine own throat.

DESDEMONA

Can you inquire him out, and be edified by report?

Clown

I will catechise the world for him; that is, make questions, and by them answer.

DESDEMONA

Seek him, bid him come hither: tell him I have moved my lord on his behalf, and hope all will be well.

Clown

To do this is within the compass of man's wit: and therefore I will attempt the doing it.
Exit

DESDEMONA

Where should I lose that handkerchief, Emilia?

EMILIA

I know not, madam.

DESDEMONA

Believe me, I had rather have lost my purse
Full of crusadoes: and, but my noble Moor
Is true of mind and made of no such baseness

I don't know where he's staying. If I were to make it up and say where he is staying then I'd be lying.

DESDEMONA

Can you ask around and find out?

Clown

I will examine the world for him; I will
Create questions and get them answered.

DESDEMONA

Find him and tell him to come here. Tell him I have spoken to my husband on his behalf, and everything is going to be alright.

Clown

That is within the possibility of a man's intelligence. I can do that.
Exit

DESDEMONA

Where do you think I have lost my handkerchief, Emilia?

EMILIA

I don't know, madam.

DESDEMONA

Believe me, I would rather have lost my purse
Full of gold coins than that, but my noble Moor
Doesn't get jealous so will not think anything suspicious of me.

As jealous creatures are, it were enough

To put him to ill thinking.

EMILIA

Is he not jealous?

DESDEMONA

Who, he? I think the sun where he was born

Drew all such humours from him.

EMILIA

Look, where he comes.

DESDEMONA

I will not leave him now till Cassio

Be call'd to him.

Enter OTHELLO

How is't with you, my lord

OTHELLO

Well, my good lady.

Aside

O, hardness to dissemble!--

How do you, Desdemona?

DESDEMONA

Well, my good lord.

OTHELLO

Give me your hand: this hand is moist, my lady.

EMILIA

Does he not get jealous?

DESDEMONA

Who, Othello? I think all the sun in the country

where he was born

Dried up all those traits from him.

EMILIA

Look, here he comes.

DESDEMONA

I won't leave him alone until he gives Cassio his job back.

Enter OTHELLO

How are you, my lord?

OTHELLO

Well, my good lady.

Aside

Oh, it's so difficult to pretend!

How are you, Desdemona?

DESDEMONA

Well, my good lord.

OTHELLO

Give me your hand. Your hand is moist, my lady.

DESDEMONA

It yet hath felt no age nor known no sorrow.

OTHELLO

This argues fruitfulness and liberal heart:
Hot, hot, and moist: this hand of yours requires
A sequester from liberty, fasting and prayer,
Much castigation, exercise devout;
For here's a young and sweating devil here,
That commonly rebels. 'Tis a good hand,
A frank one.

DESDEMONA

You may, indeed, say so;
For 'twas that hand that gave away my heart.

OTHELLO

A liberal hand: the hearts of old gave hands;
But our new heraldry is hands, not hearts.

DESDEMONA

I cannot speak of this. Come now, your promise.

OTHELLO

What promise, chuck?

DESDEMONA

I have sent to bid Cassio come speak with you.

DESDEMONA

It's moist because it's inexperienced and hasn't known sorrow.

OTHELLO

This is a sign of being fertile and shows you've got a good heart.
Hot, hot, and moist. This hand of yours requires
Locking up, fasting, and prayer,
It needs telling off and religious exercise to stave off temptation, because there's a sweating young devil here,
And you will rebel sooner or later. It's a nice hand. An open one.

DESDEMONA

You would say that.
It was this hand that gave away my heart.

OTHELLO

A free hand that gives itself away. In the olden days, hands and hearts were given together, but now hands are given without hearts.

DESDEMONA

I don't know anything about that. Don't forget your promise.

OTHELLO

What promise, dear?

DESDEMONA

I have sent for Cassio to come and talk to you.

OTHELLO I have a salt and sorry rheum offends me; Lend me thy handkerchief.	**OTHELLO** I am getting a bad cold. Lend me you handkerchief.
DESDEMONA Here, my lord.	**DESDEMONA** Here, my lord.
OTHELLO That which I gave you.	**OTHELLO** The one I gave you.
DESDEMONA I have it not about me.	**DESDEMONA** I don't have it with me.
OTHELLO Not?	**OTHELLO** No?
DESDEMONA No, indeed, my lord.	**DESDEMONA** No I don't, my lord.
OTHELLO That is a fault. That handkerchief Did an Egyptian to my mother give; She was a charmer, and could almost read The thoughts of people: she told her, while she kept it, 'Twould make her amiable and subdue my father Entirely to her love, but if she lost it Or made gift of it, my father's eye Should hold her loathed and his spirits should hunt After new fancies: she, dying, gave it me; And bid me, when my fate would have me	**OTHELLO** That's a mistake. An Egyptian gave that handkerchief to my mother. She was a witch and she could almost read People's minds. She told my mother that as long as she kept it with her then my father would always love her and desire her. But if she lost it or gave it away to anybody else, my father would start hating her and looking at other women. She gave it to me when she was dying, And told me that when it was my turn to marry I should give it to my wife. I did so, and pay attention to this.

wive,

To give it her. I did so: and take heed on't;

Make it a darling like your precious eye;

To lose't or give't away were such perdition

As nothing else could match.

DESDEMONA

Is't possible?

OTHELLO

'Tis true: there's magic in the web of it:

A sibyl, that had number'd in the world

The sun to course two hundred compasses,

In her prophetic fury sew'd the work;

The worms were hallow'd that did breed the

silk;

And it was dyed in mummy which the skilful

Conserved of maidens' hearts.

DESDEMONA

Indeed! is't true?

OTHELLO

Most veritable; therefore look to't well.

DESDEMONA

Then would to God that I had never seen't!

OTHELLO

Ha! wherefore?

DESDEMONA

Why do you speak so startingly and rash?

OTHELLO

Value it as much as you value your eyesight. To lose it or give it away would be an unspeakable loss.
A loss like no other.

DESDEMONA

Is that possible?

OTHELLO

It is true. There's magic in its fabric. A two-hundred-year-old witch sewed it while she was under a spell.
The worms that made the silk were sacred.
It was dyed in fluid from mummies and skilfully coloured with the extract of virgins' hearts.

DESDEMONA

Really! Is that true?

OTHELLO

Absolutely true. Take good care of it.

DESDEMONA

Then I wish to God I had never seen it!

OTHELLO

Ha! Why?

DESDEMONA

Why are you speaking to me so angrily?

OTHELLO

Is't lost? is't gone? speak, is it out
o' the way?

DESDEMONA

Heaven bless us!

OTHELLO

Say you?

DESDEMONA

It is not lost; but what if it were?

OTHELLO

How!

DESDEMONA

I say, it is not lost.

OTHELLO

Fetch't, let me see't.

DESDEMONA

Why, so I can, sir, but I will not now.

This is a trick to put me from my suit:

Pray you, let Cassio be received again.

OTHELLO

Fetch me the handkerchief: my mind misgives.

DESDEMONA

Come, come;

You'll never meet a more sufficient man.

Is it lost? Is it gone? Tell me. Is it missing?

DESDEMONA

God help me!

OTHELLO

What did you say?

DESDEMONA

It's not lost, but what if it were?

OTHELLO

What?

DESDEMONA

I said it's not lost.

OTHELLO

Go and get it. Let me see it.

DESDEMONA

I can, sir, but I don't want to now.

This is a trick to distract me from my mission to

get you to see Cassio. Please hire him again.

OTHELLO

Go and get the handkerchief. My mind is

unsettled.

DESDEMONA

Come on.

You couldn't meet a more capable man.

OTHELLO

The handkerchief!

DESDEMONA

I pray, talk me of Cassio.

OTHELLO

The handkerchief!

DESDEMONA

A man that all his time

Hath founded his good fortunes on your love,

Shared dangers with you,--

OTHELLO

The handkerchief!

DESDEMONA

In sooth, you are to blame.

OTHELLO

Away!

Exit

EMILIA

Is not this man jealous?

DESDEMONA

I ne'er saw this before.

Sure, there's some wonder in this

handkerchief:

I am most unhappy in the loss of it.

OTHELLO

The handkerchief!

DESDEMONA

I am asking you to talk to me about Cassio.

OTHELLO

The handkerchief!

DESDEMONA

He's a man that has counted on your friendship

and loved you.

He has shared dangers with you.

OTHELLO

The handkerchief!

DESDEMONA

I don't know what is wrong with you.

OTHELLO

Away!

Othello exits

EMILIA

And you claim Othello isn't jealous?

DESDEMONA

I've never seen him behave like this before.

There must be something special about that

handkerchief.

I am really unhappy that I've lost it.

EMILIA	**EMILIA**
'Tis not a year or two shows us a man:	It takes longer than a year or two to show us
They are all but stomachs, and we all but food;	what men are really like. They are all the same.
To eat us hungerly, and when they are full,	They are stomachs and we are food. They eat
They belch us. Look you, Cassio and my	us hungrily and when they are full they belch
husband!	us.
	Oh look, Cassio and my husband!
Enter CASSIO and IAGO	*Enter CASSIO and IAGO*
IAGO	**IAGO**
There is no other way; 'tis she must do't:	There is no other way. She must do it.
And, lo, the happiness! go, and importune her.	How lucky that she's here! Go and ask her.
DESDEMONA	**DESDEMONA**
How now, good Cassio! what's the news with	Hello, Cassio. How are you?
you?	
CASSIO	**CASSIO**
Madam, my former suit: I do beseech you	Madam, about my former request. I am
That by your virtuous means I may again	begging you to use your good nature to help
Exist, and be a member of his love	me get back on his good side.
Whom I with all the office of my heart	I honour him with all my heart. I cannot cope
Entirely honour: I would not be delay'd.	with any delay in this.
If my offence be of such mortal kind	If my offence was so bad that my services past
That nor my service past, nor present sorrows,	and present,
Nor purposed merit in futurity,	Nor my future good intentions, are not good
Can ransom me into his love again,	enough to gain his forgiveness then I would
But to know so must be my benefit;	rather know so that I can get used to it
So shall I clothe me in a forced content,	And find something else to do and get on with
And shut myself up in some other course,	my life.
To fortune's alms.	
DESDEMONA	**DESDEMONA**
	Sorry, dear Cassio!

Alas, thrice-gentle Cassio!
My advocation is not now in tune;
My lord is not my lord; nor should I know him,
Were he in favour as in humour alter'd.
So help me every spirit sanctified,
As I have spoken for you all my best
And stood within the blank of his displeasure
For my free speech! you must awhile be
patient:
What I can do I will; and more I will
Than for myself I dare: let that suffice you.

IAGO

Is my lord angry?

EMILIA

He went hence but now,
And certainly in strange unquietness.

IAGO

Can he be angry? I have seen the cannon,
When it hath blown his ranks into the air,
And, like the devil, from his very arm
Puff'd his own brother:--and can he be angry?
Something of moment then: I will go meet
him:
There's matter in't indeed, if he be angry.

DESDEMONA

I prithee, do so.

This is not a good time for me.
Othello is not himself. I wouldn't recognise him
if his appearance had changed as much as his
mood has.
Every blessed spirit has heard me argue your
case.
I have really annoyed him and made him angry
at me
For speaking up for you! You must be patient
for a little while longer.
I will do whatever I can to help you – more than
I'd do for myself. I hope that's good enough for
you.

IAGO

Is Othello angry?

EMILIA

He's just left and was acting strangely. He was
upset about something.

IAGO

Can he even get angry? I have seen a cannon
blow his soldiers to bits and kill his own
brother, yet I have never seen him angry.
Is he really upset?
It must be something very important that has
bothered him. I will go and talk to him. There
must be something seriously wrong if he's
angry.

DESDEMONA

Please do.

Exit IAGO	*Exit IAGO*
Something, sure, of state,	It must be something political,
Either from Venice, or some unhatch'd	Either from Venice or maybe some dangerous
practise	plot
Made demonstrable here in Cyprus to him,	That he's found out about. One that is planned
Hath puddled his clear spirit: and in such cases	here in Cyprus.
Men's natures wrangle with inferior things,	Maybe that has ruined his good mood. When
Though great ones are their object. 'Tis even	things like this happen
so;	Men usually react badly, especially to small
For let our finger ache, and it indues	things
Our other healthful members even to that	Even when they have other important matters
sense	to worry about. That's just how it is. It's like
Of pain: nay, we must think men are not gods,	when you hurt your finger; it makes the rest of
Nor of them look for such observances	your body hurt too.
As fit the bridal. Beshrew me much, Emilia,	We must not think that all men are perfect,
I was, unhandsome warrior as I am,	And we shouldn't expect them to always be as
Arraigning his unkindness with my soul;	polite as they were on our wedding day.
But now I find I had suborn'd the witness,	Forgive me, Emilia.
And he's indicted falsely.	I am not experienced in this and thought he
	was being really unkind. I realise now that I am
	being unfair.
	I have falsely accused him of being mean.
EMILIA	**EMILIA**
Pray heaven it be state-matters, as you think,	Let's hope to God it is political, just like you've
And no conception nor no jealous toy	said,
Concerning you.	And not something to do with you that has
	made him feel jealous.
DESDEMONA	**DESDEMONA**
Alas the day! I never gave him cause.	Oh no! I have never given him reason to feel
	like that.

EMILIA

But jealous souls will not be answer'd so;

They are not ever jealous for the cause,

But jealous for they are jealous: 'tis a monster

Begot upon itself, born on itself.

DESDEMONA

Heaven keep that monster from Othello's mind!

EMILIA

Lady, amen.

DESDEMONA

I will go seek him. Cassio, walk hereabout:

If I do find him fit, I'll move your suit

And seek to effect it to my uttermost.

CASSIO

I humbly thank your ladyship.

Exeunt DESDEMONA and EMILIA

Enter BIANCA

BIANCA

Save you, friend Cassio!

CASSIO

What make you from home?

How is it with you, my most fair Bianca?

I' faith, sweet love, I was coming to your house.

EMILIA

But jealous people do not think like that. They never have a reason for their jealousy. They're jealous just because they're jealous. It's a monster that just grows from nothing.

DESDEMONA

I hope God keeps that monster from Othello's mind!

EMILIA

Amen.

DESDEMONA

I will go and look for him. Stay nearby, Cassio. If I find him in a better mood then I'll ask him again about you and try my best to get him to agree.

CASSIO

Thank you so much.

Exit DESDEMONA and EMILIA

Enter BIANCA

BIANCA

Hello, Cassio!

CASSIO

What are you doing so far from home?

How are you, my beautiful Bianca?

I was just about to come visit you at your house.

BIANCA	**BIANCA**
And I was going to your lodging, Cassio.	And I was on my way to your house, too.
What, keep a week away? seven days and nights?	Why have you kept away from me all week?
	Seven days and seven nights?
Eight score eight hours? and lovers' absent hours,	A hundred and sixty-eight hours? Lovers' hours are so much longer than regular hours.
More tedious than the dial eight score times?	
O weary reckoning!	What a long time to wait!
CASSIO	**CASSIO**
Pardon me, Bianca:	Please forgive me, Bianca:
I have this while with leaden thoughts been press'd:	I have had a lot of things on my mind these last few days,
But I shall, in a more continuate time,	But I will make it up to you soon.
Strike off this score of absence. Sweet Bianca,	Sweet Bianca,
Giving her DESDEMONA's handkerchief	*Giving her DESDEMONA's handkerchief*
Take me this work out.	Take this and copy it for me.
BIANCA	**BIANCA**
O Cassio, whence came this?	Oh Cassio, where did this come from?
This is some token from a newer friend:	This looks like a gift from another woman. Now I understand why you've been distant. Has it come to this? Well, well.
To the felt absence now I feel a cause:	
Is't come to this? Well, well.	
CASSIO	**CASSIO**
Go to, woman!	Come on, woman!
Throw your vile guesses in the devil's teeth, From whence you have them. You are jealous now	You can throw your accusations back to the evil place where you got them from.
	You are jealous.
That this is from some mistress, some	You think that I have got this as a souvenir from another mistress to remember her by.

remembrance:

No, in good troth, Bianca.

BIANCA

Why, whose is it?

CASSIO

I know not, sweet: I found it in my chamber.

I like the work well: ere it be demanded--

As like enough it will--I'ld have it copied:

Take it, and do't; and leave me for this time.

BIANCA

Leave you! wherefore?

CASSIO

I do attend here on the general;

And think it no addition, nor my wish,

To have him see me woman'd.

BIANCA

Why, I pray you?

CASSIO

Not that I love you not.

BIANCA

But that you do not love me.

I pray you, bring me on the way a little,

And say if I shall see you soon at night.

CASSIO

I swear I haven't, Bianca.

BIANCA

Well whose is it then?

CASSIO

I don't know, sweetheart. I found it in my bedroom.

I really like the embroidery. Before someone claims it, which I am sure they will, please copy it for me.

Take it and do it, and leave me alone for a bit.

BIANCA

Leave you! why?

CASSIO

I'm here to see the general.

I don't think it will be helpful, nor do I, for him to see me with a woman.

BIANCA

Why not?

CASSIO

It's not that I don't love you.

BIANCA

But you don't love me.

Please, just walk with me for a little while, and tell me if you will see me tonight.

CASSIO

'Tis but a little way that I can bring you;

For I attend here: but I'll see you soon.

BIANCA

'Tis very good; I must be circumstanced.

Exeunt

I can only walk with you for a little while

because I have to be here.

But I will see you soon.

BIANCA

Fine. It will have to do.

Exit

PART 22: ANALYSING ACT 3 SCENE 4

Themes: Appearance vs Reality, Womanhood and Sexuality, Loyalty, Prejudice, Jealousy, Manhood and Honour.

The position of the handkerchief as the most important symbol in the play becomes even more apparent as the drama continues to unfold in Act 3 Scene 4. Desdemona is the focus in this scene that begins with her powerless in the company of a riddling clown. Although he provides some comic relief, the language of the clown represents how language can be misconstrued and how Desdemona will be the victim. Once the clown leaves, Desdemona turns to Emilia for help in seeking the lost handkerchief, but Emilia chooses to be duplicitous in order to please her husband.

DESDEMONA

Where should I lose that handkerchief, Emilia?

EMILIA

I know not, madam.

For Emilia, the handkerchief is a symbol of her loyalty to Iago. Rather than portray Emilia as a villain, the lack of **loyalty** displayed by Emilia towards Desdemona demonstrates a level of ignorance towards her husband's true nature and intentions.

When Othello enters the scene, Desdemona notices that Othello appears to be troubled but there appears to be a huge distance in their understanding of one another. Desdemona is convinced that Othello is incapable of jealousy and Othello is convinced that Desdemona has been unfaithful. This theme of **distrust** and **jealousy** continues in the scene as Othello attempts to prove Desdemona's infidelity through veiled references to her sexuality by claiming her hands are 'hot' and 'moist' (an indication of lust) and repetitively requesting use of the handkerchief after initially appearing to re-establish their bond by fondly referring to her as 'chuck'. Othello's furious and repetitive demands to produce the handkerchief highlight his paranoid jealousy and the importance of the handkerchief as an emblem of Desdemona's chastity and Iago's reputation. With Desdemona's failure to produce the handkerchief, Othello adds to her torment of losing it by lamenting its importance leading Desdemona to panic and lie about its whereabouts and change the topic of conversation to Cassio's case and character thus (unknowingly) confirming Iago's claims and cementing her fate. The handkerchief as a symbol of love has now switched to become a symbol of betrayal and Othello leaves the scene furious.

Emilia recognises Othello's behaviour and attempts to convince Desdemona that all men are capable of jealousy. Through a metaphor about food, Emilia reveals her true thoughts about men:

EMILIA

'Tis not a year or two shows us a man:

They are all but stomachs, and we all but food;

To eat us hungerly, and when they are full,

They belch us. Look you, Cassio and my husband!

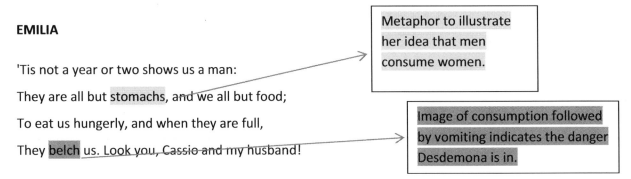

Metaphor to illustrate her idea that men consume women.

Image of consumption followed by vomiting indicates the danger Desdemona is in.

A later reference to jealousy as a 'monster' echoes Iago's earlier comment about the 'green-eyed monster'. Unfortunately, regardless of her apparent disdain of the behaviour of men in support of her friend, the similarity between her language and Iago's (alongside her denial of knowledge about the whereabouts of the handkerchief) highlights the fact that she is yet another person in Desdemona's life that cannot be trusted.

In order to provide contrast to jealousy being a male trait as well as a contrast to the virtuous Desdemona, Shakespeare introduces a prostitute named Bianca to the play. Again, light relief is provided to the audience as the comic language (Bianca: 'This is some token from a newer friend:/To the felt absence now I feel a cause:/Is't come to this? Well, well'. Cassio: 'Go to, woman!') exchanged between Bianca and Cassio mirrors Othello's mistake with Bianca's mistake that Cassio is unfaithful, leading to a sense of bathos. The irony of the scene is that all the jealousy is expressed over fabricated events centred on a handkerchief.

The chaotic world of the play becomes even more evident to the audience as there appear to be two separate time frames operating simultaneously. Cassio appears to have been on the island for a week whereas the events of the play have represented three days up to this point. This seems to add to the ridiculousness of the idea that Desdemona has had any time to commit adultery. Structurally, the scene is brief and clear in that it attends to a number of plot details, such as the fact that Iago stands back and observes as the whereabouts of the handkerchief is revealed and Othello plays the role of prosecutor at a trial. In terms of stagecraft, the reappearance of a clown is a diversion to allow Desdemona time to send for Cassio. It is also Shakespeare's attempt to provide some comic relief after the intensity of the previous scene.

ORIGINAL TEXT:	MODERN TRANSLATION:
SCENE I. Cyprus. Before the castle.	**SCENE I. Cyprus. Before the castle.**
Enter OTHELLO and IAGO	*Enter OTHELLO and IAGO*
IAGO	**IAGO**
Will you think so?	Do you think so?
OTHELLO	**OTHELLO**
Think so, Iago!	Yes I think so, Iago!
IAGO	**IAGO**
What,	What,
To kiss in private?	Just because they kissed in private?
OTHELLO	**OTHELLO**
An unauthorized kiss.	It was an illicit kiss.
IAGO	**IAGO**
Or to be naked with her friend in bed	Or maybe she was just naked in bed with him
An hour or more, not meaning any harm?	for an hour or more, but maybe they didn't
	do anything?
OTHELLO	**OTHELLO**
Naked in bed, Iago, and not mean harm!	Naked in bed, Iago, and not get up to
It is hypocrisy against the devil:	something! That's hypocrisy against the devil.
They that mean virtuously, and yet do so,	Those that intend to be innocent yet act in
The devil their virtue tempts, and they tempt	ways that aren't only tempt the devil, and
heaven.	they tempt heaven to judge them.
IAGO	**IAGO**

So they do nothing, 'tis a venial slip: But if I give my wife a handkerchief,--	If they didn't do anything then it is just a small sin. But if I gave my wife a handkerchief...
OTHELLO What then?	**OTHELLO** Then what?
IAGO Why, then, 'tis hers, my lord; and, being hers, She may, I think, bestow't on any man.	**IAGO** Well, then, it's hers, and because it belongs to her, She can give it to anybody she wants.
OTHELLO She is protectress of her honour too: May she give that?	**OTHELLO** She also has a reputation. Can she give that away too?
IAGO Her honour is an essence that's not seen; They have it very oft that have it not: But, for the handkerchief,--	**IAGO** Her reputation is something that cannot really be seen. Most people don't deserve their reputations. But a handkerchief...
OTHELLO By heaven, I would most gladly have forgot it. Thou said'st, it comes o'er my memory, As doth the raven o'er the infected house, Boding to all--he had my handkerchief.	**OTHELLO** God, I wish I could just forget all about it. What you've told me is constantly on my mind. He had my handkerchief.
IAGO Ay, what of that?	**IAGO** Yes, so what?
OTHELLO That's not so good now.	**OTHELLO** That's bad.
IAGO	**IAGO**

What,

If I had said I had seen him do you wrong?

Or heard him say,--as knaves be such abroad,

Who having, by their own importunate suit,

Or voluntary dotage of some mistress,

Convinced or supplied them, cannot choose

But they must blab—

OTHELLO

Hath he said any thing?

IAGO

He hath, my lord; but be you well assured,

No more than he'll unswear.

OTHELLO

What hath he said?

IAGO

'Faith, that he did--I know not what he did.

OTHELLO

What? what?

IAGO

Lie—

OTHELLO

With her?

IAGO

With her, on her; what you will.

What if I said that I had actually seen him do something that would hurt you? Or what if I had heard him say something – as idiots do – about having seduced a married woman?

Men like him can't help blabbing about it.

OTHELLO

Has he said anything?

IAGO

He has, my lord,

But he'd deny it.

OTHELLO

What has he said?

IAGO

He said he did, but I don't actually know what he's done.

OTHELLO

What? what?

IAGO

Lie...

OTHELLO

With her?

IAGO

With her, on top of her, everything else.

OTHELLO

Lie with her! lie on her! We say lie on her, when they belie her. Lie with her! that's fulsome.

--Handkerchief--confessions--handkerchief!—

To confess, and be hanged for his labour;-- first, to be hanged, and then to confess.--I tremble at it. Nature would not invest herself in such shadowing passion without some instruction. It is not words that shake me thus. Pish! Noses, ears, and lips. --Is't possible?--Confess--handkerchief!--O devil!—

Falls in a trance

IAGO

Work on,

My medicine, work! Thus credulous fools are caught;

And many worthy and chaste dames even thus,

All guiltless, meet reproach. What, ho! my lord!

My lord, I say! Othello!

Enter CASSIO

How now, Cassio!

CASSIO

What's the matter?

OTHELLO

In bed with her! On top of her!

That's evidence.

Handkerchief – confessions – handkerchief!

To confess and be hanged for it. I will kill him first, then he will confess. I am shaking with rage.

I would not be shaking like this if I didn't know it was true. It's more than just hearing the words making me shake like this. Noses, ears, and lips – is it possible? Confess – handkerchief! Oh, devil!

Falls in a trance

IAGO

Work on,

My evil poison, keep working! This is how gullible fools are caught.

Lots of innocent men and women have been punished in this way.

Wake up, my lord!

My lord, wake up! Othello!

Enter CASSIO

How now, Cassio!

CASSIO

What's happened?

IAGO

My lord is fall'n into an epilepsy:

This is his second fit; he had one yesterday.

CASSIO

Rub him about the temples.

IAGO

No, forbear;

The lethargy must have his quiet course:

If not, he foams at mouth and by and by

Breaks out to savage madness. Look he stirs:

Do you withdraw yourself a little while,

He will recover straight: when he is gone,

I would on great occasion speak with you.

Exit CASSIO

How is it, general? have you not hurt your head?

OTHELLO

Dost thou mock me?

IAGO

I mock you! no, by heaven.

Would you would bear your fortune like a man!

OTHELLO

A horned man's a monster and a beast.

IAGO

Othello has had a fit.

This is the second time. He had one yesterday.

CASSIO

Rub his temples.

IAGO

No, stop.

The fit must take its natural course.

If not then he will foam at the mouth and break out into a dangerous madness. Look, he's coming round.

Just leave us alone for a little while.

He will recover soon. When he leaves it is important that I talk to you.

Exit CASSIO

How are you? Have you hurt your head?

OTHELLO

Are you making fun of me?

IAGO

I am not! God, no.

I wish you could take this bad news like a man!

OTHELLO

A man who has been cheated on is no longer a man. He's like an animal.

IAGO

There's many a beast then in a populous city,

And many a civil monster.

OTHELLO

Did he confess it?

IAGO

Good sir, be a man;

Think every bearded fellow that's but yoked

May draw with you: there's millions now alive

That nightly lie in those unproper beds

Which they dare swear peculiar: your case is

better.

O, 'tis the spite of hell, the fiend's arch-mock,

To lip a wanton in a secure couch,

And to suppose her chaste! No, let me know;

And knowing what I am, I know what she shall

be.

OTHELLO

O, thou art wise; 'tis certain.

IAGO

Stand you awhile apart;

Confine yourself but in a patient list.

Whilst you were here o'erwhelmed with your

grief--

A passion most unsuiting such a man--

Cassio came hither: I shifted him away,

And laid good 'scuse upon your ecstasy,

IAGO

Then there are a lot of animals in this city,

And there are many monsters.

OTHELLO

Did he confess?

IAGO

Good sir, be a man;

Think of it like this: every married man has

been cheated on. We are all in the same

situation. Millions of men sleep with wives

that cheat on them. They think they are

faithful.

You are better off knowing.

It is worse than hell to kiss your wife

and think she is innocent when she is actually

a whore!

No, I'd rather know.

And just as well as I know myself, I will know

her and what she is capable of.

OTHELLO

Oh, you are wise, that's definite.

IAGO

Go and stand somewhere else for a while.

Calm down, control yourself, and hide. While

you were passed out with grief

A state which doesn't suit a man like you,

Cassio was here. I managed to get him to go

away and I made up an excuse for your

Bade him anon return and here speak with me;
The which he promised. Do but encave yourself,
And mark the fleers, the gibes, and notable scorns,
That dwell in every region of his face;
For I will make him tell the tale anew,
Where, how, how oft, how long ago, and when
He hath, and is again to cope your wife:
I say, but mark his gesture. Marry, patience;
Or I shall say you are all in all in spleen,
And nothing of a man.

OTHELLO

Dost thou hear, Iago?
I will be found most cunning in my patience;
But--dost thou hear?--most bloody.

IAGO

That's not amiss;
But yet keep time in all. Will you withdraw?

OTHELLO retires

Now will I question Cassio of Bianca,
A housewife that by selling her desires
Buys herself bread and clothes: it is a creature
That dotes on Cassio; as 'tis the strumpet's plague
To beguile many and be beguiled by one:

condition. I told him to come back later and speak to me.
He promised he would. So hide here
And watch him as he sneers, mocks, and scorns,
The traits live in every part of his face.
I will make him tell me the story again. The one about how he has often, and will again, have your wife.

I am telling you, watch his face, but stay calm. Don't allow anger to consume you or you are not a man.

OTHELLO

Do you hear me, Iago?
I will control myself and be patient.
Do you hear me? I will kill him.

IAGO

That's fine.
But you need to keep calm for now. Will you go and hide?

OTHELLO hides

Now I'll ask Cassio about Bianca, A housewife turned prostitute who sold herself to buy food and clothing.
She is disgusting
and dotes on Cassio. That's the curse of being a whore

He, when he hears of her, cannot refrain
From the excess of laughter. Here he comes:

Re-enter CASSIO

As he shall smile, Othello shall go mad;
And his unbookish jealousy must construe
Poor Cassio's smiles, gestures and light behavior,
Quite in the wrong. How do you now, lieutenant?

CASSIO

The worser that you give me the addition
Whose want even kills me.

IAGO

Ply Desdemona well, and you are sure on't.
Speaking lower
Now, if this suit lay in Bianco's power,
How quickly should you speed!

CASSIO

Alas, poor caitiff!

OTHELLO

Look, how he laughs already!

IAGO

Have as many men as you can but fall in love
with one. As soon as he hears her name he
will not be able to control his laughter. Here
he is.

Re-enter CASSIO

Othello will go mad when he sees him
laughing. His naïve jealousy will misconstrue
Poor Cassio's laughter and behaviour to be
aimed at Desdemona.
How are you, lieutenant?

CASSIO

Worse now you've called me by the title I no
longer have.
I'm dying to get it back.

IAGO

Just keep asking Desdemona and it will be
yours once again.
Speaking lower
If it were up to Bianca, you'd already have
your job back!

CASSIO

Poor thing!

OTHELLO

Look at him laughing already!

IAGO

I never knew woman love man so.	I have never known a woman love a man so much.
CASSIO	**CASSIO**
Alas, poor rogue! I think, i' faith, she loves me.	I know. The poor thing! I really think she loves me.
OTHELLO	**OTHELLO**
Now he denies it faintly, and laughs it out.	Now he's trying to deny it and is laughing it off.
IAGO	**IAGO**
Do you hear, Cassio?	Do you know what, Cassio?
OTHELLO	**OTHELLO**
Now he importunes him To tell it o'er: go to; well said, well said.	Now he is asking him for the story again. Go on, tell it.
IAGO	**IAGO**
She gives it out that you shall marry hey: Do you intend it?	She is telling everybody that you are going to marry her. Is that what you are going to do?
CASSIO	**CASSIO**
Ha, ha, ha!	Ha, ha, ha!
OTHELLO	**OTHELLO**
Do you triumph, Roman? do you triumph?	Are you laughing because you think you have won?
CASSIO	**CASSIO**
I marry her! what? a customer! Prithee, bear some charity to my wit: do not think it so unwholesome. Ha, ha, ha!	I am not going to marry her! What? A whore! Please! Give me some credit. Don't think I don't have standards. Ha, ha, ha!

OTHELLO	**OTHELLO**
So, so, so, so: they laugh that win.	So, so, so, so. The winner will have the last laugh.
IAGO	**IAGO**
'Faith, the cry goes that you shall marry her.	Honestly, the gossip is that you are going to marry her.
CASSIO	**CASSIO**
Prithee, say true.	You must be joking.
IAGO	**IAGO**
I am a very villain else.	I am a villain if I am lying.
OTHELLO	**OTHELLO**
Have you scored me? Well.	Have you marked me as a fool? Well.
CASSIO	**CASSIO**
This is the monkey's own giving out: she is persuaded I will marry her, out of her own love and flattery, not out of my promise.	The monkey has spread the rumours herself. She is in love with me and is flattering herself if she thinks I will marry her. I haven't promised her.
OTHELLO	**OTHELLO**
Iago beckons me; now he begins the story.	Iago wants me to come closer. Now he's telling the story.
CASSIO	**CASSIO**
She was here even now; she haunts me in every place. I was the other day talking on the sea-bank with certain Venetians; and thither comes the bauble, and, by this hand, she falls me thus about my neck—	She was here just now. She hangs around everywhere I am all the time. I was at the beach the other day talking to some Venetians, and she comes along and drapes herself all over me, hugging and kissing me.

OTHELLO

Crying 'O dear Cassio!' as it were: his gesture imports it.

CASSIO

So hangs, and lolls, and weeps upon me; so hales, and pulls me: ha, ha, ha!

OTHELLO

Now he tells how she plucked him to my chamber. O,
I see that nose of yours, but not that dog I shall throw it to.

CASSIO

Well, I must leave her company.

IAGO

Before me! look, where she comes.

CASSIO

'Tis such another fitchew! marry a perfumed one.
Enter BIANCA

What do you mean by this haunting of me?

BIANCA

Let the devil and his dam haunt you! What did you mean by that same handkerchief you gave me even now?

OTHELLO

Crying 'Oh, Cassio,' if his gestures are anything to go by.

CASSIO

She hangs all over me and cries.
She's always shaking me and pulling me close. Ha, ha, ha!

OTHELLO

Now he is telling him about her taking him to my bedroom.
I am going to feed that nose of yours to the dogs.

CASSIO

Well, I am going to have to get rid of her.

IAGO

Look out! Here she comes.

CASSIO

It is a whore smothered in cheap perfume.
Enter BIANCA

What do you think you are doing, stalking me like this?

BIANCA

Damn you!
Why did you give me that handkerchief?

I was a fine fool to take it. I must take out the work?--A likely piece of work, that you should find it in your chamber, and not know who left it there!

This is some minx's token, and I must take out the work? There; give it your hobby-horse: wheresoever you had it, I'll take out no work on't.

CASSIO

How now, my sweet Bianca! how now! how now!

OTHELLO

By heaven, that should be my handkerchief!

BIANCA

An you'll come to supper to-night, you may; an you will not, come when you are next prepared for.

Exit

IAGO

After her, after her.

CASSIO

'Faith, I must; she'll rail in the street else.

IAGO

Will you sup there?

CASSIO

I was an idiot to take it off you. You want me to copy the pattern? A likely story that you found it in your bedroom, and that you don't know who left it there! This is some other tart's love token, and you want me to copy its pattern for you? Give it back to your mistress, whoever she is. I am not going to do anything with it.

CASSIO

Come on, my sweet Bianca! Come on, come on now!

OTHELLO

My God, that's my handkerchief!

BIANCA

If you want to come and have dinner with me tonight, then you can. If you don't want to, then come when you like.

Exit

IAGO

Go after her.

CASSIO

Yes, I'll have to or she'll shout in the streets.

IAGO

Will you have supper there?

CASSIO

'Faith, I intend so.	Yes, I suppose so.
IAGO	**IAGO**
Well, I may chance to see you; for I would very fain speak with you.	Well, I may bump into you again. I need to speak to you.
CASSIO	**CASSIO**
Prithee, come; will you?	Please come with me; will you?
IAGO	**IAGO**
Go to; say no more.	Go on after her; say no more.
Exit CASSIO	*Exit CASSIO*
OTHELLO	**OTHELLO**
[Advancing] How shall I murder him, Iago?	[coming forward] How shall I murder him, Iago?
IAGO	**IAGO**
Did you perceive how he laughed at his vice?	Did you watch how he laughed about his behaviour?
OTHELLO	**OTHELLO**
O Iago!	Oh Iago!
IAGO	**IAGO**
And did you see the handkerchief?	And did you see the handkerchief?
OTHELLO	**OTHELLO**
Was that mine?	Was that mine?
IAGO	**IAGO**

Yours by this hand: and to see how he prizes the foolish woman your wife! she gave it him, and he hath given it his whore.

OTHELLO

I would have him nine years a-killing. A fine woman! a fair woman! a sweet woman!

IAGO

Nay, you must forget that.

OTHELLO

Ay, let her rot, and perish, and be damned to-night; for she shall not live: no, my heart is turned to stone; I strike it, and it hurts my hand. O, the world hath not a sweeter creature: she might lie by an emperor's side and command him tasks.

IAGO

Nay, that's not your way.

OTHELLO

Hang her! I do but say what she is: so delicate with her needle: an admirable musician: O! she will sing the savageness out of a bear: of so high and plenteous wit and invention:--

IAGO

She's the worse for all this.

It was yours, I swear. Do you see how much your foolish wife actually means to him! She gave it to him, and he has given it his whore.

OTHELLO

I want to kill him slowly. Oh she's a fine woman! A fair woman! A sweet woman!

IAGO

No, you must forget that.

OTHELLO

Yes, let her rot, and die, and be damned tonight because she will not live beyond that. My heart has turned to stone. I strike it and it hurts my hand. Oh, there's not a sweeter person in the world. She'd be able to manipulate an emperor.

IAGO

But that's not how you are going to have things.

OTHELLO

Hang her! I am only saying what she is. She is so delicate with her sewing; she's an admirable musician; oh, she could sing a savage bear to calm. She is so intelligent and creative.

IAGO

She's worse for stooping this low then.

OTHELLO	**OTHELLO**
O, a thousand thousand times: and then, of so gentle a condition!	Oh, she's a thousand times worse. But she's so gentle!
IAGO	**IAGO**
Ay, too gentle.	Yes, a bit too gentle.
OTHELLO	**OTHELLO**
Nay, that's certain: but yet the pity of it, Iago! O Iago, the pity of it, Iago!	Yes, that's definitely true. It is dreadful, Iago! Oh Iago, it is dreadful, Iago!
IAGO	**IAGO**
If you are so fond over her iniquity, give her patent to offend; for, if it touch not you, it comes near nobody.	If you still feel so fond of her, then why not just let her cheat on you? If it doesn't offend you, then it won't offend anybody else.
OTHELLO	**OTHELLO**
I will chop her into messes: cuckold me!	I will chop her up into tiny pieces. How dare she cheat on me!
IAGO	**IAGO**
O, 'tis foul in her.	Oh, It is disgusting of her.
OTHELLO	**OTHELLO**
With mine officer!	And with my officer!
IAGO	**IAGO**
That's fouler.	That's even worse.
OTHELLO	**OTHELLO**
Get me some poison, Iago; this night: I'll not expostulate with her, lest her body and beauty unprovide my mind again: this night, Iago.	Get me some poison, Iago. Tonight. I will not delay what I need to do just in case her body and beauty makes me change my mind. Tonight, Iago.

IAGO

Do it not with poison, strangle her in her bed, even the bed she hath contaminated.

OTHELLO

Good, good: the justice of it pleases: very good.

IAGO

And for Cassio, let me be his undertaker: you shall hear more by midnight.

OTHELLO

Excellent good.

A trumpet within

What trumpet is that same?

IAGO

Something from Venice, sure. 'Tis Lodovico, Come from the duke: and, see, your wife is with him.

Enter LODOVICO, DESDEMONA, and Attendants

LODOVICO

Save you, worthy general!

OTHELLO

With all my heart, sir.

IAGO

Don't do it with poison. Strangle her in bed – the bed that she has contaminated.

OTHELLO

Good idea. That is appropriate justice. Very good.

IAGO

As for Cassio, let me deal with him. I will kill him. You will hear from me by midnight.

OTHELLO

Excellent.

A trumpet can be heard

What's that trumpet for?

IAGO

I think it is something from Venice. It's Lodovico,
He has come from the duke. Your wife is with him.

Enter LODOVICO, DESDEMONA, and Attendants

LODOVICO

Greetings, worthy general!

OTHELLO

Greetings with all my heart, sir.

LODOVICO

The duke and senators of Venice greet you.

Gives him a letter

OTHELLO

I kiss the instrument of their pleasures.

Opens the letter, and reads

DESDEMONA

And what's the news, good cousin Lodovico?

IAGO

I am very glad to see you, signior

Welcome to Cyprus.

LODOVICO

I thank you. How does Lieutenant Cassio?

IAGO

Lives, sir.

DESDEMONA

Cousin, there's fall'n between him and my lord

An unkind breach: but you shall make all well.

OTHELLO

Are you sure of that?

DESDEMONA

My lord?

LODOVICO

The duke and senators of Venice greet you.

Gives him a letter

OTHELLO

I will do whatever they request of me.

Opens the letter, and reads

DESDEMONA

And what's the news, good cousin Lodovico?

IAGO

I am very glad to see you, sir.

Welcome to Cyprus.

LODOVICO

Thank you. How is Lieutenant Cassio?

IAGO

He's alive, sir.

DESDEMONA

Cousin, there's been a fall out between him

and Othello

It's an unfortunate rift but you will sort it.

OTHELLO

Are you sure of that?

DESDEMONA

Excuse me?

OTHELLO

[Reads] 'This fail you not to do, as you will--'

LODOVICO

He did not call; he's busy in the paper.

Is there division 'twixt my lord and Cassio?

DESDEMONA

A most unhappy one: I would do much

To atone them, for the love I bear to Cassio.

OTHELLO

Fire and brimstone!

DESDEMONA

My lord?

OTHELLO

Are you wise?

DESDEMONA

What, is he angry?

LODOVICO

May be the letter moved him;

For, as I think, they do command him home,

Deputing Cassio in his government.

DESDEMONA

OTHELLO

[Reads] 'This you must not fail to do, if you...'

LODOVICO

He wasn't talking to you; he's engrossed in

the paper.

Is there a conflict between my lord and

Cassio?

DESDEMONA

Yes, unfortunately: I would do anything to

bring them back together again for the sake

of the love I have for Cassio.

OTHELLO

Damn everything!

DESDEMONA

My lord?

OTHELLO

Are you wise?

DESDEMONA

Why is he angry?

LODOVICO

Maybe the letter has upset him.

I think they are calling him home and

replacing him with Cassio.

DESDEMONA

Trust me, I am glad on't.

OTHELLO

Indeed!

DESDEMONA

My lord?

OTHELLO

I am glad to see you mad.

DESDEMONA

Why, sweet Othello,--

OTHELLO

[Striking her] Devil!

DESDEMONA

I have not deserved this.

LODOVICO

My lord, this would not be believed in Venice,

Though I should swear I saw't: 'tis very much:

Make her amends; she weeps.

OTHELLO

O devil, devil!

If that the earth could teem with woman's

tears,

Each drop she falls would prove a crocodile.

Out of my sight!

Trust me, I am glad about it.

OTHELLO

I bet you are!

DESDEMONA

My lord?

OTHELLO

I am glad to see you are crazy enough to

admit it.

DESDEMONA

What do you mean, sweet Othello?

OTHELLO

[Striking her] You devil!

DESDEMONA

I haven't done anything to deserve this.

LODOVICO

My lord, nobody in Venice would believe you

capable of this,

Even if I should swear I saw it. It's too much.

She's crying. Apologise to her.

OTHELLO

Oh you devil, you devil!

Her tears are not real tears.

Get out of my sight!

DESDEMONA I will not stay to offend you. *Going* **LODOVICO** Truly, an obedient lady: I do beseech your lordship, call her back. **OTHELLO** Mistress! **DESDEMONA** My lord? **OTHELLO** What would you with her, sir? **LODOVICO** Who, I, my lord? **OTHELLO** Ay; you did wish that I would make her turn: Sir, she can turn, and turn, and yet go on, And turn again; and she can weep, sir, weep; And she's obedient, as you say, obedient, Very obedient. Proceed you in your tears. Concerning this, sir,--O well-painted passion!-- I am commanded home. Get you away; I'll send for you anon. Sir, I obey the mandate, And will return to Venice. Hence, avaunt!	**DESDEMONA** I will not offend you by staying. *Going* **LODOVICO** She is such an obedient lady. I beg you to call her back. **OTHELLO** Mistress! **DESDEMONA** My lord? **OTHELLO** What do you want her for, sir? **LODOVICO** Who, me? **OTHELLO** Yes, you asked me to call her back. Sir, she can turn and leave as many times as she likes. And she can cry, sir, she can cry. And she's obedient, as you say, very obedient. You carry on crying. Oh, what fake emotion! I am being ordered home. Get away from me. I will send for you later. Sir, I will obey the order, And return to Venice. Go away Desdemona, vanish!

Exit DESDEMONA	*Exit DESDEMONA*
Cassio shall have my place. And, sir, tonight, I do entreat that we may sup together: You are welcome, sir, to Cyprus.--Goats and monkeys!	Cassio can have my job. Tonight, sir, I invite you to have dinner with me. Welcome to Cyprus. Horny animals!
Exit	*Othello exits*
LODOVICO	**LODOVICO**
Is this the noble Moor whom our full senate Call all in all sufficient? Is this the nature Whom passion could not shake? whose solid virtue The shot of accident, nor dart of chance, Could neither graze nor pierce?	Is this really the same noble moor whom the senate Considers so capable of his job? Is this the guy who's supposed to never get emotional about anything? The guy who never reacts No matter what happens?
IAGO	**IAGO**
He is much changed.	He has changed a lot.
LODOVICO	**LODOVICO**
Are his wits safe? is he not light of brain?	Is his mind stable? Has he lost his mind?
IAGO	**IAGO**
He's that he is: I may not breathe my censure What he might be: if what he might he is not, I would to heaven he were!	That's just how he is. I will not say anything negative About what he might be like. If he isn't the person you thought then I wish to god he were!
LODOVICO	**LODOVICO**
What, strike his wife!	He hit his wife!

IAGO

'Faith, that was not so well; yet would I knew

That stroke would prove the worst!

LODOVICO

Is it his use?

Or did the letters work upon his blood,

And new-create this fault?

IAGO

Alas, alas!

It is not honesty in me to speak

What I have seen and known. You shall observe him,

And his own courses will denote him so

That I may save my speech: do but go after,

And mark how he continues.

LODOVICO

I am sorry that I am deceived in him.

Exeunt

IAGO

That's true. That wasn't very nice. But I wish that was the worst thing he is capable of!

LODOVICO

Is this what he's like?

Or did the letter make him angry and create this new fault in his personality?

IAGO

It's bad!

It would be disloyal of me to discuss what I have seen and what I know.

Watch him,

And you will see exactly what he is like

Then I won't have to tell you. Just follow him

And see how he behaves.

LODOVICO

I am sorry that I was wrong about him.

They exit

PART 24: ANALYSING ACT 4 SCENE 1

Themes: Appearance vs Reality, Jealousy, Manhood and Honour, Womanhood and Sexuality.

Iago's manipulation intensifies in this scene as he continues to torment Othello and delights in the pleasure of adding to his suffering by repeatedly making reference to the handkerchief and to Cassio's apparent confession of a sexual affair with Desdemona: : '...heard him say...with her, on her; what you will.' . Othello repetitively raves in response ('Lie with her! lie on her! We say lie on her, when they belie her. Lie with her!), focuses obsessively on the handkerchief (repats the noun three times), loses the ability to speak (Pish! Noses, ears, and lips. --Is't possible?--Confess—handkerchief!--O devil!—), and ultimately suffers a fit.Othello is no longer speaking in verse shown byhis phrases becoming disconnected. Othello's language was the trait that, at the start of the play, helped him challenge prejudices and secure his honour and without the ability to speak, Othello becomes animalistic in his incoherence. The language corresponds to the action of the scene and Othello almost becomes a comic stereotype of the black man as a beast. The stereotype is further reinforced when Iago states '...he foams at the mouth and by and by/Breaks out to savage madness.' With his dignity lost, the status as military hero has gone along with his honour. Cassio's entrance at this point highlights his caring nature as he shows concern for Othello's welfare, but Iago continues to manipulate events by convincing Cassio that Othello often suffers from mental health issues as well as fits. Although there is no evidence that Othello is epileptic (other than the words of the liar, Iago), Othello's seizure would have reinforced the belief that he was somehow connected to evil.

During the Renaissance, a lack of understanding of epilepsy led to the formulation of superstitious views of the disease. Sufferers were believed to be possessed and/or connected to witchcraft. Once again, Iago maintains control by acting as a concerned friend, mexperienced in Othello's apparent recurring fits and he convinces Cassio to return once Othello has recovered and left. Iago then convinces Othello to hide and listen to his conversation with Cassio in which he promises to have him confess to sleeping with Desdemona. At this point, the play once again displays comic elements with Othello's misunderstanding of Cassio as the former leader of successful armies now crouches in hiding. In a comedy, misunderstandings are usually recognised possibly giving the audience false hope that Othello may realise the truth. A Shakespearean comedy has a very different meaning from a modern comedy. Rather than focusing on generating laughs, a Shakespearean comedy was light-hearted rather than humorous and contained irony and wordplay alongside fun. The plot would usually involve a struggle of lovers to overcome problems resulting in a happy ending. Although

Othello may have almost convinced a Shakespearean audience of a happy ending, the hamartia displayed by Othello would have reminded them of his inevitable downfall.

Once Iago has convinced Othello that Cassio's laughter-filled confession is about Desdemona (it is actually about Bianca), Othello's behaviour becomes repulsive and barbaric as he threatens to kill Cassio and hits Desdemona in front of Lodovico. The very fact that Othello acts recklessly in front of an emissary from Venice reinforces the change in his character as well as his loss of honour. Othello's loss of humanity, loss of control over his public and private conduct, and his descent into savagery contrasts with Iago's complete security in his perverted triumph as he convinces Lodovico of Othello's 'changed' behaviour. Lodovico's presence immediately after Othello's writhing on the floor serves as a reminder of how much Othello has transformed. At the start of the play he stood before the senate as an eloquent orator before hitting the floor and then crouching in secret as he allows Cassio to manipulate him into hitting his wife.

The scene ends with Iago, once again, refusing to directly answer questions by manipulating his language so that he appears loyal: 'Alas, alas!/It is not honesty in me to speak/What I have seen and known. You shall observe him,'

This scene is also important for its depiction of verbal and physical violence against Desdemona, as well as crude discussions about Bianca. In contrast, the women in the scene appear strong and loyal. Bianca enters after being refered to by Cassio as a 'poor rogue', and a 'monkey' who 'haunts' him yet immediately presents herself as unaccepting of ill-treatment, 'Let the devil and his dam haunt you!' before she then offers forgiveness through '…supper to-night'. Similarly, once the verbal violence from Othello leads to physical violence, Desdemona reacts with grace as she declares that she will '…not stay to offend…' Othello. The dignity displayed by Desdemona forshadows the way she chooses to behave in death in what Iago convonces Othello is a 'contaminated' bed. Although furious, Othello struggles with the thought of killing the 'fine…sweet' Desdemona and worries that her 'body and beauty' might make him change his mind. His threats to let her 'rot, and die and be damned…', to 'chop her up', and to 'poison' her demonstrate his savagery and his descent into a fallen hero.

ORIGINAL TEXT:	MODERN TRANSLATION:
SCENE II. A room in the castle.	**SCENE II. A room in the castle.**
Enter OTHELLO and EMILIA	*Enter OTHELLO and EMILIA*
OTHELLO	**OTHELLO**
You have seen nothing then?	You haven't seen anything, then?
EMILIA	**EMILIA**
Nor ever heard, nor ever did suspect.	No, and I haven't heard anything or suspected anything.
OTHELLO	**OTHELLO**
Yes, you have seen Cassio and she together.	But you have seen Cassio and Desdemona together.
EMILIA	**EMILIA**
But then I saw no harm, and then I heard Each syllable that breath made up between them.	Yes, but I haven't seen them do anything wrong. I have heard every single word said between them.
OTHELLO	**OTHELLO**
What, did they never whisper?	Didn't they ever whisper?
EMILIA	**EMILIA**
Never, my lord.	Never, my lord.
OTHELLO	**OTHELLO**
Nor send you out o' the way?	Or send you out of the way?

EMILIA

Never.

OTHELLO

To fetch her fan, her gloves, her mask, nor nothing?

EMILIA

Never, my lord.

OTHELLO

That's strange.

EMILIA

I durst, my lord, to wager she is honest,
Lay down my soul at stake: if you think other,
Remove your thought; it doth abuse your bosom.
If any wretch have put this in your head,
Let heaven requite it with the serpent's curse!
For, if she be not honest, chaste, and true,
There's no man happy; the purest of their wives
Is foul as slander.

OTHELLO

Bid her come hither: go.

Exit EMILIA

EMILIA

Never.

OTHELLO

Not even to fetch her fan, her gloves, her mask, or anything?

EMILIA

Never, my lord.

OTHELLO

That's strange.

EMILIA

I dare bet you my soul that she's honest. If you think that she isn't then you must stop thinking that right now because you are wrong. It abuses your heart.
If some horrible person has put these thoughts in your head then
Let God punish him with the serpent's curse!
If she's not honest, faithful, and true,

Then there's no such thing as a happy husband and a faithful wife.
Saying otherwise is slander.

OTHELLO

Tell her to come here. Go.

Exit EMILIA

She says enough; yet she's a simple bawd
That cannot say as much. This is a subtle whore,
A closet lock and key of villanous secrets
And yet she'll kneel and pray; I have seen her do't.

Enter DESDEMONA with EMILIA

DESDEMONA

My lord, what is your will?

OTHELLO

Pray, chuck, come hither.

DESDEMONA

What is your pleasure?

OTHELLO

Let me see your eyes;
Look in my face.

DESDEMONA

What horrible fancy's this?

OTHELLO

[To EMILIA] Some of your function, mistress;
Leave procreants alone and shut the door;
Cough, or cry 'hem,' if any body come:
Your mystery, your mystery: nay, dispatch.

She's said enough. She's just like a dumb brothel owner.
She daren't speak the truth. Desdemona is a crafty whore,
She is a locked closet full of awful secrets
But she kneels and prays like an innocent woman. I've seen her do it.

Enter DESDEMONA with EMILIA

DESDEMONA

My lord, what do you want?

OTHELLO

Please, dear, come here.

DESDEMONA

What do you want me to do?

OTHELLO

Let me see your eyes;
Look at my face.

DESDEMONA

What horrible game are you playing?

OTHELLO

[To EMILIA] Go to your duties, mistress;
Leave us alone to have sex and shut the door;
If somebody comes then shout us.
That's your job. Now go.

DESDEMONA

Upon my knees, what doth your speech import?

I understand a fury in your words.

But not the words.

OTHELLO

Why, what art thou?

DESDEMONA

Your wife, my lord; your true

And loyal wife.

OTHELLO

Come, swear it, damn thyself

Lest, being like one of heaven, the devils themselves

Should fear to seize thee: therefore be double damn'd:

Swear thou art honest.

DESDEMONA

Heaven doth truly know it.

OTHELLO

Heaven truly knows that thou art false as hell.

DESDEMONA

To whom, my lord? with whom? how am I false?

DESDEMONA

I am on my knees begging you to tell me what your words mean.

I can tell that you are furious when you speak.

But I don't understand you.

OTHELLO

Why, who are you?

DESDEMONA

I'm your wife, my lord; your true

And loyal wife.

OTHELLO

Go on, swear that you are loyal and you will be damned to hell for being a liar. The devils will mistake you for an angel and should be too scared to grab hold of you. So go on, damn yourself by swearing you are faithful to me.

DESDEMONA

God knows the truth.

OTHELLO

God knows you are a liar and unfaithful as hell.

DESDEMONA

To whom, my lord? Who with? How am I unfaithful?

OTHELLO	**OTHELLO**
O Desdemona! away! away! away!	Oh, Desdemona! Go away! Go away! Go away!
DESDEMONA	**DESDEMONA**
Alas the heavy day! Why do you weep?	Oh, what a horrible day! Why are you crying?
Am I the motive of these tears, my lord?	Is it because of me?
If haply you my father do suspect	
An instrument of this your calling back,	If my father has ordered you back to Venice,
Lay not your blame on me: If you have lost him,	Please do not blame me. If you have lost his respect,
Why, I have lost him too.	Then he has lost respect for me too.
OTHELLO	**OTHELLO**
Had it pleased heaven	If it pleased God
To try me with affliction; had they rain'd	To make me ill
All kinds of sores and shames on my bare head.	And cover me
Steep'd me in poverty to the very lips,	In sores and shame apparent to all.
Given to captivity me and my utmost hopes,	Drenched me in poverty and sold me and all my hopes into slavery.
I should have found in some place of my soul	I would have found a way to accept it
A drop of patience: but, alas, to make me	With patience, but he has made me
A fixed figure for the time of scorn	A complete laughingstock for everyone to
To point his slow unmoving finger at!	point and laugh at!
Yet could I bear that too; well, very well:	I could even put up with that, actually.
But there, where I have garner'd up my heart,	But my wife, who I have loved with all my heart,
Where either I must live, or bear no life;	
The fountain from the which my current runs,	Who is supposed to be the bearer of my
Or else dries up; to be discarded thence!	children and my descendants,
Or keep it as a cistern for foul toads	Or I will no longer exist and will be discarded of!
To knot and gender in! Turn thy complexion there,	She has polluted herself and is now only a
Patience, thou young and rose-lipp'd	woman worthy of reproducing with disgusting toads.

cherubin,--

Ay, there, look grim as hell!

DESDEMONA

I hope my noble lord esteems me honest.

OTHELLO

O, ay; as summer flies are in the shambles,

That quicken even with blowing. O thou weed,

Who art so lovely fair and smell'st so sweet

That the sense aches at thee, would thou

hadst ne'er been born!

DESDEMONA

Alas, what ignorant sin have I committed?

OTHELLO

Was this fair paper, this most goodly book,

Made to write 'whore' upon? What

committed!

Committed! O thou public commoner!

I should make very forges of my cheeks,

That would to cinders burn up modesty,

Did I but speak thy deeds. What committed!

Heaven stops the nose at it and the moon

winks,

The bawdy wind that kisses all it meets

Is hush'd within the hollow mine of earth,

And will not hear it. What committed!

Impudent strumpet!

Look over there, goddess of patience,

Yes, look there, It's horrifying!

DESDEMONA

I hope my noble lord knows that I am faithful.

OTHELLO

Oh, yes. You're as faithful as flies in a

slaughter house,

That breed even when the wind blows on

them, you weed.

Pretending to be so beautiful and so sweet

smelling

That my senses ache when I look at you. I

wish you had never been born!

DESDEMONA

What sin have I unconsciously committed?

OTHELLO

Was this lovely paper, this beautiful book,

Made to write 'whore' on it? What sin have

you committed? What sin have you

committed? You common whore!

If I said out loud what you had done then

you'd burn up with shame.

What sin have you committed!

God has to hold his nose when he sees you.

The moon has to close its eyes. Even the

vulgar wind that touches everything it meets

is ashamed to go near you.

What sin have you committed!

You insolent whore!

DESDEMONA

By heaven, you do me wrong.

OTHELLO

Are you not a strumpet?

DESDEMONA

No, as I am a Christian:

If to preserve this vessel for my lord

From any other foul unlawful touch

Be not to be a strumpet, I am none.

OTHELLO

What, not a whore?

DESDEMONA

No, as I shall be saved.

OTHELLO

Is't possible?

DESDEMONA

O, heaven forgive us!

OTHELLO

I cry you mercy, then:

I took you for that cunning whore of Venice

That married with Othello.

Raising his voice

DESDEMONA

I swear to God that I haven't done anything wrong.

OTHELLO

Aren't you a whore?

DESDEMONA

No, I am a Christian.

If saving my body only for my husband and keeping it away from anybody else makes me not a whore then I am not a whore.

OTHELLO

What, you're not a whore?

DESDEMONA

No, and I swear it.

OTHELLO

Is it possible?

DESDEMONA

Oh, heaven help us!

OTHELLO

I beg your pardon then.

I thought you were that cunning whore of Venice

That married Othello.

Raising his voice

You, mistress, That have the office opposite to Saint Peter, And keep the gate of hell!	You, mistress, You whore-house keeper!
Re-enter EMILIA	*Re-enter EMILIA*
You, you, ay, you! We have done our course; there's money for your pains: I pray you, turn the key and keep our counsel.	You, you, yes, you! We've finished our business. Here's some money for your trouble. Lock the door and keep quiet.
Exit	*Othello exits*
EMILIA Alas, what does this gentleman conceive? How do you, madam? how do you, my good lady?	**EMILIA** What does he think you've done wrong? Are you ok? How are you my good lady?
DESDEMONA 'Faith, half asleep.	**DESDEMONA** I'm shocked.
EMILIA Good madam, what's the matter with my lord?	**EMILIA** Good madam, what's the matter with my lord?
DESDEMONA With who?	**DESDEMONA** With who?
EMILIA Why, with my lord, madam.	**EMILIA** With my lord, madam.
DESDEMONA Who is thy lord?	**DESDEMONA** Who is your lord?

EMILIA

He that is yours, sweet lady.

DESDEMONA

I have none: do not talk to me, Emilia;

I cannot weep; nor answer have I none,

But what should go by water. Prithee, tonight

Lay on my bed my wedding sheets:

remember;

And call thy husband hither.

EMILIA

Here's a change indeed!

Exit

DESDEMONA

'Tis meet I should be used so, very meet.

How have I been behaved, that he might stick

The small'st opinion on my least misuse?

Re-enter EMILIA with IAGO

IAGO

What is your pleasure, madam?

How is't with you?

DESDEMONA

I cannot tell. Those that do teach young babes

Do it with gentle means and easy tasks:

EMILIA

My lord is your lord, sweet lady.

DESDEMONA

I don't have a lord. Don't talk to me, Emilia. I

cannot even cry. I do not have anything to

say.

Tonight

Put my wedding sheets on my bed. Don't

forget.

And tell your husband to come here and see

me.

EMILIA

Things have changed!

Emilia exits

DESDEMONA

It would be acceptable for him to treat me

this way if I have done something wrong.

What could I have done so wrong to make

him have such a bad opinion of me?

Re-enter EMILIA with IAGO

IAGO

What can I do for you, madam?

What's wrong with you?

DESDEMONA

I can't tell you because I don't know. When

grown-ups teach children, they do it gently

and easily.

He might have chid me so; for, in good faith,
I am a child to chiding.

IAGO

What's the matter, lady?

EMILIA

Alas, Iago, my lord hath so bewhored her.
Thrown such despite and heavy terms upon
her,
As true hearts cannot bear.

DESDEMONA

Am I that name, Iago?

IAGO

What name, fair lady?

DESDEMONA

Such as she says my lord did say I was.

EMILIA

He call'd her whore: a beggar in his drink
Could not have laid such terms upon his callat.

IAGO

Why did he so?

DESDEMONA

I do not know; I am sure I am none such.

IAGO

He should have treated me in the same way
because I am not used to having such abuse
directed at me.

IAGO

What's the matter, lady?

EMILIA

Iago, Othello has called her a whore,

He has also thrown so much abuse at her,
things that are impossible for a true heart to
hear.

DESDEMONA

Am I really one of those?

IAGO

What, fair lady?

DESDEMONA

That name that Emilia said.

EMILIA

He called her a whore. A drunken beggar
would not even call a beggar woman such a
horrible name.

IAGO

Why did he say it?

DESDEMONA

I don't know, but I'm sure I'm not one.

IAGO

Do not weep, do not weep. Alas the day!

EMILIA

Hath she forsook so many noble matches,

Her father and her country and her friends,

To be call'd whore? would it not make one weep?

DESDEMONA

It is my wretched fortune.

IAGO

Beshrew him for't!

How comes this trick upon him?

DESDEMONA

Nay, heaven doth know.

EMILIA

I will be hang'd, if some eternal villain,

Some busy and insinuating rogue,

Some cogging, cozening slave, to get some office,

Have not devised this slander; I'll be hang'd else.

IAGO

Fie, there is no such man; it is impossible.

DESDEMONA

If any such there be, heaven pardon him!

Don't cry. Don't cry. What a day!

EMILIA

Has she really given up all those chances to marry noble men,

And given up her father, her country, and her friends

To be called a whore? Would it not make you cry?

DESDEMONA

It is just my bad luck.

IAGO

Damn him for it!

How did he get such an idea?

DESDEMONA

God knows.

EMILIA

I will bet my life on it that some evil life-long villain, some deceptive, selfish trouble-causer has suggested it to get further in his position. I'll be hanged if I am wrong.

IAGO

Don't be silly. There isn't anybody like that. It's impossible.

DESDEMONA

If there is, God pardon him!

EMILIA

A halter pardon him! and hell gnaw his bones!

Why should he call her whore? who keeps her

company?

What place? what time? what form? what

likelihood?

The Moor's abused by some most villanous

knave,

Some base notorious knave, some scurvy

fellow.

O heaven, that such companions thou'ldst

unfold,

And put in every honest hand a whip

To lash the rascals naked through the world

Even from the east to the west!

IAGO

Speak within door.

EMILIA

O, fie upon them! Some such squire he was

That turn'd your wit the seamy side without,

And made you to suspect me with the Moor.

IAGO

You are a fool; go to.

DESDEMONA

O good Iago,

What shall I do to win my lord again?

Good friend, go to him; for, by this light of

heaven,

I know not how I lost him. Here I kneel:

EMILIA

A noose around his neck should pardon him!

Let hell gnaw on his bones!

Why should he call her a whore? Who has she

been with?

Where? When? How? How is it even

possible?

The Moor is being tricked by some villain,

Some evil villain, some filthy person.

Oh God, I wish you would expose people like

this.

And put a whip in every honest person's

hands so they could whip them naked

through the entire world

From east to west!

IAGO

Speak quietly.

EMILIA

Oh, to hell with them! It was the same kind of

person who made you question my

faithfulness by suggesting I had been with the

Moor.

IAGO

You are a fool. Shut up.

DESDEMONA

Oh good Iago,

What can I do to win my husband back?

Please go to him, my good friend, I swear on

heaven that I do not know how I have lost

him. I am on my knees.

If e'er my will did trespass 'gainst his love,
Either in discourse of thought or actual deed,
Or that mine eyes, mine ears, or any sense,
Delighted them in any other form;
Or that I do not yet, and ever did.
And ever will--though he do shake me off
To beggarly divorcement--love him dearly,
Comfort forswear me! Unkindness may do much;
And his unkindness may defeat my life,
But never taint my love. I cannot say 'whore:'
It does abhor me now I speak the word;
To do the act that might the addition earn
Not the world's mass of vanity could make me.

IAGO

I pray you, be content; 'tis but his humour:
The business of the state does him offence,
And he does chide with you.

DESDEMONA

If 'twere no other—

IAGO

'Tis but so, I warrant.

Trumpets within

Hark, how these instruments summon to supper!
The messengers of Venice stay the meat;
Go in, and weep not; all things shall be well.

If I have ever done anything to betray him and destroy his love for me, either by thinking something or by actually doing something, Or if I have ever looked at, listened to, or done anything at all to hurt him that I do not know about, or if I never loved him and don't now – even though he is trying to divorce me -
then I hope I suffer!
Unkindness is powerful and his may kill me.
But I will always love him. I can't say 'whore'
It disgusts me when I say it.
I could not do what it takes to be one.
Nothing in the world would make me want to earn that name.

IAGO

Please calm down. He is just in a strange mood.
This political business is affecting him,
And he's taking it out on you.

DESDEMONA

If it's just...

IAGO

It is. I'm sure.

Trumpets sound

Listen, the trumpets are calling us to dinner!
The Venetians are waiting for their food.
Go, and don't cry. Everything will be ok.

Exeunt DESDEMONA and EMILIA	*DESDEMONA and EMILIA exit*
Enter RODERIGO	*Enter RODERIGO*
How now, Roderigo!	How are you, Roderigo?
RODERIGO	**RODERIGO**
I do not find that thou dealest justly with me.	I don't think you are being fair with me.
IAGO	**IAGO**
What in the contrary?	What's making you say that?
RODERIGO	**RODERIGO**
Every day thou daffest me with some device, Iago; and rather, as it seems to me now, keepest from me all conveniency than suppliest me with the least advantage of hope. I will indeed no longer endure it, nor am I yet persuaded to put up in peace what already I have foolishly suffered.	Every day you put me off with some silly trick instead of just finding something for me. You keep avoiding me rather than helping me progress. I will not put up with it anymore, nor will I put up with what you have already done to me.
IAGO	**IAGO**
Will you hear me, Roderigo?	Will you listen to me, Roderigo?
RODERIGO	**RODERIGO**
'Faith, I have heard too much, for your words and performances are no kin together.	I have listened to you far too much. Your words and actions just don't match up.
IAGO	**IAGO**
You charge me most unjustly.	You are unfairly accusing me.
RODERIGO	**RODERIGO**
With nought but truth. I have wasted myself out of my means. The jewels you have had	With nothing but the truth. I have wasted all my money. The jewels you have had from me

from me to deliver to Desdemona would half have corrupted a

votarist: you have told me she hath received them and returned me expectations and comforts of sudden

respect and acquaintance, but I find none.

IAGO

Well; go to; very well.

RODERIGO

Very well! go to! I cannot go to, man; nor 'tis not very well: nay, I think it is scurvy, and begin to find myself fobbed in it.

IAGO

Very well.

RODERIGO

I tell you 'tis not very well. I will make myself known to Desdemona: if she will return me my jewels, I will give over my suit and repent my unlawful solicitation; if not, assure yourself I will seek satisfaction of you.

IAGO

You have said now.

RODERIGO

Ay, and said nothing but what I protest intendment of doing.

IAGO

---

to give to Desdemona would have made a nun want to sleep with me. You told me that she has received them and that she promised to give me something in return. But I haven't got anything.

IAGO

Well, if that's what you think. Fine.

RODERIGO

If that's what I think! Fine! It's not fine, and it's not happening. It's disgusting and I am starting to think I have been tricked.

IAGO

Fine.

RODERIGO

I am telling you it is not fine. I will tell Desdemona exactly how I feel. If she returns my jewels then I will leave her alone and apologise. If not, then I will challenge you to a fight.

IAGO

You have said what you wanted to say.

RODERIGO

Yes, and I haven't said anything that I am not intending to do.

IAGO

Why, now I see there's mettle in thee, and even from this instant to build on thee a better opinion than ever before. Give me thy hand, Roderigo: thou hast

taken against me a most just exception; but yet, I protest, I have dealt most directly in thy affair.

RODERIGO

It hath not appeared.

IAGO

I grant indeed it hath not appeared, and your suspicion is not without wit and judgment. But, Roderigo, if thou hast that in thee indeed, which I have greater reason to believe now than ever, I mean purpose, courage and valour, this night show it: if thou the next night following enjoy not Desdemona, take me from this world with treachery and devise engines for my life.

RODERIGO

Well, what is it? is it within reason and compass?

IAGO

Sir, there is especial commission come from Venice

to depute Cassio in Othello's place.

RODERIGO

Is that true? why, then Othello and Desdemona return again to Venice.

Well, now I can see that you have some courage, and I have instantly gained more respect for you than I had before. Give me your hand, Roderigo. You have complained about me and that is understandable, but I insist that I have done everything that I can.

RODERIGO

It doesn't look like it.

IAGO

I admit that it doesn't look like I have done much, and your suspicion is a smart one. But, Roderigo, if you are as courageous as you say, and I believe that now more than I did before, then just wait a little bit longer.
If you are not having sex with Desdemona by tomorrow night, then I suggest you find some way to kill me.

RODERIGO

Well, what do I have to do? Is it reasonable and possible?

IAGO

Sir, a special letter has come from Venice that is asking for Othello to be replaced by Cassio.

RODERIGO

Is that true? Well then, Othello and Desdemona will be returning to Venice.

IAGO

O, no; he goes into Mauritania and takes away with him the fair Desdemona, unless his abode be lingered here by some accident: wherein none can be

so determinate as the removing of Cassio.

RODERIGO

How do you mean, removing of him?

IAGO

Why, by making him uncapable of Othello's place;

knocking out his brains.

RODERIGO

And that you would have me to do?

IAGO

Ay, if you dare do yourself a profit and a right. He sups to-night with a harlotry, and thither will I go to him: he knows not yet of his horrorable fortune. If you will watch his going thence, which

I will fashion to fall out between twelve and one, you may take him at your pleasure: I will be near to second your attempt, and he shall fall between

us. Come, stand not amazed at it, but go along with me; I will show you such a necessity in his death that you shall think yourself bound to put it on

him. It is now high suppertime, and the night grows to waste: about it.

IAGO

Oh, no. He is going to Mauritania and taking the beautiful Desdemona with him. That's unless his stay here is prolonged by some accident. The best thing to do is to get rid of Cassio.

RODERIGO

What do you mean, get rid of him?

IAGO

I mean make him unable to take Othello's place.

Knock his brains out.

RODERIGO

And you want me to do that?

IAGO

Yes, if you want to do yourself a favour.

He's eating his dinner with a prostitute tonight, and I will be going to visit him. He doesn't know what he's been appointed as yet. If you stay and watch him, I will arrange for him to leave between twelve and one, and then you can attack him as you please. I will be nearby to support you, and he will fall between us. Come on, don't stand there in a daze. Come with me. I will give you some good reasons to kill him so you feel honour bound to do it.

It's nearly dinner time, and the night is going to waste. Let's go.

RODERIGO

I will hear further reason for this.

IAGO

And you shall be satisfied.

Exeunt

RODERIGO

I want to know the reasons.

IAGO

You will and you will be satisfied by them.

They all exit.

PART 26: ANALYSING ACT 4 SCENE 2

Themes: Appearance vs Reality, Jealousy, Manhood and Honour, Womanhood and Sexuality.

In his desperation, Othello begins this scene by interrogating Emilia (like a witness to a crime) about Desdemona's behaviour. Othello is resolute but composed in his language and appears to have recovered his rhetorical talent as he attempts to extract the 'truth' from Emilia and directs her to bring Desdemona to him, 'Bid her come hither: go.'. Emilia finally reveals her loyalty to Desdemona by insisting that her behaviour is auspicious. Emilia's epithet for a rogue when she refers to an 'eternal villain' having slandered Desdemona is a serious description but an accidental description of her own husband. Had Othello mentioned the handkerchief at this point, Emilia would have recognised the dishonesty of her husband and been able to clear Desdemona and implicate Iago. Unfortunately, Othello in his paranoia believes that Emilia is also deceived by Desdemona's ability to be a 'subtle whore' just like a 'simple bawd' would be and Shakespeare effectively conveys a sense of impending and inevitable doom when Othello sends Emilia to collect Desdemona.

Othello's jealousy and obsession intensifies with the return of Desdemona to the stage and a request that Emilia stand guard as he interrogates her. It is immediately apparent that Othello and Desdemona no longer understand one another as she reveals that she '...understand[s] a fury in [his] words./But not the words.' In an emotionally charged interview, Desdemona declares her fidelity and states that she is 'loyal' resulting in a barrage of exaggerated accusations and insults from Othello. He refers to Desdemona as 'false', a 'public commoner', an 'Impudent stumpet', and a 'whore'. His anger intensifies as he calls her a prostitute and throws money at her, highlighting attitudes towards women at the time and re-visiting the importance of chastity. The insult 'whore' was the most common term of abuse directed at women during the seventeenth century. Prostitution was widespread and London was a prime location for the sex trade. Being labelled a whore was a serious and dangerous accusation as it could lead to the downfall of an entire family. Women were guilty until proven innocent and Othello uses this as justification as to why Desdemona must die. A Shakespearean audience might have struggled to sympathise with a woman who had already brought shame on her family by eloping against her father's consent. In stark contrast to how she may appear, Desdemona calls Othello her 'noble lord' and refuses to criticise him instead hoping that she may 'win' him again. By the time Othello has finished abusing her, , Desdemona appears exhausted and unable to cry but desperately attempts to symbolically strengthen her marriage by putting her wedding night sheets back on the bed. Historically in some cultures, wedding sheets stained with the blood of a virginal bride would be hung out on a balcony to prove the bride's purity. Desdemona still loves her husband and is desperate to remind Othello of her chastity and of her honour to him. Her attitude toward her chastity is representative of the audience's expectation of women at the time. Chastity is worth more than life. Emilia, on the other hand, does not advocate fidelity and instead chooses to suggest that women are the same as men and are unfaithful.

Iago returns to the stage at Desdemona's request as she is desperate to discover why Othello is behaving in the way that he is. Iago continues to show his powers of manipulation as he dismisses his wife's comment that an 'eternal villain' is responsible for Othello's behaviour and manages to convince Desdemona that Othello is troubled by political affairs. Iago's cruelty is highlighted when he asks Desdemona not to 'weep' as he knows that she has worse yet to come. As Desdemona and Emilia exit, Roderigo returns to the stage angry that he is yet to enjoy Desdemona's company and demanding a return of the jewels he has given to Iago in payment. Roderigo poses a real challenge to Iago's plot and acts as a reminder of Iago's pleasure in manipulating everybody over what seems to be a long time prior to his determination to see Othello's demise. At this point, the audience are given some false hope, yet again, that Iago's plot could be uncovered. The steadily mounting tension continues as Iago decides to combine his two plots and use Roderigo in the plan to kill Cassio.

ORIGINAL TEXT:	MODERN TRANSLATION:
SCENE III. Another room In the castle. *Enter OTHELLO, LODOVICO, DESDEMONA,* *EMILIA and Attendants*	**SCENE III. Another room In the castle.** *Enter OTHELLO, LODOVICO, DESDEMONA,* *EMILIA and Attendants*
LODOVICO I do beseech you, sir, trouble yourself no further .	**LODOVICO** Please don't go to any more trouble.
OTHELLO O, pardon me: 'twill do me good to walk.	**OTHELLO** Oh, excuse me but nothing will make me feel better.
LODOVICO Madam, good night; I humbly thank your ladyship.	**LODOVICO** Madam, good night. Thank you.
DESDEMONA Your honour is most welcome.	**DESDEMONA** You are very welcome.
OTHELLO Will you walk, sir? O,--Desdemona,--	**OTHELLO** Will you walk with me, sir? Oh, Desdemona...
DESDEMONA My lord?	**DESDEMONA** Yes, my lord?
OTHELLO	**OTHELLO**

Get you to bed on the instant; I will be returned forthwith: dismiss your attendant there: look it be done.	Get to bed right now. I will be there soon. Send your maid Emilia away. Make sure you do as you're told.
DESDEMONA	**DESDEMONA**
I will, my lord.	I will, my lord.
Exeunt OTHELLO, LODOVICO, and Attendants	*OTHELLO, LODOVICO, and Attendants exit*
EMILIA	**EMILIA**
How goes it now? he looks gentler than he did.	How are things now? He looks calmer than he did.
DESDEMONA	**DESDEMONA**
He says he will return incontinent: He hath commanded me to go to bed, And bade me to dismiss you.	He says he'll be back soon. He has ordered me to go to bed. And he has asked me to dismiss you.
EMILIA	**EMILIA**
Dismiss me!	Dismiss me!
DESDEMONA	**DESDEMONA**
It was his bidding: therefore, good Emilia,. Give me my nightly wearing, and adieu: We must not now displease him.	That's what he said. Therefore, good Emilia, Get me my nightgown and goodnight. We must not do anything to upset him.
EMILIA	**EMILIA**
I would you had never seen him!	I wish you'd never laid eyes on him!
DESDEMONA	**DESDEMONA**
So would not I my love doth so approve him, That even his stubbornness, his cheques, his frowns--	I don't. I love him so much.

Prithee, unpin me,--have grace and favour in them.

EMILIA

I have laid those sheets you bade me on the bed.

DESDEMONA

All's one. Good faith, how foolish are our minds!
If I do die before thee prithee, shroud me
In one of those same sheets.

EMILIA

Come, come you talk.

DESDEMONA

My mother had a maid call'd Barbara:
She was in love, and he she loved proved mad
And did forsake her: she had a song of 'willow;'
An old thing 'twas, but it express'd her fortune,
And she died singing it: that song to-night
Will not go from my mind; I have much to do,
But to go hang my head all at one side,
And sing it like poor Barbara. Prithee, dispatch.

EMILIA

Shall I go fetch your night-gown?

I love him even when he is being stubborn, and harsh, and mean.
Please help me unpin this.

EMILIA

I have made your bed with those sheets you asked for.

DESDEMONA

It doesn't matter. How silly are our minds!
If I die before you, please wrap me in one of those sheets.

EMILIA

Stop saying silly things.

DESDEMONA

My mother had a maid called Barbara. She was in love but her lover turned out to be mad
And left her. She sang a song about a willow.
It was an old song that reminded her of her life.
And she died singing it. That song is in my head tonight
I cannot get it out of my mind.
I feel like going and hanging my head down and singing that song, just like poor Barbara.
Please, hurry up.

EMILIA

Shall I go and get your nightgown?

DESDEMONA

No, unpin me here.

This Lodovico is a proper man.

EMILIA

A very handsome man.

DESDEMONA

He speaks well.

EMILIA

I know a lady in Venice would have walked barefoot to Palestine for a touch of his nether lip.

DESDEMONA

[Singing] The poor soul sat sighing by a sycamore tree,

Sing all a green willow:

Her hand on her bosom, her head on her knee,

Sing willow, willow, willow:

The fresh streams ran by her, and murmur'd her moans;

Sing willow, willow, willow;

Her salt tears fell from her, and soften'd the stones;

Lay by these:--

Singing

Sing willow, willow, willow;

Prithee, hie thee; he'll come anon:--

Singing

DESDEMONA

No, unpin me here.

Lodovico is an attractive man.

EMILIA

A very handsome man.

DESDEMONA

He speaks well.

EMILIA

I know a lady in Venice who would have done anything for a kiss from him.

DESDEMONA

[Singing] The poor soul sat singing by a sycamore tree,

Everyone sing the green willow:

Her hand on her bosom, her head on her knee,

Sing willow, willow, willow:

The fresh streams ran by her, and murmured her moans;

Sing willow, willow, willow;

Her salt tears fell from her, and softened the stones;

Put these away.

Singing

Sing willow, willow, willow;

Please, hurry; he'll come right away:--

Singing

Sing all a green willow must be my garland.

Let nobody blame him; his scorn I approve,-

Nay, that's not next.--Hark! who is't that knocks?

EMILIA

It's the wind.

DESDEMONA

[Singing] I call'd my love false love; but what said he then?
Sing willow, willow, willow:
If I court moe women, you'll couch with moe men!
So, get thee gone; good night Ate eyes do itch;
Doth that bode weeping?

EMILIA

'Tis neither here nor there.

DESDEMONA

I have heard it said so. O, these men, these men!
Dost thou in conscience think,--tell me, Emilia,--
That there be women do abuse their husbands
In such gross kind?

EMILIA

Everyone sing a green willow must be my garland.

Let nobody blame him; I approve of his hate,-

No, that's not how it goes. Listen! Who is knocking?

EMILIA

It's the wind.

DESDEMONA

[Singing] I told my lover that he didn't love me; but what
said did he say?
Sing willow, willow, willow:
If I chase more women, you'll sleep with more men!
Go away now; good night. My eyes itch;
Does that mean I am about to cry?

EMILIA

No. It doesn't mean anything.

DESDEMONA

I have heard someone say what it means. Oh, these men, these men!
Do you honestly think, and you must tell me,
That there are women who cheat on their husbands
In such a disgusting way?

EMILIA

There be some such, no question.

DESDEMONA

Wouldst thou do such a deed for all the world?

EMILIA

Why, would not you?

DESDEMONA

No, by this heavenly light!

EMILIA

Nor I neither by this heavenly light;
I might do't as well i' the dark.

DESDEMONA

Wouldst thou do such a deed for all the world?

EMILIA

The world's a huge thing: it is a great price.
For a small vice.

DESDEMONA

In troth, I think thou wouldst not.

EMILIA

In troth, I think I should; and undo't when I had done. Marry, I would not do such a thing for a joint-ring, nor for measures of lawn, nor for gowns, petticoats, nor caps, nor any petty exhibition; but for the whole world,--why,

There are definitely some women like that, no doubt.

DESDEMONA

Would you ever do such a thing for all the world?

EMILIA

Why, wouldn't you?

DESDEMONA

Not a slight chance!

EMILIA

I wouldn't either.
I might do it easier in the dark.

DESDEMONA

Could you really do such a thing for all the world?

EMILIA

The world's huge. It is a great price.
For a small vice.

DESDEMONA

I don't believe you. I don't think you would.

EMILIA

I believe I would. I would then undo it later after I had done it. Seriously, I wouldn't do it for a ring, or for a property, or for dresses, petticoats, hats, or anything else superficial. But for the world?

228

who would not make her husband a cuckold
to make him a monarch? I should venture
purgatory for't.

DESDEMONA

Beshrew me, if I would do such a wrong
For the whole world.

EMILIA

Why the wrong is but a wrong i' the world:
and having the world for your labour, tis a
wrong in your own world, and you might
quickly make it right.

DESDEMONA

I do not think there is any such woman.

EMILIA

Yes, a dozen; and as many to the vantage as
would store the world they played for.
But I do think it is their husbands' faults
If wives do fall: say that they slack their duties,
And pour our treasures into foreign laps,
Or else break out in peevish jealousies,
Throwing restraint upon us; or say they strike
us,
Or scant our former having in despite;
Why, we have galls, and though we have some
grace,
Yet have we some revenge. Let husbands
know
Their wives have sense like them: they see
and smell

Who wouldn't cheat on their husband to
make him the king? I would risk going to hell
for that.

DESDEMONA

Shame on me if I ever did such a horrible
thing for the world.

EMILIA

A bad action is only wrong in this world.
Once you've won the whole world, you have
only committed a sin in your world. It's yours
so you can just make it right again.

DESDEMONA

I do not think there is a woman like that in
existence.

EMILIA

Yes there is. There are loads of them – as
many as there are women in the world.
But I do think it is the husbands' fault
if the wife cheats.
What if they have neglected them and are
sleeping with other women?

They may get insanely jealous and start
keeping us from going anywhere. They might
hit us.
They might reduce our money out of spite.
We have gall as well as grace, and we need to
get our own back sometimes.
Husbands need to know that their wives are
no different to them.

And have their palates both for sweet and sour,
As husbands have. What is it that they do
When they change us for others? Is it sport?
I think it is: and doth affection breed it?
I think it doth: is't frailty that thus errs?
It is so too: and have not we affections,
Desires for sport, and frailty, as men have?
Then let them use us well: else let them know,
The ills we do, their ills instruct us so.

DESDEMONA

Good night, good night: heaven me such uses send,
Not to pick bad from bad, but by bad mend!
Exeunt

They see and smell. They have the same tastes.
They are sensitive to sweet and sour.
Just like their husbands. Why do they change us for other women?
Is it for fun?
I think it is. And isn't it our affection for them that allows them to do it?
I think so. Isn't it our weakness that allows them to do it?
I think so. Don't we have desires, and don't we want to have fun like men do?
They should be good to us or we will show them that the bad things we do are learned from them.

DESDEMONA

Good night, good night. I hope God teaches me how to use bad examples as lessons. I want to learn from the bad and improve myself!
They all exit.

PART 28: ANALYSING ACT 4 SCENE 3

Themes: Appearance vs Reality, Womanhood and Sexuality, Jealousy.

Othello's demand that Desdemona go to bed without him shows that his desire for her has vanished and he no longer sees their bed as a symbol of their love but as a symbol of dishonour. This contrasts directly with Act 2 Scene 3 where Othello calms the conflict and lovingly leads his wife to bed, 'Come, my dear love.'. Desdemona remains obedient as well as loyal as she retires to bed and continues to declare her love for her husband as Emilia states that she wishes Desdemona had never met Othello. There is a hint that Desdemona believes Othello may kill her as she requests her bed sheets be used as a 'shroud' for her should she 'die'. This devotion to her husband, even though it could cost Desdemona her life, contrasts with Iago's description of female loyalty throughout the play. Desdemona proves herself to be the ideal woman of the time bothered more about her chastity than her life. Feminist critical reading focuses on the passivity of Desdemona in the moments leading up to her death. Her change from assertive heroine to passive victim presents her as a paradoxical and complex character. She has become increasingly vulnerable until eventually becoming the atypical submissive woman in order to prove her love for Othello. Her refusal to blame her husband for his behaviour and her forgiveness further presents her as accepting of her fate as an accused female.

This is the first and only scene where Desdemona makes reference to her mother by telling the story of her mother's maid, Barbary. Barbary appears as a parallel for Desdemona and Othello in that her name means foreigner and links to the word Barbarian as well as echoes Iago's description of Othello as a 'Barbary horse'. Desdemona shares Barbary's 'Willow Song' which echoes the story of Ophelia's tragic drowning surrounded by willows in *Hamlet* after being rejected by her lover. This reflects Desdemona's melancholic mood and ideas about the fatalism of love and foreshadows her tragic end. Emilia understands Desdemona's torment and also knows that the loss of her handkerchief has caused her grief as she witnessed Othello using its absence to accuse Desdemona of infidelity. Knowing where the handkerchief is and not revealing the truth suggests that Emilia chooses to protect her husband rather than her lady. Unfortunately, Emilia's actions show an acceptance of Desdemona and Othello's fate.

Although Desdemona's faithfulness is unquestionable and she hopes her love recoverable, as Emilia undresses her for bed they both discuss how attractive Lodovico is. Emilia deliberately encourages this conversation based on her beliefs that female chastity is exaggerated. Like Iago, Emilia has a cynical view of relationships and believes adultery is a 'small vice'. This shocking admittance (though seemingly untrue based on her earlier admittance of being virtuous when proclaiming she wouldn't commit adultery for a 'joint-ring') serves as a reminder to the audience of the different codes of sexual conduct for men and women. Society had high expectations of women, therefore Emilia need to be virtuous in order to successfully defend Desdemona in death. Their discussion of how they view Lodovico as a 'proper man' hints at the possibility that women have the ability to be unfaithful especially at points of crisis in their marriage, but the dismissal of such behaviour as 'abuse' of a 'gross kind' reaffirms the fact that they are loyal . Of course, their discussion could also imply that Desdemona, having just been violently criticised by her husband, is starting to imagine what life could have been like without Othello and that Emilia wants her to seek happiness elsewhere. She continues to encourage Desdemona to speak openly about her thoughts as she believes Desdemona is superior to Othello in the first place. For the first time in the play, Desdemona is actually imagining what it might be like to be unfaithful as Emilia provides the societal acknowledgement, and reality, that women have needs and desires similar to men. The contrast in the female characters' thoughts about marriage and fidelity provide the audience with two very different women. Emilia is practical and unafraid to suggest that female infidelity could be justified whereas Desdemona is a romantic who places loyalty to her husband above everything. The scene ends with Emilia's speech about husbands echoing Iago's speech about wives, both of which Desdemona dismisses.

ORIGINAL TEXT:	MODERN TRANSLATION:
SCENE I. Cyprus. A street.	**SCENE I. Cyprus. A street.**
Enter IAGO and RODERIGO	*Enter IAGO and RODERIGO*
IAGO	**IAGO**
Here, stand behind this bulk; straight will he come:	Here, stand behind this wall. He will be here straight away.
Wear thy good rapier bare, and put it home:	Get your sword out, and then stick it in him as far as it will go.
Quick, quick; fear nothing; I'll be at thy elbow:	Be quick. Don't be scared. I'll be right next to you.
It makes us, or it mars us; think on that,	This will either make us or break us. Think about that. Be strong.
And fix most firm thy resolution.	
RODERIGO	**RODERIGO**
Be near at hand; I may miscarry in't.	Stay near me. I might mess up.
IAGO	**IAGO**
Here, at thy hand: be bold, and take thy stand.	I am right next to you. Be brave, and get ready.
Retires	*Iago moves*
RODERIGO	**RODERIGO**
I have no great devotion to the deed;	I have no real reason to do this.
And yet he hath given me satisfying reasons:	But he has given me some reasons to justify it.
'Tis but a man gone. Forth, my sword: he dies.	It is only one man down. My sword comes out, and he dies.

IAGO

I have rubb'd this young quat almost to the sense,

And he grows angry. Now, whether he kill Cassio,

Or Cassio him, or each do kill the other,

Every way makes my gain: live Roderigo,

He calls me to a restitution large

Of gold and jewels that I bobb'd from him,

As gifts to Desdemona;

It must not be: if Cassio do remain,

He hath a daily beauty in his life

That makes me ugly; and, besides, the Moor

May unfold me to him; there stand I in much peril:

No, he must die. But so: I hear him coming.

Enter CASSIO

RODERIGO

I know his gait, 'tis he.--Villain, thou diest!

Makes a pass at CASSIO

CASSIO

That thrust had been mine enemy indeed,

But that my coat is better than thou know'st

I will make proof of thine.

Draws, and wounds RODERIGO

RODERIGO

IAGO

I have rubbed this young spot until he's about to burst.

And he is getting angrier. Whether he kills Cassio,

Or Cassio kills him, or they kill each other, it is all in my favour. If Roderigo survives, he will ask me to give him back the gold and jewellery that I stole from him,

And said I gave to Desdemona as gifts.

That can't happen. If Cassio lives,

He is so handsome that he makes me look ugly. Besides, the Moor might tell him about all the lies I have told him. That would be really dangerous for me.

No, he has to die. I can hear him coming.

Enter CASSIO

RODERIGO

I know the sound of his walk. It's him. Die villain!

Makes a pass at CASSIO

CASSIO

That thrust might have really hurt me,

But I have a really good coat on, better than you thought.

Now I am going to test yours.

Draws, and wounds RODERIGO

RODERIGO

O, I am slain!

IAGO from behind wounds CASSIO in the leg, and exit

CASSIO

I am maim'd for ever. Help, ho! murder! murder!

Falls

Enter OTHELLO

OTHELLO

The voice of Cassio: Iago keeps his word.

RODERIGO

O, villain that I am!

OTHELLO

It is even so.

CASSIO

O, help, ho! light! a surgeon!

OTHELLO

'Tis he:--O brave Iago, honest and just,
That hast such noble sense of thy friend's wrong!
Thou teachest me. Minion, your dear lies dead,
And your unblest fate hies: strumpet, I come.
Forth of my heart those charms, thine eyes, are blotted;

He's killed me!

IAGO from behind wounds CASSIO in the leg, and exit

CASSIO

I am crippled forever. Help! Murder! Murder!

Falls

Enter OTHELLO

OTHELLO

That's Cassio's voice. Iago has kept his word.

RODERIGO

Oh, what a villain I am!

OTHELLO

That's the truth.

CASSIO

Oh, help me! Get me a light! Get me a surgeon!

OTHELLO

It's him! Brave Iago, you are so honest and trustworthy. You are noble enough to put my grievance first!
You put me to shame. Whore, your lover is dead now,
And your own horrible fate will soon be here. I am coming.

Thy bed, lust-stain'd, shall with lust's blood be spotted.	I have shut all the beautiful memories and your pretty eyes out of my heart. Your bed, which is stained with lust, will soon be stained with your blood.
Exit *Enter LODOVICO and GRATIANO*	*Exit* *Enter LODOVICO and GRATIANO*
CASSIO What, ho! no watch? no passage? murder! murder!	**CASSIO** What, help! Where is the guard? No one passing? Murder! Murder!
GRATIANO 'Tis some mischance; the cry is very direful.	**GRATIANO** Something is wrong. The shout sounds very serious.
CASSIO O, help!	**CASSIO** Oh, help!
LODOVICO Hark!	**LODOVICO** Listen!
RODERIGO O wretched villain!	**RODERIGO** I am a disgusting villain!
LODOVICO Two or three groan: it is a heavy night: These may be counterfeits: let's think't unsafe To come in to the cry without more help.	**LODOVICO** Two or three men are groaning. It's a really dark night. These could be fake cries. Let's stay safe and not go towards the shouts until we have more help.
RODERIGO Nobody come? then shall I bleed to death.	**RODERIGO** Nobody's coming? I am going to bleed to death.

LODOVICO

Hark!

Re-enter IAGO, with a light

GRATIANO

Here's one comes in his shirt, with light and weapons.

IAGO

Who's there? whose noise is this that ones on murder?

LODOVICO

We do not know.

IAGO

Did not you hear a cry?

CASSIO

Here, here! for heaven's sake, help me!

IAGO

What's the matter?

GRATIANO

This is Othello's ancient, as I take it.

LODOVICO

The same indeed; a very valiant fellow.

IAGO

What are you here that cry so grievously?

LODOVICO

Listen!

Re-enter IAGO, with a light

GRATIANO

Someone is coming, with a light and a weapon.

IAGO

Who's there? Who is crying murder?

LODOVICO

We don't know.

IAGO

Did you not hear someone shouting?

CASSIO

Here, here! For God's sake, help me!

IAGO

What's the matter?

GRATIANO

This is Othello's ensign, I think.

LODOVICO

It is. He's a good man.

IAGO

Who is shouting so badly?

CASSIO

Iago? O, I am spoil'd, undone by villains!
Give me some help.

IAGO

O me, lieutenant! what villains have done
this?

CASSIO

I think that one of them is hereabout,
And cannot make away.

IAGO

O treacherous villains!
What are you there? come in, and give some
help.

To LODOVICO and GRATIANO

RODERIGO

O, help me here!

CASSIO

That's one of them.

IAGO

O murderous slave! O villain!

Stabs RODERIGO

RODERIGO

O damn'd Iago! O inhuman dog!

CASSIO

Iago? I have been destroyed by villains! Help
me.

IAGO

Oh dear, lieutenant! What villains have done
this?

CASSIO

I think that one of them is still here, and can't
get away.

IAGO

Oh the treacherous villains!
Who are you? Come and help me.

To LODOVICO and GRATIANO

RODERIGO

Oh, help me!

CASSIO

That's one of them.

IAGO

Oh you murderous slave! Oh you villain!

Stabs RODERIGO

RODERIGO

Oh damned Iago! You inhuman dog!

IAGO

Kill men i' the dark!--Where be these bloody thieves?--

How silent is this town!--Ho! murder! murder!--

What may you be? are you of good or evil?

LODOVICO

As you shall prove us, praise us.

IAGO

Signior Lodovico?

LODOVICO

He, sir.

IAGO

I cry you mercy. Here's Cassio hurt by villains.

GRATIANO

Cassio!

IAGO

How is't, brother!

CASSIO

My leg is cut in two.

IAGO

Marry, heaven forbid!

Light, gentlemen; I'll bind it with my shirt.

IAGO

Kill men in the dark, do you? Where are these murdering thieves?

This is a quiet town! Murder! Murder!

Who is that? Are you good or evil?

LODOVICO

You can decide for yourself.

IAGO

Lodovico?

LODOVICO

That's me.

IAGO

I beg your pardon. Cassio is here and he's been hurt by villains.

GRATIANO

Cassio!

IAGO

How are you, brother?

CASSIO

My leg has been cut in two.

IAGO

God forbid!

Bring me some light, gentlemen; I'll bind the wound with my shirt.

Enter BIANCA	*Enter BIANCA*
BIANCA	**BIANCA**
What is the matter, ho? who is't that cried?	What is the matter? Who was doing all the shouting?
IAGO	**IAGO**
Who is't that cried!	Who is shouting?
BIANCA	**BIANCA**
O my dear Cassio! my sweet Cassio! O Cassio, Cassio, Cassio!	Oh, my dear Cassio! My sweet Cassio! Oh, Cassio, Cassio, Cassio!
IAGO	**IAGO**
O notable strumpet! Cassio, may you suspect Who they should be that have thus many led you?	You notorious whore! Cassio, do you have any suspicions Who might have stabbed you?
CASSIO	**CASSIO**
No.	No.
GRATIANO	**GRATIANO**
I am to find you thus: I have been to seek you.	I am sorry to find you in this mess. I've been looking for you.
IAGO	**IAGO**
Lend me a garter. So. O, for a chair, To bear him easily hence!	Lend me one of your garters. We need a chair so we can carry him easily!
BIANCA	**BIANCA**
Alas, he faints! O Cassio, Cassio, Cassio!	He's fainted! Cassio, Cassio, Cassio!

IAGO

Gentlemen all, I do suspect this trash

To be a party in this injury.

Patience awhile, good Cassio. Come, come;

Lend me a light. Know we this face or no?

Alas my friend and my dear countryman

Roderigo! no:--yes, sure: O heaven! Roderigo.

GRATIANO

What, of Venice?

IAGO

Even he, sir; did you know him?

GRATIANO

Know him! ay.

IAGO

Signior Gratiano? I cry you gentle pardon;

These bloody accidents must excuse my

manners,

That so neglected you.

GRATIANO

I am glad to see you.

IAGO

How do you, Cassio? O, a chair, a chair!

GRATIANO

Roderigo!

IAGO

Everybody listen, I do suspect this trash has

something to do with this trouble. Just have

patience. Come on.

Give me the light. Do we know who this is?

Oh, this is my friend and my dear countryman

Roderigo! No, can't be. Yes, it is. Oh God!

Roderigo.

GRATIANO

What, from Venice?

IAGO

Yes, it's him. Do you know him?

GRATIANO

Yes, I know him!

IAGO

Gratiano? I beg your pardon.

These horrible matters must excuse my

manners towards you.

GRATIANO

I am glad to see you.

IAGO

How are you, Cassio? A chair, a chair!

GRATIANO

Roderigo!

IAGO	**IAGO**
He, he 'tis he.	It's him. It's him.
A chair brought in	*A chair brought in*
O, that's well said; the chair!	Oh, that's good timing.
GRATIANO	**GRATIANO**
Some good man bear him carefully from hence;	Get somebody to carry him away from here.
I'll fetch the general's surgeon.	I'll get the general's surgeon.
To BIANCA	*To BIANCA*
For you, mistress,	As for you, mistress,
Save you your labour. He that lies slain here, Cassio,	Don't bother. The man lying here hurt, Cassio,
Was my dear friend: what malice was between you?	Was my dear friend: what was the problem between you?
CASSIO	**CASSIO**
None in the world; nor do I know the man.	Nothing at all; I don't know the man.
IAGO	**IAGO**
[To BIANCA] What, look you pale? O, bear him out o' the air.	[To BIANCA] What, why do you look so pale? Get him out into the fresh air.
CASSIO and RODERIGO are borne off	*CASSIO and RODERIGO are carried off*
Stay you, good gentlemen. Look you pale, mistress?	Stay, good gentlemen. Why do you look so pale, mistress?
Do you perceive the gastness of her eye?	Do you see how guilty she looks?

Nay, if you stare, we shall hear more anon.

Behold her well; I pray you, look upon her:

Do you see, gentlemen? nay, guiltiness will speak,

Though tongues were out of use.

Enter EMILIA

EMILIA

'Las, what's the matter? what's the matter, husband?

IAGO

Cassio hath here been set on in the dark

By Roderigo and fellows that are scaped:

He's almost slain, and Roderigo dead.

EMILIA

Alas, good gentleman! alas, good Cassio!

IAGO

This is the fruit of whoring. Prithee, Emilia,

Go know of Cassio where he supp'd to-night.

To BIANCA

What, do you shake at that?

BIANCA

He supp'd at my house; but I therefore shake not.

Watch her, we will get more information.

Keep an eye on her. I ask you, watch her.

Can you see, gentlemen? The guilty say a lot when they are silent.

Enter EMILIA

EMILIA

What's the matter? What's the matter, husband?

IAGO

Cassio has been attacked here in the dark by Roderigo and some other men who have escaped.

He's nearly dead, and Roderigo is dead.

EMILIA

Oh no, good gentleman! Oh no, good Cassio!

IAGO

This is what happens when you visit whores.

Please, Emilia,

Go and ask Cassio where he had dinner tonight.

To BIANCA

What, does that worry you?

BIANCA

He had dinner at my house, but I am not worried.

IAGO	**IAGO**
O, did he so? I charge you, go with me.	Oh, did he? I am arresting you, come with me.
EMILIA	**EMILIA**
Fie, fie upon thee, strumpet!	Shame on you, whore!
BIANCA	**BIANCA**
I am no strumpet; but of life as honest As you that thus abuse me.	I am not a whore, I am as honest as you – the person abusing me.
EMILIA	**EMILIA**
As I! foh! fie upon thee!	As I? Shame on you!
IAGO	**IAGO**
Kind gentlemen, let's go see poor Cassio dress'd. Come, mistress, you must tell's another tale. Emilia run you to the citadel, And tell my lord and lady what hath happ'd. Will you go on? I pray.	Kind gentlemen, let's go and make sure poor Cassio's wounds are dressed. Come on, mistress, you can tell us another story. Emilia run ahead to the castle, And tell Othello and Desdemona what has happened. Will you please go now?
Aside	*Aside*
This is the night That either makes me or fordoes me quite.	This is the night That will either make or break me.
Exeunt	*Exit*

PART 30: ANALYSING ACT 5 SCENE 1

Themes: Appearance vs Reality, Womanhood and Sexuality, Manhood and Honour, Jealousy, Prejudice.

This short scene begins in darkness with Iago in control explaining to Roderigo that this night '...makes us or it mars us...' suggesting that the fate of themselves and others is in their control. The night-time setting mirrors the opening of the play and, therefore, reminds the audience of Iago's use of the cover of darkness to conceal his actions. In fact, most of the violent occurances (the brawl; destruction of Cassio's reputation; the stabbings; and later the death of Desdemona) all take place at night suggesting that evil was always going to win adnIago appears to know this when he confesses at the end of the scene, 'This is the night/That either makes me or fordoes me quite'. Iago's dishonesty, manipulation, and depravity has reached its peak. He doesn't just want to destroy Othello, he wants to destroy anybody and everybody who poses a problem to his plan. He is now worried that Othello may 'unfold' him to Cassio and feels threatened. He believes he is in danger and will do anything to protect himself. However, his cowardice is also apparent as he sends Roderigo into conflict first before then attacking Cassio from behind, blaming Roderigo, and then stabbing Roderigo to death before he can reveal his plan. Roderigo, after questioning his involvement, allows jealousy and the false hope of the reward of Desdemona's love to encourage him to kill Cassio. Iago, having promised to defend Roderigo, reveals just how abhorrent he is by betraying another soldier. Roderigo dies lonely, unloved, pathetic, and penniless but not before recognising Iago's villainy when he proclaims, 'O damned Iago! O inhuman dog!'. Roderigo's use of animal imagery mirrors Iago's earlier insults and reminds the audience of how Iago has dehumanised Othello. Ironically, it is Iago who carries and casts light on the wounded Cassio and Roderigo, symbolising the deceptive role he has over those in 'darkness'. Meanwhile, Lodovico and Graziano (Brabantio's brother; Desdemona's uncle) tend to the surviving Cassio as Iago reveals Roderigo as the attacker and uses misogynisitic stereotypes to implicate Bianca in the plot when he states that he suspects '...this trash/To be a party in this injury'. The abuse Bianca suffers in this scene mirrors the downfall of Desdemona and suggests that women suffer because love makes them helpless.

Emilia, unhappy with Bianca's lifestyle and attitude towards Iago, provokes her into an argument before Bianca dares to suggest that they are similar in their honesty. Emilia's loyalty to her husband is once again reinforced with her defence of him and her refusal to reveal the whereabouts of the handkerchief. Shakespeare's choice to include the female conflict appears to suggests that stereotype and prejudices affect everyone. Just as the men entertain prejudices and stereotypes

245

against women, so do the women in the play. Therefore suggesting that women themselves behave and conduct themselves reflects an internalised acceptance of society's expectations of them.

Everything that happens in this scene reflects the extent that Iago will go in order to stop Othello discovering the truth. He arrests the innocent Bianca, 'I charge you, go with me' and suggests that he and others tend to the wounded Cassio, "…let's go and see poor Cassio dress'd'. The events and reactions also serve as a reminder that Iago is still seen to be 'honest'. Nobody suspects him.

Although desperately attempting to keep control, Iago is becoming reactive in order to cover his tracks. Fortunately for him, Othello misinterprets the events, reacts admiringly to Iago, then finalises his violent plans to kill Desdemona in their bed. He struggles with his decision until he remembers the handkerchief and makes comparisons between its strawberry spotted appearance and what will become the blood-stained sheets of murder. The symbol of fidelity, passion, and love now becomes symbolic of infidelity and death. The scene ends how it begins with Iago making reference to a '…night that either makes me, or fordoes me quite'.

ORIGINAL TEXT:	MODERN TRANSLATION:
SCENE II. A bedchamber in the castle:	SCENE II. A bedchamber in the castle:
DESDEMONA in bed asleep;	DESDEMONA in bed asleep;
a light burning.	a light burning.
Enter OTHELLO	*Enter OTHELLO*
OTHELLO	**OTHELLO**
It is the cause, it is the cause, my soul,--	This is the reason. This is the reason, my love.
Let me not name it to you, you chaste stars!--	Don't ask me to say it out loud to you, perfect
It is the cause. Yet I'll not shed her blood;	stars.
Nor scar that whiter skin of hers than snow,	This s the reason. I will not shed her blood,
And smooth as monumental alabaster.	Nor leave any marks on her pure white skin,
Yet she must die, else she'll betray more men.	That is as smooth as marble.
Put out the light, and then put out the light:	But she has to die, or she will continue to
If I quench thee, thou flaming minister,	cheat.
I can again thy former light restore,	Extinguish the light first, and then kill her.
Should I repent me: but once put out thy light,	I fi extinguish the light of the candle then I can
Thou cunning'st pattern of excelling nature,	always light it again if I regret it, but once I
I know not where is that Promethean heat	put out your light,
That can thy light relume. When I have pluck'd	You beautiful deceptive woman,
the rose,	I don't know of any way to restore your life.
I cannot give it vital growth again.	Once I have plucked a rose
It must needs wither: I'll smell it on the tree.	I cannot make it grow again.
	It will just wither and die. I will smell it on the
	tree instead.
Kissing her	*Kissing her*

Ah balmy breath, that dost almost persuade Justice to break her sword! One more, one more.	Ah that sweet breath almost convinces me not to kill you and carry out justice!
Be thus when thou art dead, and I will kill thee,	One more kiss, one more.
And love thee after. One more, and this the last:	If you are this beautiful when you are dead, I'll kill you and still love you afterward. One more, and this is the last kiss.
So sweet was ne'er so fatal. I must weep,	Something this sweet has never been so fatal. I must cry.
But they are cruel tears: this sorrow's heavenly;	But these are cruel tears. This act is necessary.
It strikes where it doth love. She wakes.	I have to punish the one I love. She's waking up.

DESDEMONA

Who's there? Othello?

OTHELLO

Ay. Desdemona.

DESDEMONA

Will you come to bed, my lord?

OTHELLO

Have you pray'd to-night, Desdemona?

DESDEMONA

Ay, my lord.

OTHELLO

If you bethink yourself of any crime
Unreconciled as yet to heaven and grace,
Solicit for it straight.

DESDEMONA

Who's there? Othello?

OTHELLO

Yes, Desdemona.

DESDEMONA

Will you come to bed, my lord?

OTHELLO

Have you prayed tonight, Desdemona?

DESDEMONA

Yes, my lord.

OTHELLO

If you can think of any crime that you haven't confessed to God, then you need to pray for that now.

DESDEMONA	**DESDEMONA**
Alas, my lord, what do you mean by that?	Oh, my lord, what do you mean by that?
OTHELLO	**OTHELLO**
Well, do it, and be brief; I will walk by:	Well, do it, and be quick. I will wait over here.
I would not kill thy unprepared spirit;	I do not want to kill your unprepared soul. No,
No; heaven forfend! I would not kill thy soul.	heaven forbid! I don't want to kill your soul.
DESDEMONA	**DESDEMONA**
Talk you of killing?	Are you talking about killing me?
OTHELLO	**OTHELLO**
Ay, I do.	Yes. I am
DESDEMONA	**DESDEMONA**
Then heaven	Then heaven
Have mercy on me!	Have mercy on me!
OTHELLO	**OTHELLO**
Amen, with all my heart!	Amen, from the bottom of my heart!
DESDEMONA	**DESDEMONA**
If you say so, I hope you will not kill me.	If you really feel like that, then I hope you
	won't kill me.
OTHELLO	**OTHELLO**
Hum!	Whatever!
DESDEMONA	**DESDEMONA**
And yet I fear you; for you are fatal then	You are scaring me. You are dangerous when
When your eyes roll so: why I should fear I	you roll your eyes like that,
know not,	I don't know why I should be so scared
Since guiltiness I know not; but yet I feel I fear.	because I haven't done anything wrong. But I
	am scared.

OTHELLO

Think on thy sins.

DESDEMONA

They are loves I bear to you.

OTHELLO

Ay, and for that thou diest.

DESDEMONA

That death's unnatural that kills for loving.

Alas, why gnaw you so your nether lip?

Some bloody passion shakes your very frame:

These are portents; but yet I hope, I hope,

They do not point on me.

OTHELLO

Peace, and be still!

DESDEMONA

I will so. What's the matter?

OTHELLO

That handkerchief which I so loved and gave

thee

Thou gavest to Cassio.

DESDEMONA

No, by my life and soul!

Send for the man, and ask him.

OTHELLO

OTHELLO

Think about your sins.

DESDEMONA

My only sin was loving you.

OTHELLO

Yes, and that's why you have to die.

DESDEMONA

It is unnatural to kill me for loving you. Why

are you chewing on your lip like that?

Your whole body is shaking with emotion.

These are bad signs, but I really hope

That they don't predict my future.

OTHELLO

Quiet, and be still!

DESDEMONA

I will. What's the matter?

OTHELLO

That handkerchief which I loved so much and

gave to you

You gave it to Cassio.

DESDEMONA

No, I swear on my life and soul!

Send for him and ask him.

OTHELLO

Sweet soul, be careful.

Sweet soul, take heed,

Take heed of perjury; thou art on thy

deathbed.

DESDEMONA

Ay, but not yet to die.

OTHELLO

Yes, presently:

Therefore confess thee freely of thy sin;

For to deny each article with oath

Cannot remove nor choke the strong

conception

That I do groan withal. Thou art to die.

DESDEMONA

Then Lord have mercy on me!

OTHELLO

I say, amen.

DESDEMONA

And have you mercy too! I never did

Offend you in my life; never loved Cassio

But with such general warranty of heaven

As I might love: I never gave him token.

OTHELLO

By heaven, I saw my handkerchief in's hand.

O perjured woman! thou dost stone my heart,

And makest me call what I intend to do

Be careful of lying when you're on your

deathbed.

DESDEMONA

Yes, but I am not dead yet.

OTHELLO

Yes, but you will be soon.

Therefore, confess your sins freely.

Denying any sin under oath will not convince

me to believe you, nor will it remove the

thought that is tormenting me. You are going

to die.

DESDEMONA

Then God have mercy on me!

OTHELLO

Amen to that.

DESDEMONA

And you have mercy on me too! I have never

done anything to offend you in my life. I have

never loved Cassio

I have only ever treated him the same way as

I would treat others.

I have never given him anything as a sign of

love.

OTHELLO

I saw him holding my handkerchief in his

hand.

A murder, which I thought a sacrifice: I saw the handkerchief.	You lying woman! You have turned my heart to stone. And you're making me say this s murder, when it is actually a sacrifice. I saw the handkerchief.
DESDEMONA He found it then; I never gave it him: send for him hither; Let him confess a truth.	**DESDEMONA** Then he must have found it. I never gave it to him: send for him; Let him tell you the truth.
OTHELLO He hath confess'd.	**OTHELLO** He has already confessed.
DESDEMONA What, my lord?	**DESDEMONA** What, my lord?
OTHELLO That he hath used thee.	**OTHELLO** He's already confessed to having sex with you.
DESDEMONA How? unlawfully?	**DESDEMONA** Having sex with me?
OTHELLO Ay.	**OTHELLO** Yes.
DESDEMONA He will not say so.	**DESDEMONA** He would not say that.
OTHELLO No, his mouth is stopp'd; Honest Iago hath ta'en order for't.	**OTHELLO** No, He won't be able to say anything anymore. Honest Iago has made sure of it.

DESDEMONA	**DESDEMONA**
O! my fear interprets: what, is he dead?	Oh! I am scared. Is he dead?
OTHELLO	**OTHELLO**
Had all his hairs been lives, my great revenge Had stomach for them all.	If he had as many lives as he had hair on his head, I would have killed each one in revenge.
DESDEMONA	**DESDEMONA**
Alas! he is betray'd and I undone.	Oh no! He has been betrayed and I have been ruined.
OTHELLO	**OTHELLO**
Out, strumpet! weep'st thou for him to my face?	Shut up, whore! Are you really crying about him to my face?
DESDEMONA	**DESDEMONA**
O, banish me, my lord, but kill me not!	Oh, send me away, my lord, but don't kill me!
OTHELLO	**OTHELLO**
Down, strumpet!	Get down, whore!
DESDEMONA	**DESDEMONA**
Kill me to-morrow: let me live to-night!	Kill me tomorrow: let me live tonight!
OTHELLO	**OTHELLO**
Nay, if you strive—	No, if you struggle...
DESDEMONA	**DESDEMONA**
But half an hour!	Just half an hour!
OTHELLO	**OTHELLO**
Being done, there is no pause.	While I am doing this, I can't pause.
DESDEMONA	**DESDEMONA**

But while I say one prayer!	Just let me say one more prayer!
OTHELLO	**OTHELLO**
It is too late.	It is too late.
He stifles her	*He smothers her*
EMILIA	**EMILIA**
[Within] My lord, my lord! what, ho! my lord, my lord!	[Offstage] My lord, my lord! Hello! My lord, my lord!
OTHELLO	**OTHELLO**
What noise is this? Not dead? not yet quite dead? I that am cruel am yet merciful; I would not have thee linger in thy pain: So, so.	What's that noise? Aren't you dead yet? I know I am cruel but I don't want you to suffer.
EMILIA	**EMILIA**
[Within] What, ho! my lord, my lord!	[Offstage] Hello! my lord, my lord!
OTHELLO	**OTHELLO**
Who's there?	Who's there?
EMILIA	**EMILIA**
[Within] O, good my lord, I would speak a word with you!	[Offstage] Oh, good my lord, I need to speak to you!
OTHELLO	**OTHELLO**
Yes: 'tis Emilia. By and by. She's dead. 'Tis like she comes to speak of Cassio's death.-- The noise was here. Ha! no more moving? Still as the grave. Shall she come in? were't	Yes, it is Emilia. Just a minute. She's dead. Emilia has probably come to tell me that Cassio has died. It was a loud fight. Ha! You're not moving anymore. You're as still as a grave. Shall I let

good?--

I think she stirs again:--no. What's best to do?

If she come in, she'll sure speak to my wife:

My wife! my wife! what wife? I have no wife.

O insupportable! O heavy hour!

Methinks it should be now a huge eclipse

Of sun and moon, and that the affrighted globe

Should yawn at alteration.

EMILIA

[Within] I do beseech you

That I may speak with you, O, good my lord!

OTHELLO

I had forgot thee: O, come in, Emilia;

Soft; by and by. Let me the curtains draw.

Where art thou?

Unlocks the door

Enter EMILIA

What's the matter with thee now?

EMILIA

O, my good lord, yonder's foul murders done!

OTHELLO

What, now?

EMILIA

---

her in? Is that a good idea? I think she's moving again. No. What should I do?

If she comes in she will try to speak to my wife.

My wife! my wife! what wife? I don't have a wife.

Oh, this is unbearable! What a horrible hour! There should now be a world-wide eclipse of the sun and moon, now that Desdemona is dead.

EMILIA

[Offstage] Please,

I need to speak to you, Oh, my good lord!

OTHELLO

I'd forgotten about you: Come in, Emilia;

Let me draw the curtains.

Where are you?

Unlocks the door

Enter EMILIA

What's the matter with you now?

EMILIA

Oh, my good lord, terrible murders have been committed!

OTHELLO

What, just now?

EMILIA

But now, my lord.	Yes, just now, my lord.
OTHELLO	**OTHELLO**
It is the very error of the moon;	It is because of the full moon.
She comes more nearer earth than she was wont,	If she comes too close to the earth
And makes men mad.	she drives men crazy.
EMILIA	**EMILIA**
Cassio, my lord, hath kill'd a young Venetian Call'd Roderigo.	Cassio, my lord, has killed a young Venetian named Roderigo
OTHELLO	**OTHELLO**
Roderigo kill'd!	Roderigo has been killed!
And Cassio kill'd!	And Cassio has been killed!
EMILIA	**EMILIA**
No, Cassio is not kill'd.	No, Cassio is not dead.
OTHELLO	**OTHELLO**
Not Cassio kill'd! then murder's out of tune,	Cassio's not dead!
And sweet revenge grows harsh.	then the wrong murder has been committed,
	And sweet revenge has gone wrong.
DESDEMONA	**DESDEMONA**
O, falsely, falsely murder'd!	Oh, I have been murdered unfairly!
EMILIA	**EMILIA**
Alas, what cry is that?	Oh, whose cry is that?
OTHELLO	**OTHELLO**
That! what?	That? what?
EMILIA	**EMILIA**

Out, and alas! that was my lady's voice.	Oh no! That was my lady's voice.
Help! help, ho! help! O lady, speak again!	Help! Help, hello! Help! Oh lady, speak again!
Sweet Desdemona! O sweet mistress, speak!	Sweet Desdemona! Oh sweet mistress, speak!
DESDEMONA	**DESDEMONA**
A guiltless death I die.	I die an innocent woman.
EMILIA	**EMILIA**
O, who hath done this deed?	O, who has done this?
DESDEMONA	**DESDEMONA**
Nobody; I myself. Farewell	Nobody; I have done this to myself. Goodbye.
Commend me to my kind lord: O, farewell!	Give my love to my husband: Oh, goodbye!
Dies	*Desdemona dies*
OTHELLO	**OTHELLO**
Why, how should she be murder'd?	How could she have been murdered?
EMILIA	**EMILIA**
Alas, who knows?	My God, who knows?
OTHELLO	**OTHELLO**
You heard her say herself, it was not I.	You heard her say herself, that it wasn't me.
EMILIA	**EMILIA**
She said so: I must needs report the truth.	She said so: I have to tell the truth.
OTHELLO	**OTHELLO**
She's, like a liar, gone to burning hell:	She's a liar, and she's gone to burn in hell:
'Twas I that kill'd her.	It was me that killed her.
EMILIA	**EMILIA**

O, the more angel she,

And you the blacker devil!

OTHELLO

She turn'd to folly, and she was a whore.

EMILIA

Thou dost belie her, and thou art a devil.

OTHELLO

She was false as water.

EMILIA

Thou art rash as fire, to say

That she was false: O, she was heavenly true!

OTHELLO

Cassio did top her; ask thy husband else.

O, I were damn'd beneath all depth in hell,

But that I did proceed upon just grounds

To this extremity. Thy husband knew it all.

EMILIA

My husband!

OTHELLO

Thy husband.

EMILIA

That she was false to wedlock?

OTHELLO

Oh, then she's an angel,

And you are worse than the devil!

OTHELLO

She cheated on me, and she was a whore.

EMILIA

You are slandering her, you devil.

OTHELLO

She was a liar.

EMILIA

You are being too hot-headed by accusing her of being unfaithful. Oh, she was completely faithful!

OTHELLO

Cassio had sex with her; ask your husband. If I didn't have a good reason to do this, then I will be going to hell.

Your husband knew all about it.

EMILIA

My husband!

OTHELLO

Yes, your husband.

EMILIA

He said that she was unfaithful?

OTHELLO

Ay, with Cassio. Nay, had she been true,

If heaven would make me such another world

Of one entire and Perfect chrysolite,

I'ld not have sold her for it.

EMILIA

My husband!

OTHELLO

Ay, 'twas he that told me first:

An honest man he is, and hates the slime

That sticks on filthy deeds.

EMILIA

My husband!

OTHELLO

What needs this iteration, woman? I say thy

husband.

EMILIA

O mistress, villany hath made mocks with love,

My husband say that she was false!

OTHELLO

He, woman;

I say thy husband: dost understand the word?

My friend, thy husband, honest, honest Iago.

EMILIA

Yes, with Cassio. If she had been faithful to

me, I would never have given her up. Even if

God had given me a gem the size of the whole

world, I wouldn't have swapped her for it.

EMILIA

My husband!

OTHELLO

Yes, it was him that told me first:

He's an honest man, and he hates disgusting

and filthy behaviour.

EMILIA

My husband!

OTHELLO

Why do you keep repeating yourself, woman?

I've said your husband.

EMILIA

Oh, my mistress, a villain has made a mockery

of your marriage.

My husband said she was unfaithful?

OTHELLO

Yes, woman;

I've said your husband: do you not

understand me?

My friend, your husband, honest, honest Iago.

EMILIA

If he say so, may his pernicious soul Rot half a grain a day! he lies to the heart: She was too fond of her most filthy bargain.	If he has said that, then I hope his malicious soul rots forever! He has lied to the core. She was too fond of her filthy marriage to do that.
OTHELLO Ha!	**OTHELLO** Ha!
EMILIA Do thy worst: This deed of thine is no more worthy heaven Than thou wast worthy her.	**EMILIA** Do your worst: This deed of yours is not worthy of heaven Just like you were not worthy of her.
OTHELLO Peace, you were best.	**OTHELLO** You had better be quiet.
EMILIA Thou hast not half that power to do me harm As I have to be hurt. O gull! O dolt! As ignorant as dirt! thou hast done a deed-- I care not for thy sword; I'll make thee known, Though I lost twenty lives.--Help! help, ho! help! The Moor hath kill'd my mistress! Murder! murder!	**EMILIA** You do not have enough power to hurt me more than I have been hurt already. Oh you gullible fool! You are as ignorant as dirt! You have done something... I am not afraid of your sword. I am going to tell everybody what you've done, Even if I lose twenty lives doing it. Help! Help! Hello! Help! The Moor has murdered my mistress! Murder! Murder!
Enter MONTANO, GRATIANO, IAGO, and others	*Enter MONTANO, GRATIANO, IAGO, and others*
MONTANO	**MONTANO**

What is the matter? How now, general!

EMILIA

O, are you come, Iago? you have done well,
That men must lay their murders on your
neck.

GRATIANO

What is the matter?

EMILIA

Disprove this villain, if thou be'st a man:
He says thou told'st him that his wife was
false:
I know thou didst not, thou'rt not such a
villain:
Speak, for my heart is full.

IAGO

I told him what I thought, and told no more
Than what he found himself was apt and true.

EMILIA

But did you ever tell him she was false?

IAGO

I did.

EMILIA

You told a lie, an odious, damned lie;
Upon my soul, a lie, a wicked lie.

What is the matter? What's happened,
general?

EMILIA

O, are you here, Iago? You have done well,
Men should blame their murders on you.

GRATIANO

What is the matter?

EMILIA

Tell this villain that he's wrong, if you're a
man.
He says you told him that his wife was
unfaithful:
I know you didn't say that. You're not that
much of a villain.
Speak; I am too emotional to say anything
else.

IAGO

I told him what I thought, and I didn't tell him
anything that he didn't find out was true.

EMILIA

But did you ever tell him she was unfaithful?

IAGO

I did.

EMILIA

You told a lie, a sick and evil lie;
I swear on my life it was a lie.

She false with Cassio!--did you say with Cassio?	She said she slept with Cassio! Did you say with Cassio?
IAGO	**IAGO**
With Cassio, mistress. Go to, charm your tongue.	Yes, with Cassio, mistress. Now shut up.
EMILIA	**EMILIA**
I will not charm my tongue; I am bound to speak:	I will not shut up; I have to speak out:
My mistress here lies murder'd in her bed,--	My mistress has been murdered in her own bed...
All	**All**
O heavens forfend!	Oh, heaven forbid!
EMILIA	**EMILIA**
And your reports have set the murder on.	And your lies have caused this murder.
OTHELLO	**OTHELLO**
Nay, stare not, masters: it is true, indeed.	No, don't stare, gentlemen: it is true, indeed.
GRATIANO	**GRATIANO**
'Tis a strange truth.	It's a strange truth then.
MONTANO	**MONTANO**
O monstrous act!	Oh, what a monstrous act!
EMILIA	**EMILIA**
Villany, villany, villany!	Evil, evil, evil!
I think upon't, I think: I smell't: O villany!--	If I think about it, I can smell it. Oh, evil!
I thought so then:--I'll kill myself for grief:--	I suspected this. I will kill myself with grief.
O villany, villany!	Oh, evil, evil!
IAGO	**IAGO**

What, are you mad? I charge you, get you home.

EMILIA

Good gentlemen, let me have leave to speak:
'Tis proper I obey him, but not now.
Perchance, Iago, I will ne'er go home.

OTHELLO

O! O! O!

He falls on the bed

EMILIA

Nay, lay thee down and roar;
For thou hast kill'd the sweetest innocent
That e'er did lift up eye.

OTHELLO

[Rising] O, she was foul!
I scarce did know you, uncle: there lies your niece,
Whose breath, indeed, these hands have newly stopp'd:
I know this act shows horrible and grim.

GRATIANO

Poor Desdemona! I am glad thy father's dead:
Thy match was mortal to him, and pure grief
Shore his old thread in twain: did he live now,
This sight would make him do a desperate turn,
Yea, curse his better angel from his side,
And fall to reprobation.

What, are you crazy? I am ordering you to go home.

EMILIA

Good gentlemen, please allow me to speak:
I know I should obey him, but not now.
Maybe I will never go home, Iago.

OTHELLO

Oh! Oh! Oh!

He falls on the bed

EMILIA

Yes, go on, moan.
You have killed the sweetest and most innocent person that ever lived.

OTHELLO

[Rising] Oh, she was filthy!
I barely knew you, uncle Gratiano: here is your niece lying here dead.
I have killed her with these hands.

I know this looks terrible.

GRATIANO

Poor Desdemona! I am glad your father's dead:
Your marriage killed him, and pure grief
cut his soul in half. If he were alive now,
this sight would make him do something desperate,

Yes, he would abandon the kind side of himself
And do something evil.

OTHELLO

'Tis pitiful; but yet Iago knows
That she with Cassio hath the act of shame
A thousand times committed; Cassio confess'd it:
And she did gratify his amorous works
With that recognizance and pledge of love
Which I first gave her; I saw it in his hand:
It was a handkerchief, an antique token
My father gave my mother.

OTHELLO

It is pitiful; but Iago knows
That she committed this shameful act with Cassio
A thousand times. Cassio confessed it all to him.
And she rewarded his sexual actions with a token of love that I gave her to show my love. It was my first gift to her. I saw it in his hand. It was a handkerchief. A family antique that my father gave to my mother.

EMILIA

O heaven! O heavenly powers!

EMILIA

Oh God! O God!

IAGO

Come, hold your peace.

IAGO

Shut up.

EMILIA

'Twill out, 'twill out: I peace!
No, I will speak as liberal as the north:
Let heaven and men and devils, let them all,
All, all, cry shame against me, yet I'll speak.

EMILIA

It will come out. It will come out. I will not shut up! I will speak freely and truthfully. Let God, and men, and devils punish me, I will still speak out.

IAGO

Be wise, and get you home.

IAGO

Be wise, and go home.

EMILIA

I will not.

EMILIA

I will not.

IAGO offers to stab EMILIA	*IAGO offers to stab EMILIA*
GRATIANO	**GRATIANO**
Fie!	Shame on you!
Your sword upon a woman?	You've draw your sword upon a woman!
EMILIA	**EMILIA**
O thou dull Moor! that handkerchief thou speak'st of	Oh, you stupid Moor! That handkerchief that you've just mentioned was found, by me, and
I found by fortune and did give my husband;	I gave it to my husband.
For often, with a solemn earnestness,	
More than indeed belong'd to such a trifle,	He begged me to steal it so many times.
He begg'd of me to steal it.	
IAGO	**IAGO**
Villanous whore!	You villanous whore!
EMILIA	**EMILIA**
She give it Cassio! no, alas! I found it,	She did not give it to Cassio! Sadly, I found it,
And I did give't my husband.	And I gave it to my husband.
IAGO	**IAGO**
Filth, thou liest!	Filth, you are lying!
EMILIA	**EMILIA**
By heaven, I do not, I do not, gentlemen.	I swear to God, I'm not, I'm not, gentlemen.
O murderous coxcomb! what should such a fool	Oh, you murdering fool. How could such an idiot have such a good wife?
Do with so good a woman?	
OTHELLO	**OTHELLO**
Are there no stones in heaven	Are the stones in heaven only used to create thunder?
But what serve for the thunder?--Precious villain!	You absolute villain, Iago!

He runs at IAGO IAGO, from behind, stabs EMILIA, and exit	*He runs at IAGO IAGO, from behind, stabs EMILIA, and exits*
GRATIANO The woman falls; sure, he hath kill'd his wife.	**GRATIANO** The woman has fallen down; sure, he has killed his wife.
EMILIA Ay, ay: O, lay me by my mistress' side.	**EMILIA** Yes, yes. Oh, lay me by my mistress' side.
GRATIANO He's gone, but his wife's kill'd.	**GRATIANO** He's gone, but he has killed his wife.
MONTANO 'Tis a notorious villain. Take you this weapon, Which I have here recover'd from the Moor: Come, guard the door without; let him not pass, But kill him rather. I'll after that same villain, For 'tis a damned slave. *Exeunt MONTANO and GRATIANO*	**MONTANO** He is an evil villain. Take the Moor's weapon, Guard the door and do not let him out. Kill him rather than let him escape. I'll go after Iago. He's a horrible man. *MONTANO and GRATIANO exit*
OTHELLO I am not valiant neither, But ever puny whipster gets my sword: But why should honour outlive honesty? Let it go all.	**OTHELLO** I am not that much of a man if a weak kid can grab my sword. But why should my honour matter now? I'll let it all go.
EMILIA What did thy song bode, lady? Hark, canst thou hear me? I will play the swan. And die in music.	**EMILIA** What did your song mean, lady? Listen, can you hear me? I will be like a swan. And die singing.

Singing	*Singing*
Willow, willow, willow,--	Willow, willow, willow,--
Moor, she was chaste; she loved thee, cruel Moor;	Moor, she wasn't unfaithful; she loved you, cruel Moor;
So come my soul to bliss, as I speak true;	So my soul is saved, as I speak the truth;
So speaking as I think, I die, I die.	So speaking as I think, I die, I die.
Dies	*Dies*
OTHELLO	**OTHELLO**
I have another weapon in this chamber;	I have another weapon in this bedroom;
It is a sword of Spain, the ice-brook's temper:--	It is a sword from Spain. It has been hardened in ice-cold water.
O, here it is. Uncle, I must come forth.	Oh, here it is. Uncle, I am coming out.
GRATIANO	**GRATIANO**
[Within] If thou attempt it, it will cost thee dear:	[Offstage] If you attempt it, it will cost you your life.
Thou hast no weapon, and perforce must suffer.	You don't have a weapon, so you'll have to suffer.
OTHELLO	**OTHELLO**
Look in upon me then and speak with me,	Look in the room and talk to me or I will attack you even without a weapon.
Or, naked as I am, I will assault thee.	
Re-enter GRATIANO	*Re-enter GRATIANO*
GRATIANO	**GRATIANO**
What is the matter?	What is the matter?
OTHELLO	**OTHELLO**
Behold, I have a weapon;	Look, I have a weapon.
A better never did itself sustain	It is the best sword a soldier could wish for.

Upon a soldier's thigh: I have seen the day, That, with this little arm and this good sword, I have made my way through more impediments Than twenty times your stop: but, O vain boast! Who can control his fate? 'tis not so now. Be not afraid, though you do see me weapon'd; Here is my journey's end, here is my butt, And very sea-mark of my utmost sail. Do you go back dismay'd? 'tis a lost fear; Man but a rush against Othello's breast, And he retires. Where should Othello go? Now, how dost thou look now? O ill-starr'd wench! Pale as thy smock! when we shall meet at compt, This look of thine will hurl my soul from heaven, And fiends will snatch at it. Cold, cold, my girl! Even like thy chastity. O cursed slave! Whip me, ye devils, From the possession of this heavenly sight! Blow me about in winds! roast me in sulphur! Wash me in steep-down gulfs of liquid fire! O Desdemona! Desdemona! dead! Oh! Oh! Oh!	I have seen some really horrible fights with this little arm and this good sword. I have survived fights that are twenty times more terrifying that you. But, I'm being vain by boasting. Who can actually control their own fate? I couldn't do any of that now. Don't be afraid, even though I have a weapon. This is the end of my journey in life. This is the end of my life. Are you backing away from me in fear? There is no reason to fear me. You could make one move towards my chest and I'll give up. Where can I go? What do you look like now? Oh, a girl with such bad luck! You are as pale as your nightgown! When we meet for judgment, This look of yours will send me from heaven to hell. Devils will grab at me. You're cold. You're cold, my girl. You were never passionate towards other men Damned villain! Whip me, you devils. I want to be taken away from this heavenly sight! Throw me about! Burn me! Wash me in liquid fire! Oh, Desdemona! Desdemona! Dead! Oh! Oh! Oh!
Enter LODOVICO. MONTANO,	*Enter LODOVICO. MONTANO,*

CASSIO carried in a chair, and Officers with IAGO, prisoner	*CASSIO carried in a chair, and Officers with IAGO, prisoner*
LODOVICO Where is this rash and most unfortunate man?	**LODOVICO** Where is that reactive and unfortunate man?
OTHELLO That's he that was Othello: here I am.	**OTHELLO** You mean the man who used to be Othello? Here I am.
LODOVICO Where is that viper? bring the villain forth.	**LODOVICO** Where is that snake? Bring that villain here.
OTHELLO I look down towards his feet; but that's a fable. If that thou best a devil, I cannot kill thee.	**OTHELLO** I am looking at your feet to see if they are like the devil's hooves, but that's just a story. If you are the devil, I can't kill you.
Wounds IAGO	*Wounds IAGO*
LODOVICO Wrench his sword from him.	**LODOVICO** Take his sword away from him.
IAGO I bleed, sir; but not kill'd.	**IAGO** I'm bleeding, sir; but you've not killed me.
OTHELLO I am not sorry neither: I'ld have thee live; For, in my sense, 'tis happiness to die.	**OTHELLO** I am not sorry, either. I want you to live. It would be too easy for you to die.
LODOVICO O thou Othello, thou wert once so good, Fall'n in the practise of a damned slave, What shall be said to thee?	**LODOVICO** Oh Othello, you were once such a good man, but you've been tricked by this damned villain. What am I supposed to say to you?

OTHELLO	**OTHELLO**
Why, any thing:	Say anything.
An honourable murderer, if you will;	You could call me a honourable murderer, if
For nought I did in hate, but all in honour.	you want. I did not kill out of hate, but out of
	honour.
LODOVICO	**LODOVICO**
This wretch hath part confess'd his villany:	This wretch has partly confessed to his crime.
Did you and he consent in Cassio's death?	Did you and Iago conspire to kill Cassio?
OTHELLO	**OTHELLO**
Ay.	Yes.
CASSIO	**CASSIO**
Dear general, I never gave you cause.	Dear general, I never gave you any reason to
	kill me.
OTHELLO	**OTHELLO**
I do believe it, and I ask your pardon.	I believe you, and I ask for your forgiveness.
Will you, I pray, demand that demi-devil	Will you please make this half-devil tell you
Why he hath thus ensnared my soul and	why he tricked me and ruined my life?
body?	
IAGO	**IAGO**
Demand me nothing: what you know, you	Don't ask me anything. You know what you
know:	know.
From this time forth I never will speak word.	From now on, I'll never speak another word.
LODOVICO	**LODOVICO**
What, not to pray?	What, not even to pray?
GRATIANO	**GRATIANO**

Torments will ope your lips.

OTHELLO

Well, thou dost best.

LODOVICO

Sir, you shall understand what hath befall'n,

Which, as I think, you know not. Here is a

letter

Found in the pocket of the slain Roderigo;

And here another: the one of them imports

The death of Cassio to be undertook

By Roderigo.

OTHELLO

O villain!

CASSIO

Most heathenish and most gross!

LODOVICO

Now here's another discontented paper,

Found in his pocket too; and this, it seems,

Roderigo meant to have sent this damned

villain;

But that belike Iago in the interim

Came in and satisfied him.

OTHELLO

O the pernicious caitiff!

How came you, Cassio, by that handkerchief

That was my wife's?

Torture will make you speak.

OTHELLO

Well, do your best.

LODOVICO

Sir, you will understand everything that has

happened

I am certain you don't yet know. Here is a

letter

That we found in the pocket of the murdered

Roderigo.

And here is another. This one talks about

The murder of Cassio and how it should be

done by Roderigo.

OTHELLO

Oh, you villain!

CASSIO

You disgusting monster!

LODOVICO

Here's another letter found in his pocket. We

think that this one was supposed to have

been sent from Roderigo to Iago, the damned

villain.

It seems that Iago answered him by killing

him.

OTHELLO

Oh, the evil scoundrel!

How did you get your hands on my wife's

handkerchief?

CASSIO

I found it in my chamber:

And he himself confess'd but even now

That there he dropp'd it for a special purpose

Which wrought to his desire.

OTHELLO

O fool! fool! fool!

CASSIO

There is besides in Roderigo's letter,

How he upbraids Iago, that he made him

Brave me upon the watch; whereon it came

That I was cast: and even but now he spake,

After long seeming dead, Iago hurt him,

Iago set him on.

LODOVICO

You must forsake this room, and go with us:

Your power and your command is taken off,

And Cassio rules in Cyprus. For this slave,

If there be any cunning cruelty

That can torment him much and hold him

long,

It shall be his. You shall close prisoner rest,

Till that the nature of your fault be known

To the Venetian state. Come, bring him away.

OTHELLO

CASSIO

I found it in my bedroom.

And Iago has just confessed that he

deliberately dropped it there so he could

make up this story.

OTHELLO

Oh I am a fool! A fool! A fool!

CASSIO

There's more in Roderigo's letter.

He complains to Iago about how he was made

to attack me when I was on guard. That was

the incident that led to you dismissing me.

And just now he spoke.

He seemed dead, but he managed to tell us

that Iago attacked him.

LODOVICO

You must leave this room and come with us.

Your power and your status has been

removed.

Cassio now rules Cyprus. As for this slave,

If there is a horrible torture that can be done

and prolonged,

He will have it. You will remain a prisoner

until your crime is known about

by the Venetian state. Come on, take him

away.

OTHELLO

Soft you; a word or two before you go.
I have done the state some service, and they know't.
No more of that. I pray you, in your letters,
When you shall these unlucky deeds relate,
Speak of me as I am; nothing extenuate,
Nor set down aught in malice: then must you speak
Of one that loved not wisely but too well;
Of one not easily jealous, but being wrought
Perplex'd in the extreme; of one whose hand,
Like the base Indian, threw a pearl away
Richer than all his tribe; of one whose subdued eyes,
Albeit unused to the melting mood,
Drop tears as fast as the Arabian trees
Their medicinal gum. Set you down this;
And say besides, that in Aleppo once,
Where a malignant and a turban'd Turk
Beat a Venetian and traduced the state,
I took by the throat the circumcised dog,
And smote him, thus.

Stabs himself

LODOVICO
O bloody period!

GRATIANO
All that's spoke is marr'd.

OTHELLO

Wait. Please can I just speak a couple of words before you go? I have been a good soldier to the state, and they know it. But enough of that. I beg you, when you write about these awful events,

Please describe me exactly as I am. Don't elaborate or exaggerate out of spite. Please speak about someone who didn't love wisely but loved too much.

I was not easily made jealous but I was tricked and provoked to extremes.
I acted like a rich Indian who threw away a pearl richer than all his tribe. I was not easily made emotional, but I cried a lot.
I cried more than Arabian trees drop their medicinal gum. Write this down.
And also say that once in Aleppo where an evil Turk wearing a turban insulted us by beating a Venetian,
I grabbed the circumcised dog by the throat
And killed him, like this.

Stabs himself

LODOVICO
Oh, what a violent end!

GRATIANO
Everything he said is now ruined.

OTHELLO

I kiss'd thee ere I kill'd thee: no way but this; Killing myself, to die upon a kiss.	I kissed you before I killed you. There was no other way than to kill myself and die with one last kiss.
Falls on the bed, and dies	*Falls on the bed, and dies*
CASSIO	**CASSIO**
This did I fear, but thought he had no weapon; For he was great of heart.	I was afraid he'd do this. I didn't think he had a weapon, though. He was a brave man.
LODOVICO	**LODOVICO**
[To IAGO] O Spartan dog, More fell than anguish, hunger, or the sea! Look on the tragic loading of this bed; This is thy work: the object poisons sight; Let it be hid. Gratiano, keep the house, And seize upon the fortunes of the Moor, For they succeed on you. To you, lord governor, Remains the censure of this hellish villain; The time, the place, the torture: O, enforce it! Myself will straight aboard: and to the state This heavy act with heavy heart relate.	[To IAGO] Oh, you meagre dog. You are more evil than sadness, hunger, or the sea! Look at the tragedy on that bed. This is your doing. You make me sick to look at. Hide it. Gratiano, the house is yours. And take all the Moor's possessions. You are their heir. To you, Lord Governor, Remains the punishment of this evil villain. Decide the time, the place, and the torture. Then carry it out! I am going back to Venice to tell them about these extremely sad events with a very heavy heart.
Exeunt	*They all exit.*

PART 32: ANALYSING ACT 5 SCENE 2

Themes: Appearance vs Reality, Womanhood and Sexuality, Manhood and Honour, Jealousy, Prejudice.

The tragic climax of the play begins with a dignified poetic soliloquy from Othello which eventually wakes Desdemona and provides a stark contrast to the incomprehensible, frantic, and insulting Othello of the previous act.

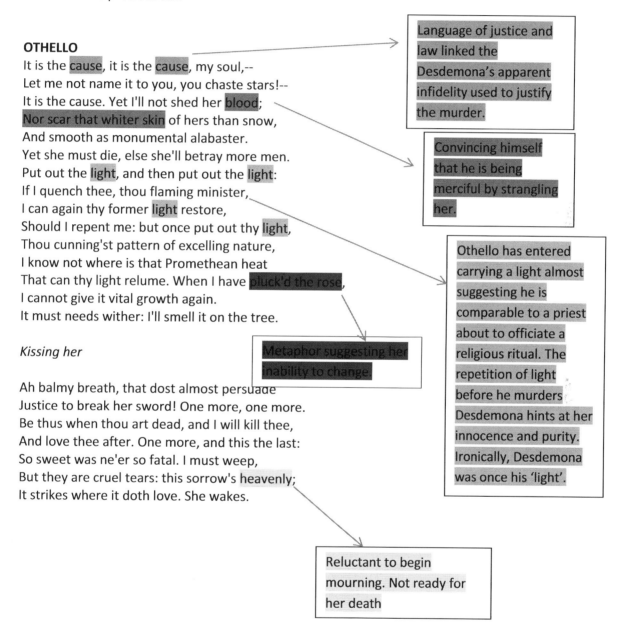

OTHELLO
It is the cause, it is the cause, my soul,--
Let me not name it to you, you chaste stars!--
It is the cause. Yet I'll not shed her blood;
Nor scar that whiter skin of hers than snow,
And smooth as monumental alabaster.
Yet she must die, else she'll betray more men.
Put out the light, and then put out the light:
If I quench thee, thou flaming minister,
I can again thy former light restore,
Should I repent me: but once put out thy light,
Thou cunning'st pattern of excelling nature,
I know not where is that Promethean heat
That can thy light relume. When I have pluck'd the rose,
I cannot give it vital growth again.
It must needs wither: I'll smell it on the tree.

Kissing her

Ah balmy breath, that dost almost persuade
Justice to break her sword! One more, one more.
Be thus when thou art dead, and I will kill thee,
And love thee after. One more, and this the last:
So sweet was ne'er so fatal. I must weep,
But they are cruel tears: this sorrow's heavenly;
It strikes where it doth love. She wakes.

Language of justice and law linked the Desdemona's apparent infidelity used to justify the murder.

Convincing himself that he is being merciful by strangling her.

Othello has entered carrying a light almost suggesting he is comparable to a priest about to officiate a religious ritual. The repetition of light before he murders Desdemona hints at her innocence and purity. Ironically, Desdemona was once his 'light'.

Metaphor suggesting her inability to change.

Reluctant to begin mourning. Not ready for her death

He appears completely rational and righteous despite the fact that he has been deceived and is about to commit a motiveless crime. Having arrived with a candle to light the darkness and regained the beauty of language, the audience could be forgiven for assuming there is still some hope left. Unfortunately, the candle is present to metaphorically remind the audience of the imminent ending of Desdemona's life ('put out the light') and serves the purpose of lighting the dark room in which Desdemona is sleeping.

In terms of stagecraft, the bed is now the most visual and important symbol of all the action that is about to take place as a result of Othello's belief that the bed has been defiled. He makes it clear to the audience that he will not defile it further by shedding Desdemona's blood, but will smother her instead. His reluctance to spill any blood almost suggests a regret at either having taken Desdemona's virginity (and regretting awakening her sexuality) or not having taken it (they were interrupted on both attempts to consummate marriage) as well as reminding the audience of his physical attraction to her white skin which is as 'smooth as monumental alabaster'. Ironically, the important white handkerchief is said to have been dyed with the blood of dead virgins, something Othello now doesn't want to completely mirror in shedding the blood of his wife.

Iago's deceptive web continues to succeed as Othello refuses to accept Desdemona's pleas of innocence once he reveals he has seen Cassio with the handkerchief. Consumed by jealousy, he refuses to allow her to prove her innocence and becomes infuriated by her tears as he believes she is weeping for the injured Cassio. He is reminded of what he believes is a sense of duty ('...she'll betray more men') and smothers Desdemona with a pillow after insisting she confess her sins to God. Othello is no longer the independent, powerful leader from the start of the play but is now under Iago's complete control. The brutality of the murder is emphasised by the slow pace of the start of the scene building up to the murder.

Emilia's arrival reminds the audience that she possesses the power to reveal the truth. She arrives just in time to hear Desdemona loyally praise her husband and risk her soul by falsely clearing him of her murder before she dies. Othello has completely lost all sense of reality and he struggles to differentiate between the voices of Desdemona and Emilia, 'That! What?'. Once again, repetition of interrogatives is used to build up to a climactic moment as Emilia seems stunned at her husband's involvement in the crime and Othello struggles to believe his dishonesty:

Emilia

'O, who hath done this deed?'[....]

Othello:

Why, how should she be murder'd?'

Emilia

Alas, who knows?'

In an act too late to save Desdemona, Emilia risks her own life and vindicates her by confessing that Iago '...lies to the heart' before announcing that Othello has '...killed [her] mistress' and demanding that Iago disprove what Othello has revealed. Iago attempts to control Emilia but she feels she has nothing to lose because she has betrayed him for the right reason. The violence that Iago displays towards Emilia when he 'offers to stab' her and refers to her as a 'villainous whore!' and 'filth' contrasts with Othello's final moments with Desdemona and proves Iago's villainy. Othello's stabbing of Iago leads to the death of another female character (Iago kills Emilia) who reminds the audience of the futility of love by revisiting the 'Willow Song' in her final moments and announcing that Desdemona loved the '...cruel Moor'. Defiant to the very end, Iago regains control of the situation and the characters by refusing to speak about his motives.

Othello's final speech is public so cannot be considered a soliloquy. Delivered in verse to reflect some of his former nobility and containing a list of similes and metaphors ('like a base Indian, threw a pearly away...Drop tears as fast as Arabian trees...a malignant and a turban'd Turk....circumcised dog.'), his statement is an inner reflection on himself delivered in the third person. The beauty and elegance of his final words could be considered a last attempt by Othello to present himself positively in public. His acceptance of Cassio's innocence and his plea for pardon helps him recover some of his status. He admits he has been a 'fool! fool! Fool!' and appears determined through use of repetition to influence the way he will be remembered. He compares himself to the 'base Judean' who sacrificed the most precious jewel in the world therefore redeeming Desdemona of the crime she has been accused of. He poses the problem of whether he will be remembered as a Venetian Christian who made a mistake or as an ethnic outsider who didn't belong in the first place before stabbing himself, thus regaining control over his end. Suicide is a sin in Christianity; however, Othello's choice to end his own life reflects the beliefs of Ancient Greeks and Romans who saw suicide as a noble and patriotic way of avoiding disgrace. Othello is seen to sacrifice his life in response to having committed unforgiveable crimes. By comparing his death to that of a Turk, Othello defines himself as somebody trying to be accepted but knows he will always be seen as an outsider by others. Lodovico announces that Iago will be punished but that the sight he leaves behind 'poisons sight' and must be reported in Venice 'with a heavy heart'.

PART 33: The Assessment Objectives

Assessment Objectives*

AO1	Articulate informed, personal and creative responses to literary texts, using associated concepts and terminology, and coherent, accurate written expression.
AO2	Analyse ways in which meanings are shaped in literary texts.
AO3	Demonstrate understanding of the significance and influence of the contexts in which literary texts are written and received.
AO4	Explore connections across literary texts.
AO5	Explore literary texts informed by different interpretations.

*This table contains public sector information licensed under the Open Government Licence v3.0.

Section B will always have a statement which you need to evaluate based on your knowledge and analysis of the text.

Even though it says 'to what extent' you do not need to provide a balanced argument. It is much more important to have a CLEAR line of argument. If in doubt use the statement as your line of argument by turning it into a question. Some example statements turned into questions are listed below:

- 'Othello's foolishness rather than Iago's cleverness leads to the tragedy of Shakespeare's Othello.' (Does Othello's foolishness rather than Iago's cleverness lead to the tragedy of Shakespeare's Othello?)
- 'Othello's race is a key factor in the tragedy of the play' (Is Othello's race a key factor in the tragedy of the play?)
- 'Shakespeare's play Othello demonstrates the weakness of human judgement' (Does the play Othello demonstrate the weakness of human judgement?)
- 'Women are the innocent victims of the play's tragedy' (Are women the innocent victims of the play's tragedy?)
- 'Irony is a powerful dramatic device used by Shakespeare to heighten the tragic dimension of his play Othello.' (Is irony a powerful dramatic device used by Shakespeare to heighten the tragic dimension of the play?)
- 'Othello is a true tragic hero' (Is Othello a true tragic hero?)
- 'Othello is essentially a noble character, flawed by insecurity and a nature that is naive and unsophisticated.' (Is Othello a noble character, flawed by insecurity and a nature that is naïve and unsophisticated?)
- 'The play fundamentally revolves around how social order is disrupted and restored' (Does the play fundamentally revolve around the disruption and restoration of social order?)

Suggested timing of the response is 45 mins.

Suggested structure is as follows:

INTRODUCTION	- Opening line that engages with the words/ideas of the statement. Use the same wording (A01)
	- Establish a clear line of argument. What will you argue and aim to prove? (A01)

	- Outline your main points (aim for 3 main) and be concise. No more that 6-7 sentences (A01) - Reference tragic elements (A04)
SECTION 1	- Strong topic sentence that outlines your first line of argument (A01) - Focus on the writer's methods and use short quotations (or paraphrase) or reference structural devices (A02) - Link to tragic elements (A04) - Explain how different audiences may view the play/characters (A03) - Explain a critical interpretation (A03) - Link back to main question and make a link to next point (A05) Don't forget: focus on the writer for A03 'Shakespeare suggests...' and use adverbs to suggest your personal attitude for A01
SECTION 2	REPEAT ABOVE BUT WITH STRONG TOPIC SENTENCE 2
SECTION 3	REPEAT ABOVE BUT WITH STRONG TOPIC SENTENCE 3
CONCLUSION	- A strong conclusion will always mirror the points in the introduction but will establish your opinion - Use vocabulary that signals a conclusion eg. 'to conclude' or 'ultimately' (A01)

Some tips and reminders:

- ✓ Plan your topic sentences.
- ✓ Be tentative if you cannot prove a claim you make (use modal verbs such as 'may', 'might', 'could'). Being tentative is also a higher level skill.
- ✓ Use adverbial phrases to suggest a line of argument ('arguably, 'significantly', 'crucially', 'clearly').
- ✓ Use analytical verbs ('suggests', 'implies', 'connotes', 'highlights', 'presents', 'symbolises').
- ✓ Make sure you are concise (especially with topic sentences). The easiest way to be concise is to ensure you are using appositional phrases (adding an additional clause that gives further information about a noun phrase) eg. The playwright William Shakespeare often explored ideas of love and hate.
- ✓ ALWAYS proofread your work!

PART 35: Example Essay Ciara Rock:

Differing attitudes to love and marriage are depicted throughout the play

To what extent do you agree with this view?

Various attitudes concerning love are depicted throughout the play; Othello's passionate yet naïve attitude conflicts with Iago's perverse and calculating view of love and marriage. It could be argued that Shakespeare presents these contrasting attitudes in order to represent the struggle between good and evil onstage which will ultimately bring about the downfall of our tragic hero.

Shakespeare exposes the audience to Brabantio's patriarchal attitudes towards marriage in Act 1 Scene II, notably before the introduction and demonstration of Othello and Desdemona's love. This manipulation of structure therefore elevates his views, allowing the audience to make judgements on their love before witnessing it. With spitting anger which can be felt through monosyllabic words such as *'O thou foul thief,'* Brabantio presents an opinion of marriage, one which favours convenience and values wealth rather than passion and connection, and can related with the popular, stereotypical beliefs of the Jacobean period. In fact, he is unable to comprehend why Desdemona has *'shunned The wealthy curled darlings'* of Venice and declares it unnatural for her to seek *'the sooty bosom of such a thing'*. The adjective *'sooty'* brings to mind the derogatory associations with Othello's race; 'moors' were widely believed to possess a *'soul black like his face'*, and therefore a devilish and demonic descent from the *'burning brimstone'* of hell, whilst also making reference to Brabantio's perception of the dirty and unclean nature of their relationship. Thus, his logical conclusion from the news that his only daughter has married *'the Moor'* is that she is *'in the chains of magic'* from Othello's *'practices of cunning hell'*. This repulsion towards an inter-racial marriage would have been found within most of the Jacobean audience, and therefore the prejudices of contemporaneous society are epitomised in Brabantio's outburst.

The passionate connection presented between Othello and Desdemona, who defy all convention and expectation to consolidate their love in marriage, is portrayed as the purest form of love – they view themselves as soulmates. A semantic field of religion is also used throughout the description of their love to depict it as holy, pure, sanctified by God and to contradict Iago's devilish and animalistic ideas: *'consecrate'*, *'peace'*, *'rites'*, *'heaven'*, *'light-wing'd toys / of feather'd Cupid'*, *'souls'*. By using the imagery of God and Cupid, Othello's view of marriage is presented as something being romantically designed by Fate, therefore suggesting it is beyond his control. However, an audience may view this attitude as naïve and ignorant to the challenges of married life, and whilst it appears certainly the most admirable expression of love in the play, this level of devotion, equality and blind romanticism ironically encourages Othello's vulnerability and susceptibility to Iago's manipulation, and is arguably the cause of Othello's downfall.

The simple honesty and purity of Othello's untainted love is conveyed by Shakespeare through a rhythmic and flowing style that is free from fragmentation, which would defer from his calm and collected nature. Equally, the faith that Desdemona inspires in her husband is impressively demonstrated through his bold statement *'my life upon her faith'*, a response to Brabantio's churlish allegation that she may deceive him. Valuing Desdemona's word as much as his own, *'Here comes the lady; let her witness it'*, Othello's wholly trusting nature in his wife is exemplified – the prepositional phrase *'upon her faith'* shows the audience that his life and being depend on her honesty, loyalty or perhaps the value she places in him. Furthermore, *'upon'* surpasses the typical attitude of a Jacobean male – Othello has passed the power to Desdemona.

The progression of the scene also exposes the rationality and order that Desdemona is able to bring to Othello, as his mind becomes disturbed when he believes she is lost. The description of his courtship with Desdemona, which he introduces as *'a round unvarnish'd tale'*, clearly shatters Brabantio and Iago's accusations that the union is a product of witchcraft or lust, and they are further undermined by the Duke's comment on the efficacy of Othello's story – *'I think this tale would win my daughter too'*. Shakespeare strengthens this spiritual side of love through Desdemona's testimony, which is delivered with 'moving lucidity'. She proves that their love is one that binds not just through the lust of the body, but also a spiritual understanding as she tells she *'saw Othello's visage in his mind'*. Her overflowing passion can be observed in her spoken desire to *'trumpet to the world'* her love for Othello, as *'trumpet'* holds connotations of a regal declaration, that is of the utmost importance. However, this could alternatively be perceived as a childish response to emotions Desdemona is not yet mature enough to process. Despite his colour and humble beginnings, she elevates Othello above herself, referring to him as *'my lord'*, allowing emphasis to fall on his mind and spirit, far from lust and material virtues. Desdemona's caring and devoted nature towards Othello may be witnessed when she pleads using the imperative *'Let me go with him'* to Cyprus as well as later in the play, *'I am not merry, but I do beguile / The thing I am, by seeing otherwise'* as she attempts to hide her concern and anxiousness when awaiting his arrival in Cyprus. These lines could arguably be viewed as a demonstration of Desdemona achieving a maturity beyond that of Brabantio, as she speaks in a cool, calm and rational manner.

Iago's soliloquies offer a valuable insight into his psychotic and perverse mind- we see him reduce love into a crude, lust-driven weakness of the will typical of an antagonist in the line *'raging motions, our carnal desires, our unbitted lusts'*. Using natural imagery, Iago suggests that our bodies are gardens are *'our wills are gardeners'* to persuade Roderigo that we need not be overwhelmed by love, but control it. Iago's character is mirrored in his attitude towards love: pragmatic, cold, and shunning all emotion except lust and anger. His misogynistic ideas are perhaps to blame for the coldness he casts towards love – that a man's head should rule his actions rather than his heart, *'but we have / reason to cool our raging motions...'*. He can only understand love to be something of *'sensuality'* and body, therefore the *'marriage of true mindes'* that Othello and Desdemona bewilders him – their relationship is only plausible in Iago's view when he envisions her as a passive animal, dominated by a more forceful one shown in the lines *'an old black ram/ Is tupping your white ewe'*. The use of binary colours in this line is possibly a reflection of Shakespeare's motif of good and evil, or alternatively, the representation of balance in Othello and Desdemona's love which brings a sense of calm and order. This emphasis of the body however does lead him to conclude that a union such as Desdemona and Othello's cannot last, as *'when she is sated with his body, she will find the error of her choice'*. Shakespeare's choice of words also draws focus to the sexual aspects of love, *'food'*, *'sated'*, saliva-inducing sibilance in *'luscious as locusts'* (also considered a delicacy), and harsh consonants that create a spitting, staccato effect when reading *'bitter as colonquintida'*. The repeated motif *'put money in thy purse'* perfectly intertwines his character and intentions with his attitude towards love- that it is a fool's emotion, which can be utilised for one's own gain.

Moreover, Iago continues to present his opinions of marriage, which arguably could reflect the views of the audience in the period. In a more jovial setting Iago teases his ideas of a wife's role, *'housewives' in your beds'*, and describes a wife's role as more of an object than a faithful and loving partner- whilst Othello seeks order, advice and comfort in Desdemona, Iago focuses on her talents in the bedroom. Whilst his complaints are hyperbolic in the efforts to amuse (*e.g. 'or else I am a Turk'*), they could be taken literally, given their speaker. For example, *'Bells in your parlours'* depicts wives as an empty vessel which produces repetitive, irritating sounds. He places them firmly in household positions- *'your parlours', 'your kitchens', 'your housewifery', 'your beds'*, presenting a particularly patriarchal argument for where a woman should belong. The repetition of the pronoun 'your' is particularly striking in his idealism of marriage- intended as a union of two partners, for him is a physical separation between the genders. Iago finishes triumphantly with the notion that wives *'go to bed to work'*, displaying his opinion that love, or lust performed through sexual acts is a wife's primary duty.

In conclusion, Shakespeare's presentation of differing attitudes to love enables him to not only explore prejudices of the time towards manhood, a woman's place and racial tension- the figure of the Moor represented not an ethnic, but a moral type, epitomising lust, witchcraft and satanic evil- but to also to facilitate the tragic end and ultimate catharsis to Othello.

Examiner Comment:

Always thorough and perceptive; ranges widely through the text. Sophisticated terminology and concepts discussed and explored in detail with a perceptive understanding of the genre and its conventions. Assured, confident writing demonstrating a secure and analytical understanding of text, character and task.

Printed in Great Britain
by Amazon